SCOTLAND YARD'S FLYING SQUAD

DICK KIRBY
has also written

Rough Justice – Memoirs of a Flying Squad officer

The Real Sweeney

You're Nicked!

Villains

The Guv'nors – Ten of Scotland Yard's Greatest Detectives

The Sweeney – The First Sixty Years of Scotland Yard's Crimebusting Flying Squad 1919–1978

Scotland Yard's Ghost Squad
The Secret Weapon against Post-War Crime

The Brave Blue Line
100 Years of Metropolitan Police Gallantry

Death on the Beat
Police Officers Killed in the Line of Duty

The Scourge of Soho
The Controversial Career of SAS Hero
Detective Sergeant Harry Challenor MM

Whitechapel's Sherlock Holmes
The Casebook of Fred Wensley OBE, KPM
Victorian Crimebuster

The Wrong Man
The Shooting of Steven Waldorf and
the Hunt for David Martin

Laid Bare
The Nude Murders and
the Hunt for 'Jack the Stripper'

London's Gangs at War

Operation Countryman
The Flawed Enquiry into London Police Corruption

Scotland Yard's Gangbuster
Bert Wickstead's Most Celebrated Cases

The Mayfair Mafia
The Lives and Crimes of the Messina Brothers

Praise for Dick Kirby's Books

'His style of writing pulls no punches and he tells it like it is. Highly recommended.'
Police History Society Journal

'Its no-nonsense portrayal of life in the police will give readers a memorable literary experience.'
Suffolk Journal

'All of the stories are told with Dick Kirby's acerbic, black humour in a compelling style, by a detective who was there.'
American Police Beat

'A series of gripping, individual stories.'
Daily Express

'A superb description of crime-busting at the front end.'
Bertram's Books

'Dick Kirby . . . knows how to bring his coppers to life on each page.'
Joseph Wambaugh, Author of *The Choirboys*

'Impeccable research, interviews and documentation, written in Kirby's delightful, conversational style.'
Police Memorabilia Collectors' Club

'Kirby writes with authority and clarity . . . highly recommended.'
Real Crime Magazine

'A well-researched book . . . written by an experienced, natural raconteur.'
History By The Yard

'He is uniquely placed to draw on those sources which really matter.'
London Police Pensioner

This book has a triple dedication:

*First, to Michael Stuart Moore QC, who came out to bat for
the Flying Squad, not once but on many occasions,
and in doing so knocked up an impressive number of runs.*

Next, to all the men and women of the Flying Squad, past and present.

*Last, and by no means least, to Ann and all the other Flying Squad wives,
who waited, wondered and worried.*

Scotland Yard's Flying Squad

100 Years of Crime Fighting

DICK KIRBY

Foreword by

JOHN O'CONNOR

Former Commander of the Flying Squad

First published in Great Britain in 2019 by
Pen & Sword True Crime
An imprint of
Pen & Sword Books Ltd
Yorkshire – Philadelphia

Copyright © Dick Kirby 2019

HB ISBN 978 1 52675 213 0
PB ISBN 978 1 52675 217 8

A CIP catalogue record for this book is
available from the British Library.

Printed and bound in the UK by TJ International Ltd, Padstow,
Cornwall.

Pen & Sword Books Limited incorporates the imprints of Atlas,
Archaeology, Aviation, Discovery, Family History, Fiction, History,
Maritime, Military, Military Classics, Politics, Select, Transport, True
Crime, Air World, Frontline Publishing, Leo Cooper, Remember
When, Seaforth Publishing, The Praetorian Press, Wharncliffe
Local History, Wharncliffe Transport, Wharncliffe True Crime
and White Owl.

For a complete list of Pen & Sword titles please contact

PEN & SWORD BOOKS LIMITED
47 Church Street, Barnsley, South Yorkshire, S70 2AS, England
E-mail: enquiries@pen-and-sword.co.uk
Website: www.pen-and-sword.co.uk

Or
PEN AND SWORD BOOKS
1950 Lawrence Rd, Havertown, PA 19083, USA
E-mail: Uspen-and-sword@casematepublishers.com
Website: www.penandswordbooks.com

Contents

About the Author

Dick Kirby was born in 1943 in the East End of London and joined the Metropolitan Police in 1967. Half of his 26 years' service as a detcctive was spent with the Yard's Serious Crime Squad and the Flying Squad.

Married, with four children and five grandchildren, Kirby lives in a Suffolk village with his wife. He writes for newspapers and magazines, reviews books, films and music and is a consultant for a television series. He also appears on radio and television and writes memoirs, biographies and true crime books – this is his eighteenth.

Kirby can be visited on his website: www.dickkirby.com.

Acknowledgements

My thanks go firstly to John O'Connor for his very kind foreword. He served as a detective sergeant and detective chief inspector in the Flying Squad, before becoming its commander; he knows what he's talking about. Also, to Brigadier Henry Wilson, Matt Jones and Tara Moran of Pen & Sword Books for their unfailing help and enthusiasm, and to George Chamier for his lynx-eyed editing.

Next, my thanks go to those indefatigable behind-the-scenes people without whose help I would have floundered badly from the start: Susi Rogol, editor of the *London Police Pensioner* magazine, Paul Bickley of the Crime Museum, New Scotland Yard, Mick Carter of the ReCIDivists' Luncheon Club.

My thanks also go to those who contributed so generously and gave so much of their time to this book: Terry Allen; Roger Baldry; Robert Bartlett; Bob Bews; Trevor Binnington; Michael Brooker; Mike Bucknole FNAVA, BA (Hons), PgC; John Bunn; Mark Burdis; Dave Butt; Mick Carroll; 'Steve Collins'; Bob Fenton QGM; Gerry Gallagher; Mick Geraghty; Mick Gray; John G. D. Grieve CBE, QPM, BA (Hons), MPhil, HonDL, Professor Emeritus; Gordon Harrison; Ron Heal; Roy Herridge, QPM; the late Bob Higgins; Terry Hobbs; Marion Jones; Peter Jones; David Kelly QPM; Alan Knapp GM; Nick Larkey; Dick Leach; Gordon Livingstone; Tony Lundy; Duncan MacRae; Iain Malone; the late Reed McGeorge; Paul Millen; Terry Mills; the late Terry O'Connell QPM; Albert Patrick; Vince Payne; Julia Pearce; Mick Petra; Arthur Porter BEM; Clive Pritchard; Peter Redford: Gordon Reynolds; Peter Rimmer; David Ryan; Jon Shatford; John Simmonds; Roger Smith; Charlie Snape; Peter Spindler BA; Tony Stevens; Michael Stuart Moore QC; Michael Stubbs; Craig Turner; Dennis Walkington; Barry Watters; Graham 'Chalky' White; Peter Wilton; Neil Wraith; Andy Yeoman and Tony Yeoman.

My thanks for the use of photographs go to: Terry Allen; Mark Burdis; Roger Charsley; Bob Fenton; Mick Gray; Marion Jones; Alan Knapp; Dick Leach; Gordon Livingstone; Nicholas Pearson OBE; Arthur Porter; John Simmonds; Michael Stuart Moore and

Tony Yeoman; others come from the author's collection. Whilst every effort has been made to trace copyright holders, Pen & Sword Books and I apologise for any inadvertent omissions.

Since this is my eighteenth book, I consider myself quite an experienced author – less experienced, to my shame, is my expertise in mastering the mysteries of cyberspace. Thankfully, Sue and Steve Cowper, my daughter and son-in-law, have persistently come galloping to my rescue to ensure that everything is readable and see-able.

To them, and the rest of my family, I owe a huge debt for their unending love, support and encouragement: my sons, Mark and Robert, my youngest daughter Barbara Jerreat, her husband Rich and their children, Sam and Annie Grace (who always puts me in my place) and the rest of my talented grandchildren, Emma Cowper B. Mus, Jessica Cowper B. Mus and Harry Cowper.

Most of all I owe to my dear wife Ann, who for over half a century has taken over the helm of my sometimes rudderless ship, to ensure that it stays on course.

Dick Kirby
Suffolk, 2018

Foreword

John O'Connor

Former Commander of the Flying Squad

There is nobody better qualified than Dick Kirby to write a book about the Flying Squad. He served on the Squad with distinction for many years and he has created a lasting tribute to the most successful and controversial department of the Metropolitan Police Service.

Dick presents his subject with impeccable research, characteristic honesty and humour. He pulls no punches and deals with both successes and problems.

The Flying Squad was created to deal with the ever-changing patterns of crime which it continues to do, to this day. There is no doubt that crime has become more violent and more dangerous for those who have to enforce the law. Like most coppers of his era, Dick despises the greedy thugs who exploit the weak and vulnerable. Clearly, the Flying Squad has played a decisive role in redressing the balance.

Many senior officers had difficulty in supporting aggressive policing but were happy to bask in the reflected glory that it produced. Following a particularly brutal and high-profile robbery, a former Commissioner said in an interview, 'You can always rely on the Flying Squad to bring home the bacon.' Therein lies the dilemma: they need the Squad to get results, but are reluctant to back them when the complaints come in.

In the early seventies Sir Robert Mark launched an unprecedented attack on the CID. He was quoted as saying that a successful police force catches more criminals than it employs. A famous photograph of Sir Robert was published with his hands together as if in prayer, with the byline, 'I don't know what they do to the enemy but they frighten the life out of me.'

The Squad survived, but its influence in the service was greatly undermined. Complaints, many of them malicious, poured in. Allegations of misconduct came from other police forces; most were unfounded. These were difficult times. Changes were inevitable, the Squad was decentralized and given the responsibility of dealing with all armed robberies. The response was remarkable and heralded the most successful period in the Squad's history.

Dick highlights the major achievements and gives credit to Criminal Intelligence and the police firearms departments with whom the Squad tackled armed robbery, head on. It gradually dawned on the criminals that armed robbery was a mugs' game.

These were halcyon days for the Squad. Coupled with the use of supergrasses, they had never been so effective. They made the fictional television series *The Sweeney* look like a picnic in the park.

The story is not yet complete, there are more successes to come. The current Flying Squad are creating legends of their own; I hope that they have a Dick Kirby to record them.

Prologue

A gang of extremely violent Jamaican Yardies had carried out a series of armed robberies, the first on 30 April 1988, when a jeweller's premises at Southall Broadway was robbed. The balaclava'd, armed attackers had abseiled through a previously weakened ceiling into the shop, letting off two shots, one of which hit the shop's owner, before decamping with property valued at £90,000. There was a further attack on another jeweller's four months later. Again, a shot was fired at the staff, and jewellery valued at £384,000 was stolen. Lastly, in October 1988, the gang robbed a branch of the Abbey National Building Society, netting the raiders £62,000.

It appeared these robberies were linked, and an investigation commenced under the codename 'Operation Ruffe' at the Barnes office of the Flying Squad.

One man, said to be the leader, came under suspicion; and as from 8 December 1988 full surveillance was carried out at his Acton address. This was exceptionally difficult since it was a particularly sensitive and vulnerable area for police to visit, plus the gang were known to use anti-surveillance techniques and scanning equipment to monitor police radio transmissions.

By Flying Squad standards, it was not a lengthy observation; at 2.50 p.m. on Wednesday, 14 December, the leader and his associate, Brian Beckford, drove to Brassie Avenue, W3, parked up and walked down to the Post Office situated in Old Oak Common Lane.

Detective Sergeants Alan Knapp and Steve Thomas were heading the Squad's surveillance team; as the two suspects entered the crowded Post Office, so Knapp followed them in. As he told me, 'The leader was wearing a threequarter-length sheepskin coat and underneath it he was carrying a sawn-off shotgun. Fortunately for me, they decided not to carry out the robbery as the Post Office was jammed with old-age pensioners drawing their Christmas money.'

The queue of customers was slow-moving; the two men signalled to each other and left, separately. It could have been the crowded Post Office that dissuaded them from carrying out a robbery there and then; equally, it could have been a 'dry-run', a tactic often favoured by armed robbers.

But at 4.33 that afternoon, from his vantage point, Thomas saw five men at the leader's address assisting each other to put on garments over the clothing in which they had arrived at the flat. The gang leader got into one car, the other four into another, and they drove to Oak Way, where the leader parked his vehicle; he then left the scene. The other vehicle continued to Brassie Avenue and parked exactly where it had stopped almost two hours previously; the four men got out and walked the 300 yards to the Post Office.

Their movements were being carefully monitored; the gang sauntered past the Post Office, then suddenly turned, pulled on balaclavas and, as three of them produced handguns, rushed into the Post Office – the police order to 'attack' was given.

Sergeants Knapp and Thomas, both armed with Smith & Wesson Model 64 revolvers, dashed forward, looked into the Post Office and saw the armed robbers and at least twenty customers, some of whom were lying on the floor. At that moment, the Post Office's audible alarm sounded.

Standing on either side of the doors, the officers shouted to the throng of pre-Christmas shoppers to stand back and take cover – Thomas had to physically drag an elderly man to the ground, to prevent him from walking into what was a potential line of fire.

And then, things happened very fast indeed.

The gang rushed out of the Post Office, firing indiscriminately towards the two officers, who from a distance of six metres and despite having shouted, 'Stop – armed police!' simply could not immediately return fire; their shots could have passed through the glass of the Post Office door, endangering the lives of the staff or customers.

So, facing a fusillade of bullets, completely exposed and with no body armour, Thomas and Knapp waited for the gang to fan out before firing all six shots from their revolvers. They then dropped to one knee in order to reload, but a shot hit Knapp in the base of his thumb which caused considerable damage; the force of it knocked the revolver from his hand and him to the ground.

Thomas had been shot in the hip; the bullet exited from his left buttock, but despite this shocking injury – it had narrowly missed his main artery and spine – and even though his gun was empty, he nevertheless started to chase Beckford, before collapsing on the pavement. Both the police and the robbers had fired twelve shots; Detective Sergeant Bob Bews, who was behind Knapp and Thomas at the time of the shooting, later discovered a bullet lodged in his clothing. Four more were found in a nearby telephone kiosk.

Two of the suspects, Andrew Clarke and Edwin McKenzie, raced off along Old Oak Common Lane towards Western Avenue. They were chased by Detective Constable Patrick Phelan, unarmed except for a police baton and well aware that two of his colleagues had been shot. Clarke discarded his gun, although Phelan could see that McKenzie was still carrying his weapon, and both men kept running. The sun had set an hour earlier, and when the robbers reached an unlit service road by a block of flats, it had gone quite dark. For a second time Phelan called upon the two men to stop, and this time, McKenzie did; he turned and pointed his Colt .45 directly at Phelan from a distance of 10 yards. Phelan moved to the building line for cover; but when the two robbers climbed over fences in a desperate attempt to escape, Phelan followed them, in those dark and isolated conditions, until McKenzie was found cowering in some rubble. His pistol was empty; all the rounds had been fired at Thomas and Knapp. Clarke, who had been shot in the throat, was chased, with enormous courage by 16-year-old Louis Bartils, and although Clarke escaped, his discarded, bloodstained jacket was recovered by the boy, who handed it to police.

Meanwhile, two other members of the gang, Beckford and Orville Murray, were sprinting towards their getaway car parked in Brassie Avenue. Running directly towards them were Detective Constables Tom Bestford and Mark Pudney, aware that their colleagues had been shot and that Beckwith – unlike them – was still armed.

Bestford rugby-tackled Murray to the ground; Pudney knocked Beckwith to the pavement. The 9mm Luger that lay between them contained six live rounds; fortunately, it had jammed.

Both Thomas and Knapp were taken to Hammersmith hospital. As Knapp told me, 'Steve said to me, "I don't know what you're doing here – I'm the one who's been shot!" I replied, "So have I!"'

The gang leader was arrested (he was later acquitted on a re-trial), and six months later, Clarke was also arrested. He had fled to Jamaica, but the date, time and flight number of his return flight was made known to the Flying Squad. Unfortunately for him, he slipped coming down the aircraft's steps and acquired a nose bleed – and providentially, the blood from his nose and the blood on the discarded jacket proved to be an exact match.

The first jury at the Old Bailey were unable to agree, but the second one, despite hearing most aggressive questioning of the officers by the defence barristers, did, and on 1 June 1990 exemplary sentences were imposed.

Edwin McKenzie, described as a self-employed musician and living apart from his wife and six children, had a liking for cannabis, since six of his eight previous convictions were for possession of that commodity; he was sentenced to 17 years' imprisonment.

Similarly, Orville Murray possessed eight convictions; several were for beating up women and damaging their property, plus more adventurous escapades such as ripping a gold medallion from a victim's neck. He received 18 years' imprisonment, as did Brian Beckford. He appeared to have an identity crisis, since he was also known as Brian Walford, Danny Beckford and Ras Napthine. His criminal past was more impressive than the others'. Having left full-time education between the ages of twelve and thirteen, he was unable to recall when he had last been in honest employment, and made up for it by taking cars which did not belong to him on nine occasions and inflicting various assaults, including one on his girlfriend, from whom he stole a gold chain.

It was not known when Andrew Clarke came to this country; he did so illegally because his real name was Romeo Dennis, and he had been convicted in Jamaica in 1972 of four cases of robbery with aggravation, for which he received 10 years' hard labour and sixteen strokes of the birch. He should have confessed all of his transgressions at the time; fifteen months later, for another three cases of robbery with aggravation, he was sentenced to a total of twenty years' imprisonment and was released on parole in 1981. Now, he received another twenty years at the Old Bailey.

His Honour Judge Laughland praised 'a display of great courage, in my view, by officers of the Metropolitan Police', and one month later, young Louis Bartils was presented with £250 by the High Sheriff of Greater London for his public-spirited action.

There was a string of commendations from the commissioner for many of the officers employed on Operation Ruffe, including high commendations for Knapp, Thomas and Phelan, and cheques from the Bow Street Reward Fund. There was another unofficial (but much prized) commendation – it came in the form of a cartoon published in the *Daily Mail* by the cartoonist JAK (Raymond Jackson), a good friend to police, depicting the shoot-out. He presented the original to Bob Bews of the Flying Squad.

On 14 May 1992, awards of the George Medal to Knapp and Thomas were gazetted, as was the award of the Queen's Commendation for Brave Conduct to Phelan.

All of the officers had exhibited enormous bravery – the injuries sustained by Knapp and Thomas would continue to plague them for years – but Operation Ruffe exemplified the reasons for the existence of the Flying Squad.

Over 70 years before those awards were bestowed, the authorities had decided that a mobile, top crime-fighting unit, made up of fearless, resolute men, was required to combat the rise of crime in London following the end of the First World War.

This book demonstrates how it came about.

CHAPTER 1

Genesis

This is not intended to be a history of Scotland Yard's Flying Squad – rather is it a collection of stories of some of the remarkable cases which the Squad dealt with during its 100-year history. But inevitably, the events which shaped the way the Squad was formed and then continued to evolve do creep into the book. I have tried to keep these historical matters to a minimum to avoid distracting the reader from some of the astonishing accounts of brilliant criminal detection and jaw-dropping bravery on the part of the Squad's detectives. I have mentioned them only where I have thought it important to do so, to provide explanations as to what happened, when, and why.

★

Before, during and after the end of the First World War in November 1918 which claimed the lives of 18 million people, not only victorious Britain but the rest of the world was in a parlous state. In March 1918, a pandemic known as Spanish 'flu swept the planet, and by the time it had been contained, two years later, 100 million people had died. The Russian Tsarist regime had been toppled by the Bolsheviks, who in July 1918 had slaughtered the imperial family, and there was a real fear that the anarchy could spread to England. In August 1918 one third of the 18,000 Metropolitan Police officers went on strike; two months later, world trade had all but collapsed; and the crime figures went through the ceiling.

Armed hold-ups became an almost daily occurrence, the number of house- and shopbreakings soared, pickpockets were an infestation and gang warfare, which had previously been confined to the race tracks, where gang members had been contemptuously known as 'pests', now flooded the streets, and pitched battles were fought. Something had to be done, and Frederick Porter Wensley was the man to do it.

By 1916, this former gardener/telegraph boy who had served in the Metropolitan Police since 1887 was a detective chief inspector at New Scotland Yard. Wensley had served for 25 years in London's East End and had been a brilliant thief-taker. He broke all of the pettifogging rules laid down by the pompous uniform superintendents in charge of their fiefdoms. He was supposed to investigate crime only in his area; if he identified the thief responsible for a felony who lived in another part of London, the regulations directed that he submit a report to the superintendent of that area, requesting permission to come and make an arrest. That consent was not always forthcoming, so this is what Wensley did. If an informant told him that an offence was being committed anywhere in the Metropolitan Police Area, Wensley went straight out and arrested the perpetrators, no matter where they were living. If he heard a gang was up to no good, he and his detectives would don disguises, acquire a horse-drawn wagon and follow them until it was time to make an arrest. He worked as an undercover officer, arrested robbers, burglars and receivers in their hundreds and murderers by the score, one of the latter a double murderer, when he was off-duty. He smashed up the ethnic Odessian and Bessarabian gangs once and for all, and put away the home-grown 'Vendettas', who had terrorized East London for twenty years for the same amount of time.

The officious superintendents were scandalized but they dared say nothing; Freemason Wensley was not only supported by no less a personage than the Assistant Commissioner (Crime), Sir Melville Macnaghten CB, KPM, but he was also much admired by the press and the judiciary. His commendations passed the three hundred mark; when the first King's Police Medal was struck in 1909 it was awarded to Wensley, the man who, twenty years previously had nailed strips of bicycle tyres to the soles of his boots in an effort to surreptitiously catch 'Jack the Ripper'.[1]

So when Macnaghten's successor, Sir Basil Thomson KCB, asked Wensley in 1916 if he thought the Criminal Investigation Department could be streamlined, made more fluid and flexible, Wensley modestly admitted – since he had been doing just that, for years – that it could. But not right then; Europe was still in the grip of a world war, with no indication as to the outcome. It was not until 22 October 1919, when the commissioner had split London into four areas with Wensley as one of the detective superintendents in charge, that his plan was put into operation.

---

[1] For further details of this extraordinary man, see *Whitechapel's Sherlock Holmes: The Casebook of Fred Wensley, OBE, KPM, Victorian Crime Buster*, Pen & Sword True Crime, 2014 and *The Sweeney: The First Sixty Years of Scotland Yard's Crimebusting Flying Squad 1919-1978*, Wharncliffe Local History, 2011

To the fury of their senior officers, he 'borrowed' a dozen of the best detectives from all over London and told them that they would go, anytime, anywhere in London where there was a prevalence of crime and hunt down, arrest, smash up and disperse the gangs. In what was called 'The Mobile Patrol Experiment', Wensley provided his men with two covered horse-drawn wagons leased from the Great Western Railway. Spyholes were cut into the canvas hoods, interchangeable boards giving the names and addresses of businesses suitable for the areas that they were going to patrol were slotted into the sides of the wagons, and as the horses clip-clopped into Whitehall they were apparently no different from any of the other thousands of wagons in the streets of London; except, of course, that these contained detectives concealed in the back. The commissioner had demanded that the Mobile Patrol's record of work should be submitted to him after twelve months to see if the experiment was sound; there was never any fear that it would not be. Seeing a team of pickpockets at work, a couple of detectives would unobtrusively slip out of the wagon and mingle with the crowd until the time was right to arrest them. Known thieves would be identified and tailed, on foot, for hours if necessary. Often, seeing thieves about to break into a car, or a shop about to be burgled, would result in the miscreants being pounced upon, apparently out of thin air.

There was only one aspect of the criminal world in which the wagons were less than useful and that was the growing emergence of 'The Motor Car Bandit'. Hooks and chains attached to high-powered vehicles would be used to rip out grilled bars on the windows of premises, before the villains loaded up with the loot and made a speedy getaway.

Wensley solved that, too; he acquired two Crossley Tenders, once owned by the Royal Flying Corps. These extraordinary looking 26 h.p. vehicles had tyres so narrow that road adhesion, especially in wet conditions, was highly treacherous; they had no front brakes; their top speed was said to be 40 mph (although 20–25 mph was a more realistic estimate); and the aerials fitted to the roof, to receive Morse transmissions from the Yard, could be raised or lowered from the back. They were later fitted with seven-valve receivers (which had a 105-mile range) and three-valve transmitters (with a 50-mile range), and under the khaki hood up to a dozen detectives could be concealed. Like the horse-drawn wagons, they utilized spyholes and interchangeable boards, and by 15 September 1920 the tenders – they were nicknamed 'Bedsteads' – were ready to go. What's more, the detectives knew exactly who they were looking for. Their informants had told them of a highly dangerous motorized gang who had been terrorizing shopkeepers and breaking into shops over a wide area, in both North and South London.

★

Police Constable 727 'P' Charles Nealon of Camberwell police station was representative of the uniform police officers of that era: tough and resolute. So when he saw William Wood, Frederick Cole and Arthur Williams breaking into the warehouse of Mr Foot, a ladies' tailor in Coldharbour Lane, Brixton one September night, he was unable to blow his whistle to summon help because he was off-duty in plain clothes – but he didn't hesitate. He rushed in to arrest them and was beaten to the ground, his assailants using an eight-sided iron jemmy and leaving him there, unconscious, in a pool of blood.

Nealon was unaware of the identities of his assailants, but the men of the Squad knew who they were. At 9.00 p.m. on 15 September, one tender under the command of Detective Inspector Charles Cooper began a patrol in the Camden Town area, with Detective Inspector Walter Hambrook in the second tender starting to patrol south of the river – both without any success. But on the second night's patrol, Hambrook – in company with Detective Inspector Albert Grosse – and other officers spotted the gang in a Ford van and followed them as they reconnoitred shops in the vicinity of Tooting High Road, until they travelled to the Elephant and Castle area. There they garaged the van and dispersed. The other tender was called in, and a combined observation was set up which lasted 31 hours, with the officers sleeping in shifts; at 4 o'clock in the morning of Saturday, 18 September the gang reappeared. The officers saw Thomas George Burfield, Henry Jackson, John Henry Morbin and George Smith – the latter carrying the eight-sided jemmy wrapped in newspaper – walking separately, a little distance apart, in the Old Kent Road. Within 45 minutes they were picked up by the Ford van and were driven, by a circuitous route over Westminster Bridge, to Parliament Square. There the van stopped, Morbin left the vehicle and whistled twice. From the shadows of Westminster Abbey, three more of the gang – Wood, Williams and Cole – emerged and got into the van.

In Victoria Street the vehicle stopped near to a silversmith's and three of the gang got out, possibly to reconnoitre the shop or perhaps to see if they were being observed – but whatever the reason, they then rejoined the others in the van, which drove off.

In Pimlico Road the van stopped outside a clothier's shop and several of the men got out, one of them grasping the jemmy, and went towards the shop. Suddenly, one of the gang leapt from the van and ran towards the others, shouting, 'Quick, it's a tumble!' – he had either seen the detectives' tender or two uniform police constables who were approaching – and there was a rush to get back on board the van, which roared away, with the tender in close pursuit. As the van drove towards Cliveden Place, the tender pulled in front of it causing it to come to a halt, whereupon two of the gang jumped from the front of the van, the other five from the back. Shouting 'Kill the bastards!', 40-year-old William Wood led the attack, wielding a heavy life-preserver[2] with which he lashed out left and right, before cracking Hambrook over the head with it; as he sank to his knees, Wood savagely kicked him. Within seconds, Wood was felled by a truncheon and, as a thunderstorm broke and lightning flashed overhead, astonished residents of Belgravia stared from their windows, roused by the yells and screams of the occupants of the tender and van. The rain poured down as the battle raged, the gang being armed with life-preservers, daggers and knuckledusters, the police with truncheons. The gang were finally knocked into submission, and a search of their van revealed a collection of iron bars, wedges – and of course, the eight-sided jemmy.

The battered burglars appeared at Westminster Police Court later that morning – most refused to give their addresses – charged with possessing housebreaking implements by night and offensive weapons, and with violently assaulting police officers. When evidence of arrest was given, the magistrate, Mr Hay Halkett, declared that the capture of the gang was 'one of the cleverest of which I've ever heard'.

Whilst they were on remand, Wood, Cole and Williams were positively identified as those who had attacked PC Nealon.

Having been found guilty, the seven men came up for judgement at the Old Bailey on 2 December 1920 before the Common Serjeant, Sir Henry Dickens, who, like his famous novelist father, tended to be a compassionate man. He demonstrated this by sentencing both Morbin and Burfield (neither of whom had previous convictions) to twelve months' imprisonment with hard labour.[3]

---

[2] Cosh
[3] Hard labour was an additional form of punishment for sentences of up two years' imprisonment. It included industrial work, oakum-picking and using a treadmill. It was abolished in 1948.

Not so the others. They had terrible records, 52-year-old Smith in particular, who was on licence following a ten-year sentence of penal servitude[4] for shopbreaking and causing grievous bodily harm to two constables. This latter he had effected with a jemmy in one hand and in the other, a condensed milk tin filled with lead weighing 4¾lb (2 kilos) with a rope through it; using these two formidable weapons, he had knocked the constables unconscious. He was described by Inspector Cooper as being 'one of the most dangerous criminals in London'.

Commenting that the attack on PC Nealon was 'the worst feature of the case', the Common Serjeant sentenced Smith, Wood and Williams each to eight years' penal servitude and, since the jury had judged them to be 'habitual criminals', that sentence was to be followed by six years' preventative detention.[5]

Williams came in for special castigation from the judge for committing gross perjury in the witness box. 'The way in which you called on the Almighty while doing it was perfectly shocking!' he was told.

'Cole is also a dangerous criminal', Cooper told the court, adding, 'and I think that Williams and Cole were the "brains" of the gang.'

Cole, however, was obviously thought not to be a habitual criminal, so he was sentenced to six years' penal servitude and Jackson, to three.

Calling the Squad before him, Sir Henry commended them for 'their courage and ability in bringing this gang to justice' and especially commended PC Nealon: 'No one could have shown higher courage.' The Commissioner agreed, highly commending Nealon, to whom he also awarded £5 which, considering a constable's weekly wage at that time was £3 5s 0d, was well worth having.

Two other matters are worth mentioning. Firstly, when the magistrate at Westminster court asked Inspector Grosse if the driver of the van had been charged, the officer artfully replied,

---

[4] The Penal Servitude Act 1857 replaced transportation; its sole purpose was not to try to reform, but to punish the prisoner. It covered terms of imprisonment from three years to life; for the first nine months of the sentence, prisoners were kept in solitary confinement and then were employed on public works or for private contractors, often in quarries. It was abolished in 1948.

[5] Under the Prevention of Crime Act 1908, persons over the age of sixteen who had been convicted of crime on three occasions and were leading a dishonest life were classed as 'habitual criminals' and, having been sentenced to penal servitude, could be sentenced to a further period of preventative detention not exceeding ten years and not less than five, for the protection of the public.

'Not at present'. In fact, he wasn't charged at all. Hambrook went rather further; referring to the driver, he wrote, 'We afterwards proved [he] was [the gang's] innocent tool.' It was quite possible that this was the earliest example of the Flying Squad using a 'participating informant', in other words a gang member who had provided police with pertinent information, taken a minor role in the offence such as look-out or driver, escaped when the gang was arrested and was never caught. It was considered to be unorthodox police work by those critical of law and order, but it would be a weapon in the Squad's armoury for years to come.

And the second matter was that four days after the Squad's arrests there appeared a piece in the *Daily Mail* by the crime correspondent, Mr G. T. Crook, who wrote, in part:

> Flying squads of picked detectives with motor transport at their disposal were based at police headquarters, ready to go anywhere at any time . . . The result of these live operations have been remarkably successful . . . scores of the most daring and dangerous criminals in London have been caught. They have been picked up by the flying squads at all hours of the day and night, some while actually engaged on a burglarious enterprise, while others have been stopped with housebreaking implements in their possession.

The name stuck. By 1921 the term 'Flying Squad' was in common usage in reports filed at Scotland Yard, where it was part of C1 Department. In Cockney rhyming slang they were known as 'The Sweeney Todd' (later abbreviated to 'The Sweeney'), 'The Odd Lot', 'The Tommy Dodds' or 'The Heavy Mob'. In the police they were simply referred to as 'The Squad'.

CHAPTER 2

Racetrack Gangs, Dips and Running-board Daring

The Squad's uses were many and varied; for some ten years they would be used intermittently to raid nightclubs and brothels and also arrest drug dealers. But one of their biggest problems were the gangsters, pickpockets and – as the late Detective Superintendent Bob Higgins would describe them to me – 'riff-raff' who infested the racecourses.

Robert Jacobs, William Hatton and Belcher Lee were 'members of an organized gang who frequent the outside of racecourses and railway stations and are a pest to society', Detective Inspector Grosse told the bench at Kingston-on-Thames police court, after the gang were seen speaking to two men in a threatening manner and demanding £1 from them. Their attempt to escape justice by boarding a ferry was thwarted, their excuse that they were there for the fishing was disbelieved and they all went to hard labour for three months.

At the same court, a year later, Aaron Jacobs, who in the past had convictions which included robbery with violence, for which he had received hard labour as well as 'a bashing' – twelve lashes with the cat o'nine tails – was overheard to say to his companions, 'If any of the fuckers are here today, they'll catch it.' After he tried to conceal a hatchet he had in his possession, and when Inspector Grosse told the Chairman of the Bench that Jacobs was looked on in the East End as 'a terror', he, too, was packed off to hard labour for three months.

Bookmakers were often too terrified to give evidence, and when Flying Squad officers at Kempton Park racecourse saw three men led by George Moss (reported to be 'a man of large stature' and of whom it was said that when he was in drink, 'He was the maddest man in South London') shake a hammer in a bookmaker's face, after which he was handed money, it was the officers who gave evidence. Inspector Grosse told the Bench at Feltham, 'The Commissioner of Police has been compelled to take action in the matter', and the man who was known in his cups as 'Mad Mossy' was sentenced to twelve months' imprisonment with hard labour.

But these were merely isolated instances. There were often pitched battles between rival gangs at the racetracks; there were many different gangs, although the two main contenders were the Italian Mob, led by Charles 'Darby' Sabini and his brothers, and their adversaries, the Birmingham Boys, whose leader was Billy Kimber. After Billy Kimber was shot by a Sabini associate, Alfie Solomon (he was acquitted), the Birmingham Boys decided that retribution was required and chose the first day of the Derby meeting in 1921 as a suitable date.

The Birmingham Boys left the meeting early in their hired charabanc and, pulling off the road in Ewell, Surrey, waited for the Sabini gang on their way back to London. When two cars appeared, the charabanc pulled out in front of them and, armed with guns, hammers, axes and house-bricks, the Birmingham Boys mercilessly set about the occupants of the cars, hacking, chopping and slicing until they suddenly realized that – due, presumably, to faulty intelligence – the men who lay on the ground with their fingers hacked off, their faces slashed and skulls cracked were not the Italian Mob at all; they were their allies, the Leeds Crowd.

It was initially thought that this had been a Sinn Féin riot, but when Inspector Stevens of the Flying Squad arrived at the scene he realized who was responsible.

The gang was found at the George and Dragon public house on Kingston Hill by a police sergeant, whose superintendent (still believing the IRA was responsible) had taken the precaution of arming him. He placed twenty-eight of the gang under arrest ('I shall shoot the first man who tries to escape!'), and twenty-three of them were convicted at Guildford Assizes of offences including committing grievous bodily harm and received sentences ranging from nine months' to three years' imprisonment.

★

Within fifteen months of joining the police, Henry Arthur Finbar Corbett – at one-eighth of an inch over the minimum height requirement of five feet eight, he was built like a tank and was known as 'Chesty' due to his punishing daily workouts – became a member of the Flying Squad before even being appointed as a detective, due to his encyclopaedic knowledge – and fanatical hatred – of pickpockets or 'dips'. He worked a lone patrol, often in disguise, and arrested groups of three, four and (on several occasions) six pickpockets, singlehandedly. William Gill, who was arrested for being a suspected person at Liverpool Street Station, told the Bench at the Guildhall Justice Rooms that whenever

Corbett saw a man with a 'black' past, he ran him in on sight; being one thus described, he was sent to hard labour for three months.

But not all officers were fortunate to be as tough as Chesty Corbett; one was kicked unconscious at a railway station and another was thrown on to the tracks. When Detective Geoffrey Pike of the Flying Squad saw Michael Gold steal a wallet from a passenger on an omnibus and followed him into a pub to arrest him, Gold said, 'Don't do that, Mr Pike and I'll give you a fiver.' His offer declined, Gold then hit and kicked the detective, who knocked him down; several onlookers grabbed hold of Pike, who shouted that he was a police officer.

'He's not!' bellowed Gold. 'He's a blackmailer!' He then head-butted Pike and kneed him in the stomach, before running off. He was chased, caught and subdued, and when he appeared before Westminster Police Court he asked for a remand, commenting sadly, 'I think my jaw is broken.'

One officer who was very tough indeed was a former Durham miner named Frederick Dew 'Nutty' Sharpe. A prolific thief-taker, he was called to Wensley's office in 1922 to be told, 'We're putting you in the Flying Squad.' It was a prudent move.

In 1927, Sharpe – by now a detective sergeant – was on patrol in a Flying Squad Lea Francis tourer when he spotted three known pickpockets by Shoreditch Church. He followed them on foot, and other pickpockets joined them until they were nine in total. Sharpe overheard them say, 'We're making for Poplar and Canning Town to work the tubs.'[1] It was a Friday, the day when dock workers from that area were paid.

The pickpockets went to a bus stop at the junction of Church Street and Bethnal Green Road, and after two buses arrived, the dips hustled the passengers without making any attempt to board the buses. But when they boarded a third bus, eight of the men sitting upstairs and the ninth, James Bryan, staying downstairs, the Squad car followed them to the bus stop at Vallance Road, and Sharpe, together with Detective Sergeant Dan Gooch, boarded the bus. When Gooch saw another of the men, Joseph Barrow, put his hand into a passenger's breast pocket, Sharpe quietly gave instructions for the bus to go straight to Bethnal Green police station, where the dips were escorted into the charge room.

'It was a good job that it wasn't an open-topped bus', lamented one of the gang, 'or we'd have been over the side like a lot of bloody monkeys!'

---

[1] Buses

At Old Street Police Court the following day, after Sharpe had given evidence of arrest, the Magistrate, Mr Ivan Snell, said:

> I have never seen this done before. I think you and the other officers ought to be congratulated on the extraordinary smartness of the capture you made. They seem to be very well known and may be presumed to be one of the worse gangs in London brought to book.

Two weeks later, at the London Sessions, the Deputy Chairman, Mr H. W. W. Wilberforce, dealt with them for being 'incorrigible rogues'[2] and imposed sentences of hard labour ranging from four to twelve months. Mr Wilberforce added his own congratulations, and when Sharpe appeared before him a week later, having this time arrested a lone pickpocket, the deputy Chairman said, with a wintry smile, 'Rather small fry for you, Sharpe?'

In the years which followed, promotion led Gooch, then Sharpe, to become head of the Flying Squad, but it was the case of the nine pickpockets that caught the public's imagination; the details of the arrests went nationwide, then worldwide.

But before the term 'Flying Squad' was on everybody's lips, a new car had to be added to the Squad's fleet.

★

The pickpockets' arrest had been aided by the officers crewing one of the 14 h.p. Lea Francis tourers. Known as 'Leafs' and capable of a top speed of 75 mph, these vehicles were fine for surveillance work or getting to a destination quickly, but all too often they came off second best when it was necessary to ram bandits' cars, which were often faster, bigger, heavier and more strongly constructed than the 'Leafs'.

The Squad acquired a black 4¼ litre Invicta, a 29.1 h.p. tourer capable of 90mph, and within days it was put to work. During the early hours of 24 July 1929, three known villains – Charles Lilley, Alfred John Head and Alfred Hayes – strongly suspected of smash and grab raids, were seen in Kennington in a powerful 30-98 h.p. Vauxhall. Police Constable 305 'CO' George 'Jack' Frost started

---

[2] Once a criminal had been convicted at the Police Court of being a suspected person under Section 4 of the Vagrancy Act 1824, he was adjudged to be a 'Rogue and a Vagabond'. If he was convicted of a further, similar offence, he could be committed to the Sessions, to be dealt with as an 'Incorrigible Rogue' and sentenced to up to twelve months' imprisonment.

up the Invicta, which was crewed by Detective Inspector Edward Ockey, then forty-seven years of age, and Detective Sergeant Ball. They were followed in a 'Leaf' by Detective Sergeant 'Jock' Weir and Detective Constables Green and Coates. The Vauxhall was soon spotted, and the two Squad vehicles began an unobtrusive tail, but when the gang stopped outside Studd & Millington's tailors shop in Victoria Street, Frost was parked 85 yards away, confident that the Invicta's acceleration could reach 60mph in 9½ seconds. Hayes and Lilley got out of the car, leaving Head at the wheel, while they went to hitch chains to the shop's barred window. At that point, Frost started the Invicta's engine, and this caused the two men to leap back into the Vauxhall, which roared away into Tothill Street; but the Invicta's acceleration was so great that within seconds the two cars were level. Travelling at 50mph in Buckingham Gate, the illuminated 'MP' sign was dropped, the gong was sounded and Ockey, shouting, 'Stop – we're police officers!' sprang from the Invicta on to the Vauxhall's running board, grabbing the driver, Head, by the collar of his jacket. Accelerating, Head bellowed, 'Knock him off!', and Hayes, who had threatened to 'brain' Ockey if he did not relinquish his grip on Head, did just that, hitting the back of Ockey's head with a jemmy while Lilley lashed out at Ockey's knuckles with an iron bar, and Ockey fell unconscious into the roadway, right in the path of the Invicta.

Frost was no more than 10 yards behind; how he managed to swerve around Ockey was nothing short of a miracle. In Buckingham Palace Road the Vauxhall shot across the junction with Grosvenor Road at almost 80mph, but as the Vauxhall slowed slightly to negotiate the right-hand bend into Pimlico Road, the Invicta suddenly accelerated, ramming the Vauxhall right on its offside and, as a tyre burst, turning it over. Imprudently, the gang decided to make a fight of it; two of them were pursued into a tenement where, using the tools with which they had attacked Ockey, they fought their way up the stairs before they were thoroughly subdued.

Ockey, meanwhile, was found by a patrolling police constable and taken to hospital. It was not until 8 August that he was able to give evidence at Westminster Police Court, and whilst Mr H. W. Wickham, counsel for the defence, rather contemptuously stated that 'this case has been very much overstated and overrated', the Police Divisional Surgeon, Dr A. M. Barlow disagreed, telling Mr Boyd, the Magistrate, 'The injury to Inspector Ockey's head was a severe one. The inspector was undoubtedly saved by his hair, which was coarse and thick and fortunately very long at the time.'

In rejecting Mr Wickham's comments, the Magistrate also refused his application for bail, and the three men were committed to the Old Bailey, where they all pleaded not guilty.

Lilley denied that he had assaulted Detective Constable Green or, indeed, any other officer. Furthermore, he stated he had not gone to the shop doorway in Victoria Street and, in any event, it had been he who had driven the Vauxhall, not Head. Neither Lilley nor his two co-defendants were believed by the jury and, said the Judge, they 'had been convicted on the clearest possible evidence'.

Detective Sergeant Weir told the court:

> These men were no doubt part of a very large gang of very desperate men who for some time past had been using this car and other cars for the purpose of shopbreaking and doing smash and grab raids in London and the suburbs. To my knowledge, this car had been used for one month. It was a very powerful car and on one occasion, the police car which was following was doing 70 miles per hour and this car left them far behind.

Sentencing the gang to penal servitude – three years for Lilley, four years for Head and five for Hayes – the Recorder of London, Sir Ernest Wild KC, said:

> The police showed considerable enterprise while their leader, Inspector Ockey, displayed great heroism. It is well that those who thought it right to undermine our police force should know what sort of man they were attacking. It is fortunate that the prisoner is not standing in the dock charged with murder. Had Ockey been killed, the prisoner would undoubtedly been hanged.

The foreman of the jury expressed 'our high admiration of the police officers in the case, especially Inspector Ockey', whom the commissioner highly commended and who was later presented with £15 from the Bow Street Reward Fund, awarded the King's Police Medal for gallantry and promoted to divisional detective inspector. Six of the other officers were commended by the commissioner, as well as being paid monetary awards, ranging from 7s 6d to 10 shillings.

There were many cases of Flying Squad running-board daring at this time – Detective Sergeant Cyril Woodcraft and another officer were both knocked off the same fast-moving car – 'You can't blame me for wanting to get away,' plaintively asked William Garner, who had been trying to break into a warehouse – but it was the Ockey case probably more than any other that brought the name of the Flying Squad to everybody's attention, and many decided to capitalize on it.

The police in Portsmouth, Brighton and Manchester decided they would have their own 'Flying Squads'; so did Paris, Cologne and Berlin. Dublin had a unit who called themselves 'The Flying Squadrons', and North Yorkshire had a fleet of Flying Squad motorcycles.

An advertisement for Austin cars told the public, 'They may be described with every justification as "The Flying Squad",' a greyhound by that name ran at White City and Edgar Wallace's play, *Flying Squad*, was shown at the Lyceum Theatre in London; it later became a film and J. Ord Hume composed 'The Flying Squad Quick March' for brass and military band.

More fast cars fitted with radio equipment were added to the Squad's fleet, and in 1929 arrests rose to 515, the personnel were increased to forty men and Walter Hambrook was promoted to detective chief inspector and became the head of the Flying Squad, which now formed part of C1 Department at Scotland Yard.

After just ten short years, the Flying Squad's star was in the ascendant; it had been crowned with success.

CHAPTER 3

Con-artists and Flying Squad Cunning

Tere was no let-up in Flying Squad officers leaping on to the running boards of bandits' cars in the 1930s. Detective Inspector William Cain and his team had followed Frank Street, William Carter and Arthur Toone for two hours on 15 March 1932 as they drove around looking at parked cars, until at 11.15 a.m., at Upper Norwood, Toone was seen to get into the car belonging to a leather goods manufacturer and drive off, with Carter and Street following in their car. Cain had already arranged to block off the road with another Squad vehicle, and now he jumped on to the running board of the car driven by Street but was pushed off by Carter. Cain dashed after the car as it tried to turn a corner, jumped on to the running board again and grabbed hold of Street, who tried several times to hit him with a spanner. The car then accelerated, mounted the pavement and crashed into a hardware shop; the men were arrested and sentenced to long terms of imprisonment. Cain and three other Squad officers later received £10 each from the Bow Street Reward Fund and Cain was awarded the King's Police Medal.

Detective Inspector Jeremiah Lynch, a native of Co. Kerry, threw up his job as a Dublin schoolmaster in 1912 to join the Metropolitan Police; a powerfully built member of the Squad, he distinguished himself time and again. In February 1932 he leapt from a moving Squad car after Sidney Farrell had carried out a smash and grab raid at Garrard's jewellers in Albemarle Street and punched him. Taken, bleeding, into Marlborough Street Police Court, Farrell said, 'I've been caught fair and square and must put up with it', adding, mournfully, 'I do ache.'

Seven months later, Lynch saw Philip Devereux – his real name was Alfred Phillips – examining shop doorways in the Strand and the West End. When Lynch stopped him, he was found to be in possession of two jemmies and keys. Additionally, Devereux attempted to withdraw an automatic pistol containing six rounds of ammunition from a shoulder holster.

'It's lucky for you, you took me by surprise and that you found it', he said, although at the Old Bailey he later denied making that comment.

Asked by prosecuting counsel why he carried a pistol, if not to resist arrest, Devereux replied, 'Unfortunately, I have always had a weakness for these things.'

It was also unfortunate that he appeared before Sir Ernest Wild KC; after Devereux was found guilty and the judge was informed that he had only been released from prison eight months previously, following his sixth conviction, Wild told the prisoner, 'Inspector Lynch is a fortunate man to be alive; Judges have to be severe in such cases' and weighed Devereux off with eight years' penal servitude. Lynch was later awarded £10 from the Bow Street Reward Fund. He also received a commissioner's commendation, to add to a total of fifty when he retired five years later.

Life is full of coincidences, and so it proved when in 1932 officers from Portsmouth CID requested help in arresting two men in London who, two weeks previously, had carried out a vicious attack on two employees of Lloyds Bank, robbing them of £23,477; one of the messengers was still in hospital. Detective Inspector Brooks of the Flying Squad was only too glad to help. One of the men arrested was named Alfred George Hinds; he joined two others in the dock at Winchester Assizes, and after they were all found guilty and the judge was informed that Hinds was 'a criminal of the most desperate type' with a long list of convictions, he was sentenced to four years' penal servitude, plus fifteen strokes of the cat. Hinds appealed on the grounds that the trial judge had misdirected the jury, but without success, and the bashing was duly carried out.

Twenty-one years passed, and now Hinds' son – also named Alfred George Hinds – was arrested for a safebreaking at Maples Store, Tottenham Court Road in which cash and jewellery worth £34,700 was stolen. The possessor of eight previous convictions (including safebreaking), Hinds, described by the trial judge as 'a most dangerous criminal' was sentenced to twelve years' preventative detention.[1]

Hinds, who maintained his innocence, appealed, stating – like his father before him – that the judge had misdirected the jury, but to no avail. Hinds had first absconded from Pentonville Remand Home at the age of seven; he later escaped from Borstal,

---

[1] Under the Criminal Justice Act 1948, preventative detention (PD) replaced penal servitude; where a person aged not less than thirty was convicted of an offence punishable with two years' imprisonment or more and had been convicted on three occasions since the age of seventeen, having served imprisonment, borstal training or corrective training, could be sentenced to a term of PD of not less than five and not more than fourteen years.

then deserted from the Army; now he resurrected his absconding skills and escaped from prison on two occasions. The common denominator was that neither offence was a Flying Squad case; but the father was taken into custody by the Squad, and it was the Squad who returned the son to prison.

At a time when Flying Squad detectives were regarded as the cream of the crop, Ted Greeno was one of those who stood head and shoulders above the rest; as Bob Higgins told me, 'He was the daddy of them all.' An able young pugilist, Greeno was fearless. He would fight anyone who challenged his authority, and when he saw gang boss Charles 'Darby' Sabini with some of the most feared Clerkenwell gangsters in tow at a racetrack, Greeno single-handedly simply told them to 'Clear off' – and they did. A great betting man, he habitually frequented racetracks; one of the reasons why he was such an extraordinarily successful detective was that when he backed winners he would lavish part of his winnings on his informants. This was a time when the price of a snippet of information from the Yard's Informants' Fund was 5s 0d – or 25 pence. Greeno would hand over £25 or £50 for top class information, and as a result, racetrack gangs were smashed up, burglars and robbers were arrested just as they were about to commit an offence and foreign thieves were quickly intercepted. The latter made sense all round, since the pickpockets and conmen who provided Greeno with information wanted foreigners like that out of the way so that they could continue their own nefarious activities.

One example (of many) came when Greeno stopped three such foreigners in the Mile End Road in the company of another visitor to these shores who was in possession of some imitation diamonds – in fact, small glass stones – whilst one of those arrested, Rose Stein, a 40-year-old Russian had in her possession a real diamond of the same size. It appeared that they were set to instigate a well-known con-trick, known as 'The Tweedle', in which a fake diamond was substituted and sold instead of the genuine article, an accusation which they all staunchly denied.

All were arrested for landing in the United Kingdom without the consent of an immigration officer. In her defence, Stein, who described herself as a widow whose two children lived in Odessa, stated that she had landed in England an hour before she was arrested; she had paid a Greek sailor £5 for travel on an unknown ship and had arrived at an unknown port.

Another Russian, 53-year-old Gedaly Brodsky, initially told Greeno that he was an Italian and that all three of them had arrived from Milan three days previously. In fact, he had two previous convictions in this country and had been recommended for deportation, as well as having a conviction in Detroit, USA from 1934.

Maurice Rosenbaum, a 39-year-old Uruguayan, had numerous convictions dating from when he was ten years of age, in Dresden, Vienna, Warsaw and Zürich. He had been expelled from Milan and Copenhagen, as well as having been deported from this country. Both Rosenbaum and Brodsky were sentenced to six months' hard labour and recommended for deportation.

Greeno was telling John Harris, the magistrate at Thames Police Court, that he had no record of convictions against Rose Stein, when a Squad officer rushed into court and handed Greeno a telegram from the French police which stated that Stein's fingerprints matched those of one Rosa Rubin, who had been sentenced for theft in Paris four years previously. Result? One month's imprisonment with hard labour – and also a recommendation for deportation.

But Greeno had dealt with a far more serious matter, four years previously. It involved a participating informant, and in such cases it was important to keep a firm grip on the informant, because it is all too easy for allegations to be made at a later stage that he was not so much participating as instigating. It was rather difficult for Greeno to keep as tight a grip as he might have wished, since the informant – who was later named in court – spent much of the time in Warsaw . . .

The informant was aware of a forgery network at three different sites in Poland which was in the process of manufacturing British National Health and Unemployment stamps, wholesale; if these were to flood the market, the economic damage to the country would be enormous.

Greeno told his informant to infiltrate the gang and inform them he was interested in buying large quantities, wholesale; it was imperative to put a big order in quickly, because if another unknown buyer were to come along first, England could still be saturated with the forgeries. One of the gang – Isek Jakob Najmark – came over to England to meet contacts. He was followed by Greeno, who saw him hand over forged Polish bonds; samples of the forgeries arrived, including a $1 bill which had been expertly converted into a $100 bill, and as the informant went to and fro, money was wired to him in Warsaw as a sign of his good faith with the gang.

And then a cable arrived from Berlin: 'Arriving Monday morning'. On 2 April 1934 at 6.00 a.m., Greeno and Detective Sergeant Bill Salisbury were waiting at Harwich Harbour to see the SS *Prague* arrive. Down the gangway came Edward Popielec and Benjamin Turek; following them was the informant, Louis Markham, who, upon seeing Greeno, nodded in the direction of the two men.

The two went to three large trunks in the customs shed; one was opened and examined by the customs officials before being shut by Turek with Popielec's assistance. Popielec superintended the loading of the trunks on to the Continental Boat Train, then the two men boarded, as did the Squad officers in a different compartment, and the train set off for Liverpool Street. Upon their arrival, they helped a porter load the trunks into a taxi with two other men – the informants – and drove off, followed by the Squad officers, also in a taxi – one used by the Flying Squad. Also following was the Squad's chief, Detective Chief Inspector Dan Gooch.

The two Poles had appeared nervous throughout the baggage inspection, and now they seemed even more apprehensive during the journey across London, constantly looking out of the taxi's rear window. When they reached Russell Square, Bloomsbury, they left the three trunks in the taxi and took a suitcase into the Imperial Hotel, then left again immediately, without it.

One of the other two occupants of the taxi was spoken to by the officers before leaving the scene, and Salisbury and Greeno stopped the two men and asked to see their passports; they were then taken to Scotland Yard, while Gooch followed on with the three trunks. 'Not my baggage!' exclaimed both men; they were thoroughly searched, but no keys were found. It was not until Salisbury examined the lining of Turek's hat that a key was revealed which fitted all three trunks. However, when they were opened, there was just clothing; nothing incriminating appeared at all.

But Greeno was not satisfied; he called for a steel rule and discovered that the trunks were two inches deeper on the outside than the inside. The false bottoms were ripped out; in one trunk were 1,909 sheets of Health, Pension and Unemployment stamps, and in the clothing was a ticket with Turek's name on it. In the second trunk were 1,307 similar sheets, and in the pocket inside the lid were business cards bearing the name of Isek Jakob Najmark. Altogether, in the three trunks there were 316,000 Health and Insurance Stamps and 303,000 Unemployment Insurance Stamps. All of them were forgeries and they had a face value of £44,700.

Told that they would be detained, Popielec exclaimed, 'My God!' and Turek replied, 'I have no baggage.'

That evening, Greeno and Salisbury met the Continental Boat Train from Harwich at Liverpool Street from which Najmark alighted and was arrested for possessing forged stamps.

He exclaimed, 'Police! My comrades were with the baggage!'

He was carrying a bag; examination of it revealed a slit inside the lining which contained six forged Unemployment Insurance Stamps and a key – it fitted the other three trunks.

The three men were charged with being in possession of forged documents, but before they could even appear in court, Detective Inspector George Hatherill (who spoke Polish as well as half a dozen other languages) flew to Warsaw, where he liaised with Dr Nagler, the head of the police, because it was essential to get the forgers' dens raided before they learned of their associates' arrests and before they could flood England with any other forged stamps. Unfortunately, the Polish police seemed less than enthusiastic, and although they arrested thirteen suspects, their premises were sealed under a magistrate's order, to be inspected only by those appointed to do so by the court. Indeed, Hatherill was told, it would be much better for him to return to England, at which time any further information would be passed on to him. Hatherill refused to go and made a nuisance of himself; as a consequence, he was interrogated from 7 o'clock one evening until 6 o'clock the following morning, on suspicion of being a spy.

Meanwhile, back in England, extraordinary measures were taken at Bow Street Court. On the prisoners' first appearance, the hearing took place in No. 2 Court, behind locked doors. None of the officials were aware of what was happening; for the first time in Bow Street's history, the gaoler and the usher were excluded. After the men were remanded, the charge sheet was taken back to Scotland Yard and the magistrate's register was placed under lock and key.

At the Old Bailey, the three men pleaded not guilty; Popielec stated that Markham and Turek had been on the train from Warsaw, and that when it stopped in Berlin, Markham had taken possession of the three trunks; he had seen them at Harwich, but had nothing to do with them. Markham had introduced him to a man named MacKay, and the four of them had travelled to London. Later, he, Turek and MacKay had travelled to the hotel in a taxi; naturally, he knew nothing of the trunks or their contents.

Turek stated, point-blank, that Markham was a police informer, and because of the implications of this, Greeno was obliged to admit that it was so but added that both Markham and MacKay were acting on the instructions of the Metropolitan Police. It was a tricky situation.

'Why then', demanded the defence, 'was Markham not giving evidence for the prosecution?' It was then suggested the whole matter was 'a frame-up'.

The three men were found guilty, and Hatherill told the court that he had traced the Mercury Press in Warsaw where the forgeries had been printed and had brought back photographs, plates and stamps. Of the men arrested, five were detained indefinitely, four were held pending further investigations and four others were released.

Greeno now told the court something of 42-year-old Najmark's history. In 1912 he had been convicted of picking pockets in Prague; between 1925 and 1926 he belonged to a band of expert swindlers who forged company shares and sold them in Paris, Berlin and Cracow.

Popielec and Turek had no previous convictions; they were each sentenced to two years' imprisonment, and Najmark who, there was no doubt, was the leader of the gang, received four years' penal servitude – all were recommended for deportation.

£1,000 was paid for the information received; Greeno and Salisbury were highly commended by the Commissioner, and Police Constable 383'CO' Bob Edney, Greeno's driver, won £10 after he bet Greeno that he would beat the Continental Boat Train from Harwich to Liverpool Street.

★

Squad officers were expected to be inventive regarding the way they gathered evidence and made arrests, and they were. Greeno was challenged in court regarding the impossibility of his observing thieves stealing furs valued at £10,000. He produced an ex-Army periscope, of the type used by First World War officers prior to 'going over the top'.

'I can see nothing through this', exclaimed the defence barrister, to which Greeno replied, 'Probably because you don't know how to use it', and passed it to the magistrate, who did.

Some officers went to extremes; Fred Sharpe was nailed up in a packing case into which eye-holes had been bored and had himself delivered to a warehouse which had been experiencing thefts. Other officers kept observation in the backs of cars, one of a pair donning a blonde ladies' wig to give the impression that they were a courting couple. Matters could get a little uncomfortable and embarrassing for the officer in drag, if the car's owner returned unexpectedly. Less ostentatious officers would limit their disguise to simply wearing a chauffeur's cap and tunic and pretending to be repairing a car. Others obtained theodolites and purported to be surveyors. But although officers used a variety of disguises – Army uniforms, clerical collars, tradesmen's working clothes – some went one step further.

In 1924, whilst a safe-blowing was being carried out, the gang had posted a lookout at a street corner who would periodically signal to the gang inside the building to let them know all was well. But at an opportune moment the lookout had a hand clapped over his mouth, was dragged round the corner and divested of his mackintosh and hat, which seconds later were donned by a Flying Squad detective, who took his place and supplied the necessary signals. It was sufficient to fool the gang, although when the officer in the case, Detective Inspector George Cornish, implied to an Old Bailey jury that the lookout, whose name was Edward Wood, had willingly passed over his garments, 'so that one of us could impersonate him, if necessary', it did seem to be stretching credulity. Then again, Wood himself topped this by stating that his arrest was a case of mistaken identity; but the jury thought otherwise, and Wood was amongst those who later collected terms of penal servitude and hard labour; Cornish, his bona fides established, went on to head the Flying Squad.

Divisional Detective Inspector Alf Dance, who served on the Squad for twenty-three years, needed no disguises at all other than his own resourcefulness. His testimony in court, regarding getting close to a pickpocket to see what he was up to, was disputed on the grounds that since Dance had arrested him on three previous occasions, the thief must have recognized him.

'He probably would have done', replied Dance, 'except that I disguised myself quickly.'

Perhaps unwisely, the pickpocket's lawyer demanded, 'Then disguise yourself quickly to me.'

With that, Dance whipped out his false teeth and screwed up his face so grotesquely that he was utterly unrecognizable; it appeared that a totally different man was standing in the witness box.

When it was thought that a thief might be secreting stolen property in his lodgings, some officers used strictly forbidden skeleton keys to gain entry during the occupier's absence. If stolen property was there, all well and good; if not, then the exercise had saved precious time waiting for the occupier to return. One officer disguised himself as a Gas Board official to gain entry to rooms; he was so confident in his duties that on several occasions he was admitted by landladies to premises where gas had not even been connected.

Police matters during the 1930s were dealt with a little differently to today. When a stolen car containing stolen furs was pursued by a Flying Squad car and crashed into an iron standard in High Street North, East Ham and the driver was killed, it was the dead man's two passengers who were charged with manslaughter.

In another 70mph Flying Squad chase through Camberwell, the occupants of the stolen car, who were also in possession of housebreaking implements by night, thoroughly upset Sir Herbert Wilberforce, the Chairman of the London Sessions, who crossly told Percy Grant and Edward Gardner, 'I'm going to pass a heavier sentence because you told a pack of lies' and awarded them fifteen and ten months' hard labour respectively.

And when a trio of safe-blowers attacked a Squad officer, mistaking him for the nightwatchman, he used his truncheon so effectively that afterwards it was said that the office walls resembled the interior of a jam sandwich – but no one was really concerned at their plight, least of all the safe-blowers. It was just as well the Independent Office for Police Conduct was not in existence, otherwise it's extremely debatable whether that officer would have been highly commended by the commissioner, or that he would have been awarded £10 by the Bow Street Reward Fund.

If those citations prompt the pseudo-intellectuals, those who've never taken their jackets off, rolled up their sleeves and 'got stuck in', to sneeringly remark, 'I suppose you think that justifies the means!' I prefer John Buchan's explanation in *The Island of Sheep*, as to how Peter Pienaar accessed the Hill of the Blue Leopard: 'He presented the world with results and left it to guess his methods.'

*

As the 1930s came to a close, it appeared that the Squad's continued presence at racetracks had paid off. Often, just the presence of a Squad tender was a sufficient deterrent; on other occasions, when a charabanc full of desperadoes intent on mischief arrived, it would be sufficient for a lone Squad officer to block their path and tell the driver, 'Turn around and clear off.' And when the Squad received a tip-off in 1936 – 'It's going to be off at Lewes, today' – the head of the Squad and seven others rushed to the track. Sixteen members of the Hoxton Gang and the Bethnal Green Mob were arrested for causing grievous bodily harm to a bookmaker's clerk and riotous assembly and were sentenced to penal servitude and hard labour for a total of 43½ years.

Just one week before the commencement of hostilities with Germany, two Flying Squad officers, John Gosling and Matthew Brinnand, received information that an IRA gang, who had already been responsible for 59 explosions in the capital, were planning to blow up Scotland Yard, Westminster Abbey and the Bank of England, with the explosives all to detonate simultaneously at 2.30 p.m. on 25 August.

That morning, they raided 32 Leinster Gardens, Bayswater, where they arrested four Irishmen, John Evans, Daniel Jordan, James O'Regan and John Gibson, who were in possession of hatboxes filled with 28lbs of potassium chlorate, gelignite and detonators fitted with alarm clocks timed to set the bombs off at 2.30 p.m., together with tradesmen's bicycles to convey them to their destinations.

But at 2.30 that afternoon a bomb left in the basket of a tradesman's bicycle in Broadgate, Coventry, exploded killing five people and leaving fifty others injured. The informant got back in touch with the Squad officers to tell them that Peter Barnes and James Richards were responsible for the murders. They raided 175 Westbourne Terrace, Paddington, where Barnes was arrested and more explosives were found. Barnes and Richards were both hanged; the other four plotters were sentenced to twenty years' penal servitude.

The curtain had come down on the 1930s Flying Squad. Now, with the arrival of the Second World War, they would face fresh difficulties.

CHAPTER 4

Wartime and the Ghost Squad

War came, and with it identity cards, rationing, ration books and evacuation – plus blackouts, dimmed headlights and air raids. Police officers who had been Army reservists were allowed to join their units, others were later allowed to join the armed services – and this left the Metropolitan Police 4,000 men short.

However, the Flying Squad was doing quite well, because its new leader was Peter Henderson Beveridge, who had joined the police following active service in France during the First World War. A red-headed Scot, he had served a tough apprenticeship in London's East End, followed by a stint with the Flying Squad, and now, to mark his debut as the Squad's detective chief inspector, he was about to score a mighty left and right with the arrest of two men who had been thorns in the side of the Metropolitan Police for some considerable time.

The first was William Charles 'Billy' Hill, who was renowned for (a) his expert use of sharp objects to hack open the faces of rival gang members and (b) his expertise in smash and grab raids, which were skilfully planned and included the use of two or sometimes three getaway cars.

Hill had been to Borstal, been birched, been sent to prison and penal servitude. During the 1930s he had teamed up with Charles 'Ruby' Sparks, a prolific criminal who had already been sentenced to three terms of penal servitude, and they, in the company of Sparks' paramour, Lillian Goldstein, aka 'The Bobbed-Haired Bandit' who was an expert and fearless driver of fast getaway cars, carried out a successful and lucrative series of smash and grabs.

That came to an end after Sparks was sentenced to five years' penal servitude in February 1939 at Kingston Assizes for burglary. However, eleven months later, he escaped from Dartmoor and met up with Hill, who in September 1939 had been released from a four-year sentence for burglary. More smash and grab raids were carried out by the duo, but on 25 June 1940, the one occasion when he was not in Sparks' company, Hill and his two associates,

Harry Bryan and George 'Square Georgie' Ball, were arrested following a smash and grab at Hemmings & Co. in Conduit Street.

Beveridge decided to have a quiet word with Hill.

The following day, Sparks was arrested near the Ritz Cinema, Neasden. Obviously, the police had received pertinent information, because the street was filled with Flying Squad officers, and although Sparks was in possession of a forged identity card in the name of Johnson and tried to bluff his way out of a decidedly tricky situation, he – and Lillian Goldstein – were arrested.

'Somebody', said Sparks later (and with complete justification), 'had really been singing. A proper tip-off, all round.'

Beveridge then decided to have a quiet word with Sparks.

Shortly afterwards, Flying Squad officers just happened to be in Mayfair when a smash and grab raid was attempted. Those arrested were Charlie Gibbs and Franny Daniels, both close associates of Billy Hill.

So what was the fate of Hill and Sparks?

Under the provisions of the Larceny Act 1916, storebreaking was a felony punishable with a maximum of fourteen years' penal servitude, so Bryan and Ball could consider themselves lucky to have received sentences of three years' imprisonment. However, Hill – the undisputed leader, with a serious criminal past – was not charged with storebreaking at all. Instead, he was charged with conspiracy and received the maximum sentence for that offence – two years' imprisonment.

And Sparks, with an even more shocking record than Hill, received a prison sentence of just twelve months, to run concurrently with his five-year sentence; the Bobbed-Haired Bandit was sentenced to six months' imprisonment for harbouring an escaped convict but only served three weeks before having her sentence substituted with a bind-over.

It's what's known as 'a little horse-trading'.

★

The Squad found themselves fully occupied dealing with the 4,584 cases of looting which had been reported in the West End, plus, due to the blackout, a rush of handbag snatches; after six months' work, the gang responsible were finally caught. Another problem was deserters who required identity cards and ration books and were ready to swap them in return for firearms. Still the smash and grab raids continued, but one case in particular was an unusual one for the Squad. This was when a young woman was approached to become a kennel maid at Wembley Dog Track in order to feed specified dogs meat laced with chloretone, a drug which affects the canine nervous system. The woman reported this to the Squad, and John Gosling and others kept observations on a very tricky gang indeed, until Montague Kosky and Leonard Jones were arrested on 4 July 1942 at a flat in Bryanston Square, where boxes of the drug were found.

'Conspiracy?' echoed Kosky, when told that was the offence for which they were being arrested. 'When nothing happens?'

'I can't understand it', lamented Jones. 'It's all like the Wizard of Oz.'

But they found it not quite as entertaining as Victor Fleming's eponymous film when they were each sentenced to two years' imprisonment.

★

When an officer commandeered a taxi to chase a stolen car, then leapt from the taxi travelling at 40mph on to the car's running board, the driver, Horace Hanson, cried to his companion, 'We're beat – Flying Squad!'

The year was 1929; the officer was Jack Capstick who, with just four years service, had been seconded to the Squad by Walter Hambrook personally. As the years went by, Capstick revelled in Squad work, being commended time and again, including a commendation for arresting five members of the feared pickpocket gang, 'The Hoxton Mob'. The person who had the greatest influence on his career was Alf Dance; rather than rush in and make an arrest, Dance would wait until he was satisfied that thieves were in possession of stolen property and then follow them to their run-in, to see if there were any more stolen goods there – or even wait until the thieves led the detectives to their receiver. Capstick learned much from his mentor (who bestowed on Capstick his nickname of 'Charlie Artful'); when he was the detective inspector at Bow Street and Dance telephoned him in January 1941 to ask if he would return to the Squad, to assist in the fight against thieves and black marketeers, Capstick was there like a shot.

For the remainder of the war Capstick and his team worked round the clock, meeting informants, keeping observations and smashing up gangs of warehousebreakers, lorry thieves and receivers. He used 'buyers' (sometimes criminals, at other times detectives) as prospective purchasers of stolen property and supplied suitably thuggish-looking Flying Squad officers to act as their minders.

Carrying out arrests during the wartime blackout was not for the faint-hearted. When Capstick and his team went to arrest a gang of shopbreakers at a house in Homerton, the Squad hit the front and back of the premises simultaneously, truncheons drawn. The first of the gang was knocked into the back of a tender, but the rest resisted arrest; during the ensuing struggle, the sides of the tender bulged in and out, as though they were made of elastic.

After four years of this type of work, Capstick left the Squad to take up the position of divisional detective inspector of 'W' Division – but not for long.

★

With the war at an end and the Metropolitan Police numbering just 14,500, crime went through the roof. The numbers of home-grown criminals were bolstered by deserters from the armed forces, and commodities such as food, liquor and clothing became the target of thieves and receivers. Lorries were hi-jacked, containers in railway sidings were broken into and forged clothing coupons flooded the market.

In the midst of this chaos, what became known as 'The Ghost Squad' was formed. Just four officers were used: Capstick, Gosling, Brinnand and Henry 'Nobby' Clark, who had served on the Squad on three occasions and was reputed to have a punch 'like the kick of a mule'. Their terms of reference were simple: to go out and get their informants to work to infiltrate and smash up the gangs, with the assurance that never would they be called upon to reveal the names of their informants. They were provided with an office, a telephone and a clapped-out Austin saloon; the rest was up to them.[1]

The Informants' Fund was doubled, then trebled. They used undercover officers, informants, participating informants and buyers. Sometimes they would infiltrate the gangs with two informants, working on the assumption that they would look after each other, provide double the work and spur each other on to greater successes. When arrests were made, the informants would be extricated, split up and sent to work with different partners on other gangs in police divisions situated a long way away.

Ghost Squad officers were not supposed to make arrests; instead, the information they received was supposed to be passed

---

[1] For further details of this extraordinary unit's exploits, see *Scotland Yard's Ghost Squad: The Secret Weapon against Post-War Crime*, Wharncliffe Local History, 2011.

on to the Flying Squad or Divisional officers, although on occasion it was inescapable that they would have to carry out arrests themselves.

This was demonstrated during an early arrest, using a 'buyer', which resulted in the capture of expertly forged clothing coupons with a face value of £25,000, the printing press responsible, a perforating machine, camera, photographic plates, inks and paper. Five men who might have been charged under the Forgery Act, which could have rendered them liable to fourteen years' penal servitude, were instead charged with conspiracy, which carried a maximum of two years' imprisonment; that was the sentence dished out to the ringleader, with other terms of imprisonment of down to nine months for the remainder.

And the 'buyer', who of necessity had to be pulled in at the same time as the others? He was marched away, ostensibly as an Army deserter, his credibility intact, especially after receiving a punch in the face from Capstick, in full view of the others, for being cheeky.

Three men were arrested by Ghost Squad officers for receiving stolen property valued at £350 and were bound over at court to keep the peace. It could be that this was a case of *quid pro quo*, because the same night, the same officers (plus a number of others) kept observation at the Cricklewood railway sidings; several lorries arrived, and over the space of half an hour a number of the occupants of those lorries vanished among the rolling stock and helped themselves to cases of whisky and carpets with a value of £15,000. As the men descended the embankment to load their booty into the waiting lorries, so the lights in a nearby builders' yard came on and the area was flooded with a mixture of Ghost and Flying Squad personnel. Four men unwisely put up resistance and suffered in consequence; two were later sentenced to five and six years' penal servitude, the others to two years each.

'Somebody must have split on us', wailed one of the gang as he was arrested, and it could be he was right; one of the other lorries and its occupants got clean away.

When a lorry driver was fingered by a Ghost Squad snout for being concerned in a garage-breaking at Wakefield and stealing a lorry, vacuum cleaners and clocks valued at £27,000, the Ghost Squad passed the information on to the police of that area to make the arrest. The reason for this was because it was not unknown for associates of the thieves to keep observation on the addresses of the loss adjusters, in order to try to identify the informant arriving there with a detective officer; they would have recognized the latter from his appearance with the prisoner in court. If that was attempted on this occasion, they were out of luck; and the 10 per cent reward of £2,700 paid to the informant was quite sufficient for him – or her – to purchase three very respectable houses for cash.

In the four years of their operations, the Ghost Squad made 727 arrests and recovered property valued at almost one quarter of a million pounds – or £10 million at today's values.

★

While the Ghost Squad was busying itself with its informers, so was the rest of the Flying Squad. Detective Inspector Len Crawford received word that a six-man gang were going to kidnap the manager of the Kentish Town branch of the Midland Bank on his way home one Friday evening. The plan was to take the manager's keys to the doors and the vault, since they felt that by Friday's close of business the strong room would be full of money.

There was a danger of the bank manager being seriously hurt if the Squad let the plan go ahead; instead, Detective Sergeant Bill Deans, who bore more than a passing resemblance to the manager, volunteered to take his place. He was well suited to the task since he had already carried out clandestine work on behalf of the Ghost Squad. Wearing clothing similar to that worn by the bank manager, plus a bowler hat which had been reinforced with padding, he left the bank and was duly followed by members of the gang; but it was not until the third Friday that the gang struck, savagely coshing Deans with a sock full of wet sand weighing 3½lb. The first blow sent the padded bowler spinning; four more blows landed on his unprotected head, and Deans was then thrown into the back of a van and relieved of the keys. The Flying Squad car which had kept vigil failed to start immediately in the freezing February weather, and the gang's van vanished, only stopping to dump Deans two miles away in the snow, tied up, with sticking plaster over his mouth and badly concussed. By the time he was found he was also suffering from exposure.

At the bank, one of the gang was seen to go to the rear door and open it with a set of keys. On arrest, his explanation, that 'Two men had promised him a hundred nicker' if he would open the door for them, was disbelieved, especially after he was searched and was found to have Deans' wristwatch in his possession. A police van was used as an impromptu interview room, five more prisoners were arrested and at the Old Bailey the gang were sentenced to penal servitude for a total of twenty-nine years.

At the time of sentencing, Deans was still on the sick-list but he was commended by the Lord Chief Justice, the Director of Public Prosecution and the commissioner, and after being handed £15 from the Bow Street Reward Fund was awarded the King's Police and Fire Services Medal.[2]

★

It was not only Deans who put himself in harm's way. When the Squad heard that there was going to be a raid on a warehouse at the newly opened Heathrow Airport in 1948, the three security guards who were going to receive drugged coffee from a member of the gang were substituted. Squad officers took their place in the warehouse, which contained goods worth £224,000 and where the strong room held jewellery worth £13,900; behind the packing cases were also concealed a large number of Flying Squad officers.

Having discarded the drugged coffee, the three 'guards' lay sprawled over a table, and at one o'clock in the morning the gang arrived. Their leader, Sammy Ross, was heard to say, 'Let's settle these geezers', and together with George Wood he went into the guards' office. The officers were slapped, had sticking plaster put over their mouths and were tied up; one was cracked over the head with a starting handle. Wood emerged with the safe keys, which he handed to Alfred Roome, who duly inserted a key into the lock.

'We're police officers of the Flying Squad – stand where you are!' came the shout, and as the Squad officers emerged from behind the packing cases, there ensued a battle royal. 'Kill the bastards – get the guns!' shouted one of the eleven-strong gang, but although there were no guns, the officers, armed only with truncheons, were attacked with a variety of weapons. Detective Chief Inspector Bob Lee's scalp was split open by Roome wielding an iron bar; in turn, Roome was so badly beaten by one of the 'guards' that he was hospitalized. One officer's nose was broken, one was slashed with a broken bottle and one's hand was shattered, whilst another's arm was broken and yet another was hit over the head with a pair of giant wire-cutters. But eventually, although three of the gang escaped, it was eight very violent robbers who lay unconscious on the floor of the warehouse.

---

[2] For further details of this (and other equally courageous acts) see *The Brave Blue Line: 100 years of Metropolitan Police Gallantry*, Wharncliffe Local History, 2011.

When the prisoners appeared at Uxbridge Court later that morning, it was hard to differentiate between them and the equally battered Squad officers. However, having pleaded guilty at the Old Bailey, the Recorder of London allowed them to share seventy-one years of penal servitude, saying, 'You went prepared for violence and you got it. You got the worst of it and you can hardly complain about that.'

The 1940s had been a particularly violent time for the Squad; the deeply unpleasant Arthur Parkyn, who was already wanted for inflicting grievous bodily harm on a police officer, was in a stolen van with his associate, Harold Berlinski. When Squad officers tried to stop them in Knightsbridge, Parkyn hit one of the officers with a hammer; Berlinski used a case opener on another, then tried to run three of the officers down before mounting the pavement and driving off, scattering pedestrians in all directions. Parkyn appeared bemused when he was charged with attempting to murder the officers because he replied, 'I didn't think it would be as bad as that.' The Lord Chief Justice thought it was, because he sentenced Parkyn and Berlinski to twelve and seven years' penal servitude, respectively.

After almost thirty years, it was decided to provide the Squad with its own identity. It had been reorganized, its staff and vehicles had increased in number, and due to the volume and importance of its work, the officer in charge would now be one with the rank of Detective Superintendent. The first was Bill 'The Cherub' Chapman – and from 28 June 1948, the Squad would be known as C8 Department.

CHAPTER 5

A New Identity

'There was quite a big organization', the newly promoted Detective Superintendent Bob Lee told Mr Justice Byrne at Hampshire Assizes on 24 April 1951, 'and the fringe of it has only been touched.'

He was right. Since 1941 there had been in the region of two hundred safebreakings, mainly at Post Offices and banks and all of them carried out by means of duplicate keys, in which more than £50,000 had been stolen. Lee had been a chief inspector at the Yard's Criminal Records Office; in that department's 'Method Index' he began to collate these offences and came to the conclusion that they had been committed by the same gang. Now, as deputy head of the Squad, he set up an operation to snare the gang; but although he was receiving reliable information he was thwarted time and again and came to the conclusion that a crooked copper at the Yard was tipping off the perpetrators.

Lee's team was hand-picked; false entries were put in the Squad's duty book, some officers were untruthfully shown as being off-duty, others were equally falsely shown to be on annual leave and others were shown to be carrying out observations miles away from the actual locations from where surveillance was being carried out.

The first arrests happened on the evening of 27 November 1950, when two men opened the front door of Barclays Bank, Waterlooville, Hampshire. Following a meeting at a Brixton pub, John William Saxton and James Thomas Howells were tailed by Squad vehicles, two vans and a car. As they headed for the A3 and the Portsmouth Road, radio transmissions failed at Cobham due to the distance from the Yard. Officers in the last vehicle had to stop at telephone boxes to relay progress reports to the Squad office.

Nevertheless, Saxton was seized by officers who had been secreted both inside and outside the bank. He was in possession of fifty-two skeleton keys, and when he put up resistance he was clumped with Inspector Philip Periam's truncheon; Howells, arrested at the same time, was in possession of six keys.

Now the rest of the arrests could be carried out, and searches of premises in London revealed a woman's muff in a wardrobe which contained twenty-five numbered keys, stamps and jewellery, a watch, two brooches and a bracelet. The lady, a post office sorter, to whom the muff belonged, and her husband were both later acquitted of any involvement in the plot; not so George Charles Allen, a locksmith employed by the Milner Safe Company.

Shown the twenty-five keys, he gasped, 'I haven't made all those!' but he admitted, 'I made one for the Kensington jewellers and another for the Golders Green Sub-Post Office, but they didn't get in there because they were disturbed.'

Also in the dock at Hampshire Assizes was Harry Bryan, former co-defendant with Billy Hill in the 1940 smash and grab case. Described by the judge as 'the brains of the conspiracy', he was sentenced to ten years' imprisonment and ordered to pay £2,000 towards the costs of the prosecution. John Arthur Wyatt ('Bryan's very able first lieutenant') was sentenced to eight years' imprisonment for conspiracy and receiving; his wife Margaret was convicted of conspiracy and placed on probation for three years.

Saxton and Howells, found guilty of conspiracy and breaking and entering the bank, were sentenced to four years' corrective training[1] and three years' imprisonment, respectively, and Allen, the locksmith – and probably the dupe of the gang – received twelve months' imprisonment.

It had been a long, complicated enquiry, and the Judge congratulated Lee 'as being worthy of the highest commendation in bringing a very dangerous gang of criminals to justice.'

★

In 1955 half a dozen Squad officers were detached from normal duties to concentrate on organized thefts of motor vehicles; this was another of Bob Lee's ideas. With experienced police constables as vehicle examiners, and operating out of premises at Chalk Farm, thirty-one arrests were made in the first year of operations. The following year, forty-one arrests were carried out, and vehicles worth £41,365 were recovered. By 1960 the Stolen Vehicle Squad (SVS) had been given its own identity – C10 Department – and of

---

[1] Under the Criminal Justice Act 1948, if a person over the age of twenty-one was convicted of an offence punishable with two years' imprisonment or more, and having been convicted on two occasions since the age of seventeen, they could be sentenced to corrective training for a period of not less than two years and not more than four.

the 14,500 vehicles stolen in 1966, all but 3,630 were recovered. Under the aegis of the Flying Squad commander, the SVS has consistently gone from one success to another.

*

Detective Sergeant Frank Davies was experiencing the first of his three tours with the Flying Squad in 1953, when he was asked if he would kill a man.

The extraordinary circumstances which gave rise to this request were as follows: Derek Howard Wright had married in 1946, and the couple had had a child but then divorced on 5 March 1953. Wright had grave concerns regarding access to his 6-year-old son, but more than anything else, he was insanely jealous and told his wife that if she contemplated marrying anybody else, her new husband would be dead within 24 hours. In fact, his wife did marry a licensee named James Edward Byrnes on 11 May, and on that day (and two days later) Wright recorded the matter in his diary:

> I found out today and I am going to kill him. There may be no more of this diary tomorrow. I am going to obtain somehow a revolver for my plan – two, if possible, and I am going to kill him. But it will have to be properly planned and executed – unless I want to go for the early morning walk and face the big drop. I must either stage a suicide or get some gelignite from somewhere and blow him to smithereens when he is in his car. I would like to think up a foolproof, lingering death . . .
>
> I am now going to do something even more drastic. I must do it, not necessarily because I am upset but simply because I said I would not stand for her going off with anyone else. She has played me up and divorced me for this clot.

It appeared that Wright was becoming more and more unhinged; he wanted a friend to acquire two revolvers and some gelignite and spoke of the possibility of throwing a grenade through Byrnes' living room window; but finally, through an intermediary, he decided to dispose of Byrnes by hiring a hitman.

On the afternoon of 27 May, at Henekey's public house, High Holborn, Wright met 'Wicker Riley', the man who was going to solve all of his problems – except, of course, that this was the pseudonym adopted by Sergeant Davies.

'You want someone taken care of for keeps?' asked Davies, to which Wright replied, 'Yes, for £150. I would do the job myself, but I would come under suspicion. As it is, they will suspect, unless you are very clever.'

As it happened, it was Wright who was not being very clever, because he wrote out a cheque for £150, then tore it in two, handing one half to Davies and retaining the other.

It was suggested that Davies should go to Stratford, East London and arrange a motoring accident, thereby killing Byrnes. Wright also said, 'I want him killed this week. If I had my way, it would be nice and slow.'

'Do you really want this man Byrnes out of the way for good?' asked Davies, to which Wright replied, 'Yes. I have waited too long.'

This seemed to be a propitious moment for Davies to introduce one of the pub's clientele who was also a colleague, saying, 'This is Detective Inspector Hislop and I am Detective Sergeant Davies of the Flying Squad, Scotland Yard. You realize now to whom you have been talking and what you have asked me to do?'

'God! What are you going to do?' gasped Wright. It was only too obvious, but after he had been formally charged he replied, 'No question of murder was ever said or intended.'

In the face of overpowering evidence, however, Wright pleaded guilty at the Old Bailey to endeavouring to persuade Davies to murder Byrnes. Sentencing him to two years' imprisonment, the judge told him, 'I do not doubt that you were keenly anxious to see your boy. You could hardly have adopted any more certain way of never seeing him at all than the one you adopted.'

He was right; proceedings were in hand to make Wright's son a ward of court.

All Wright had now was the memory of a successful career in the wartime RAF; Davies fared somewhat better, being commended by the commissioner for this case and later being awarded the MBE and becoming the Flying Squad's Commander.

But before that happened, several other officers would serve as heads of the Squad. There were a number of high value thefts as well; first the £287,000 Eastcastle Street robbery, and then gold bullion valued at £45,500 was stolen. It was known that Billy Hill was behind both jobs – indeed, he informed readers of the Sunday newspaper the *People* how both jobs had been carried out – but no one was convicted of either crime, and when the latter offence occurred during Detective Superintendent Guy Mahon's spectacularly brief tenure as head of the Squad – four months – he was replaced by Reggie Spooner.

Like Mahon, Spooner had never served on the Squad before, but he was a morale-booster and a born leader of men, so much so that when the next theft of gold bullion occurred, the Squad experienced rather more success.

★

British European Airways (BEA) had only been formed in 1946, but in August 1952 three safes were stolen from their headquarters in Ruislip, Middlesex. No sooner had John Alexander Kelly completed his sentence of thirty months' imprisonment, imposed at the Old Bailey on 20 April 1955 for feloniously receiving the safes, when he resumed his rather one-sided liaison with that company.

On the morning of 15 May 1957 Detective Sergeant James Barker and other Flying Squad officers were keeping observation on a garage at Seven Sisters Road, Tottenham, North London, when they saw three men get into a blue Bedford lorry, registration number HGO 8, and drive away. Kelly was driving, and next to him sat John Ernest Clark, together with a third man. The men were of interest to the officers; they had seen them on 26 April in the same lorry when Clark was driving and again on 9 May at the garage.

At 5.00 p.m. on 15 May, a BEA van containing 600 gold bars valued at £20,119 left Waterloo air terminal for Heathrow airport, for onward transmission to the Swiss Bank Corporation at Zürich.

By coincidence, Flying Squad officers on patrol spotted the lorry, with Kelly driving and Clark as the passenger, travelling along Millbank, but they had no idea that it was following the BEA van. They followed the lorry as far as Cheyne Walk but then lost interest and resumed their patrol, which was a pity.

Ten minutes later, the BEA van stopped at traffic lights at the junction with the Great West Road and Windmill Road, and the driver felt a slight bump. Looking into his driving mirror, he saw that the shutter at the back of the van was open and he also saw a man in the roadway holding the box containing the gold get into a blue-coloured lorry, which drove off at speed. It was certainly a well planned job; the decision to move the gold had only been made that morning.

The following day, there was the lorry, back in the yard in Tottenham. On the ground were the remains of the box which had contained the gold; inside the van were the seals which had been on the box. Of Kelly and Clark there was no sign; but a search of Kelly's home at Loughton revealed a jemmy which, in the opinion of the chief scientific officer at the laboratory, had been used to force open the box.

Nothing more happened until 18 July, when the Flying Squad received a tip-off that Clark was in a seafront pub at Ramsgate; they telephoned Kent Constabulary, asking them to detain him. A terrific fight ensued involving a dozen people in the pub in which one officer was hit over the head with a table; but Clark was brought into the local station, where he was later seen by Detective Inspector Tom Easterbrook of the Squad. Easterbrook was much admired by his colleagues, who referred to him as 'Uncle Tom'; he also knew his villains, because when Clark said to him, 'You can take me back, but it's not me you want. It's my brother John. I'm William Clark', Easterbrook replied, 'I know you and I know your brother William.'

Still keeping up the pretence, Clark said, 'I don't even know this Kelly, even if my brother John does. I've never seen a BEA van. I wouldn't know a box of gold, even if I saw one.' But luck was running out for Clark; his fingerprints proved that he was indeed John Ernest Clark, and he had left one of them on the rear of the BEA van, the driver of which, Richard Webber, positively identified him as the man who stole the gold.

If the thieves had good information, so did the Flying Squad, because on 22 August, as Kelly emerged from a swim in the sea at Saltdean Beach, Brighton, he was grabbed by Detective Sergeants Barker and Fred Lambert. Taken to a flat at Saltdean Court, Kelly said, 'This is ridiculous', but a search of the kitchen revealed a box underneath some vegetables which contained £3,999, mainly in almost new £5 notes. Its discovery failed to faze Kelly in the slightest.

'Yes, that's all right', he said. 'You don't have to worry about that. It's my savings. I have been working, you know.' And on the way to London, Kelly enquired, 'What evidence have you got against me? Do you think you've got a strong case?'

Quite obviously, they did, and 400 of the £5 notes were identified as having being retained at Martin's Bank, Lombard Street until 31 May. At the Old Bailey, Kelly's defence was that the money found at the flat was part of £4,775 which he had won at Ascot, and he called a bookmaker named Richard Anthony Cann-Lippincott (trading under the name of David Murray of Wembley), who told the court he had paid out Kelly's winnings, 'most of it in £5 notes'.

It took the jury two hours to decide otherwise; Kelly went down for seven years, and Clark for five.

★

When a Rover 90 saloon, registration number PXB 804, was stolen from Bloomsbury Square on 4 October 1955, it was, unfortunately, just one of dozens taken daily from London streets; many were taken by joy-riders and later abandoned – but not this one.

Six days later, the stolen car, its registration mark altered to PXP 804 by the simple expedient of cutting out the bottom curve of the letter 'B' and driven by John Robert Cotten aged twenty-nine, who had seven previous criminal convictions, drew up outside H. R. Drew & Son, Ltd., a jeweller's shop at 2 Hogarth Place, Earls Court. It was 12.30 p.m. when two men got out of the car and entered the shop; the first was John Cohen, aged twenty-five, who had been released from Dartmoor three weeks previously with Cotten. Cohen, who possessed eleven previous convictions, was in company with 22-year-old Ronald Thomas Parsons, who during the course of his seven previous convictions had escaped from Borstal on three occasions.

Cohen, wearing a false moustache, and Parsons, with a scarf masking his face, bolted the door, held up the staff at gunpoint and said to them, 'This is a hold up. Where are the diamonds and the cash?'

Mr Drew, the owner, was taken to the safe; two other members of staff were told to face the wall; when one of them was slow in doing so, he was pistol-whipped. They had just seized jewellery worth about £500 from the safe when two teenage girls, one of whom wanted her watch repaired, tried to enter the shop. The girls peered through the window, saw that there was a robbery in progress and rushed into a butcher's shop next door. Cohen and Parsons got back into the car and drove off; the registration number was taken and telephoned through to the Yard's Information Room, who immediately circulated it to 'All Cars'.

As the stolen car roared into Cromwell Road it was spotted by three patrol cars, but the traffic was so congested that it impaired their progress.

However, the call was also heard by the crew of a Flying Squad Rover who were on a routine patrol crossing the Serpentine Bridge in Hyde Park. The driver was Police Constable Donald Cameron, the radio operator was Detective Sergeant Ernest Cooke and the backseat passenger was Detective Sergeant Albert Chambers, who had been posted to the Flying Squad just seven months previously. Married, with a 9-year-old daughter, 39-year-old Chambers, at half an inch over six feet, was heavily built and in his eighteenth year of service. Cameron saw the stolen car being driven towards them and gave chase, but at Victoria Gate the cars were forced to stop, due to the amount of blocked traffic. The two sergeants, knowing full well that the stolen car's occupants had been involved in an armed robbery where violence had already been used, leapt from the Squad car and ran towards the Rover. Through the open driver's window, Cooke grabbed the steering wheel, but at that moment Cotten accelerated away, throwing the officer into the roadway; Chambers got back into the Squad car and Cameron took up the chase. Both cars tore down North Carriage Drive at speeds of up to 70mph, before turning south into Park Lane. As they reached the junction with Stanhope Gate, Cohen leant out of the car's window and fired twice with his .38 revolver.

'A hole appeared in the windscreen of our car', said Chambers. 'The windscreen was cracked and splintered . . . I climbed over from the back seat and knocked out the rest.'

As the stolen car veered into South Audley Street, Parsons fired at the Squad car, hitting the bonnet. As a Flying Squad driver, Cameron was used to very high speeds, but his (and all of his fellow Flying Squad drivers') main regard was the safety of other road users, both in vehicles and on foot. Of course, Parsons had no such considerations; nor did he have to contend with a broken windscreen or risk being shot at.

Seconds later, as the robbers' car turned into Curzon Street, heavy with West End lunchtime traffic, it collided with a chauffeur-driven car and a taxi, and the terrifying drive was over – but not the chase. The three men ran from the car; Parsons dashed off along Curzon Street and although chased by Cameron he escaped. Meanwhile, Cohen and Cotton ran into Hertford Street, where they split up.

Other police officers joined in the chase: Police Constable David Wood, who was on foot patrol, and Police Constable George Karn, who was on motorcycle patrol. Cohen first tried to hi-jack a lorry, then a taxi, then from a few yards away he fired directly at PC Karn but missed; Karn flung his motorcycle helmet at Cohen twice, hitting him both times, before Cohen fired at Karn again, fortunately missing him. In Charles Street Cohen fired twice at Chambers, the second shot – although Chambers was unaware of it at the time – hitting him in the arm. PC Wood caught up with Cohen and grabbed his jacket, whereupon Cohen fired at point-blank range, hitting him in the leg.

Chambers dived at Cohen and caught his ankle, and the latter went flat on the pavement.

'I pulled myself up on his legs', said Chambers, 'and twisted the gun out of his hand.'

In addition to his hands, which had been badly lacerated when he had smashed a hole in the Squad car's windscreen, and the bullet hole in his arm, Chambers later discovered three bullet holes his jacket.

With Chambers and Wood detained in St George's Hospital, a false moustache, live ammunition and a large quantity of jewellery was found on Cohen. On his way to West End Central police station he said, 'Do you think that uniformed officer is dead? He must be. I let him have it in the guts.'

When he was later seen by Detective Chief Inspector John Marner of the Flying Squad, Cohen asked, 'Was anybody killed?' Having established that nobody else had at that time been arrested, and asked if he would care to make a statement, he replied, 'I don't like ratting on people, but you may as well have the whole story.' In his statement Cohen admitted that he and Parsons had stolen the Rover and had bought two revolvers for £6, and added, 'I am thankful that nobody has been killed. I panicked and did my nut.'

Parsons was less penitent. He was seen at a hotel, was chased and dropped a tray containing five rings; he was caught by Detective Inspector Brereton, who discovered four rounds of ammunition in his pocket. When DCI Marner mentioned this to Parsons, he replied, 'You can't pin any shooting on me. I have no gun. You can only nick me for receiving the rings. A man gave them to me a short while ago.'

A flat at Redfern Road was searched and two suitcases were seized. In one of them was found twenty-three rounds of live ammunition. When Parsons was appraised of this discovery, he replied, 'The suitcases and the stuff in them are mine, but if you say you found ammunition there, you put it there. You didn't find the gun, did you?'

It was also at Redfern Road that Cotten was arrested, and he said, immediately, 'I didn't shoot anyone; I've no time for violence.'

On 8 December 1955, with Cohen pleading guilty and his co-defendants being found guilty, this charmless trio had the misfortune to be sentenced by the Lord Chief Justice, Rayner Goddard, undeniably the sternest judge to preside at the Old Bailey in recent times.

'I am sentencing you for the armed robbery at Earls Court and then shooting at the police, and shooting wildly in a public place whereby you might have killed a number of people – as many people as you had bullets', he told Cohen, and sentenced him to twenty years' imprisonment.

Addressing Parsons, Lord Goddard told him, 'You may be young but you have endangered the lives of Her Majesty's subjects', and packed him off to prison for twelve years.

'There is more good in you than the others', Lord Goddard told Cotten, and then quickly added, 'but not much. I do think you tried to stop that wild animal, Cohen, from doing any more shooting after you got out of the car', before sentencing him to ten years' imprisonment.

Calling the five officers before him, Lord Goddard said:

> I have asked you men to parade in front of me to give you the thanks of the community for your gallant and devoted sense of duty on the day in question. It takes courage of no mean order to run up and tackle desperate criminals who are in possession of firearms. The Metropolitan Police Force has reason to be proud of you and, as I say again, I thank you on behalf of the community and commend you for your gallantry.

It was the first of several commendations; more followed from the Director of Public Prosecutions, the Commissioner and the Bow Street Reward Fund, and some six months later, Chambers, Wood and Karn were each awarded the George Medal, with a British Empire Medal for gallantry for Cameron and the Queen's Commendation for Brave Conduct for Cooke.

This was a story of the most conspicuous gallantry, but it did not end there. On 6 December 1959 three prisoners escaped from Wormwood Scrubs. Two of them were captured within an hour of their escape, but four years to the day of his sentence, at 11 o'clock at night, the third escaper, Ronald Thomas Parsons, was spotted by Flying Squad officers in Tottenham Court Road and promptly arrested.

It seemed symptomatic of the Flying Squad; first, officers from that branch of the Metropolitan Police had acted with great bravery in bringing three dangerous criminals to justice – then four years later, observant officers from the same unit interrupted the unofficial parole of one of the same gang and returned him to prison.

★

The Squad prospered under Spooner; 800 arrests were carried out in 1955, and the following year, Squad arrests topped 1,000. In 1957 the Squad carried out 1,200 arrests and recovered stolen property to the value of £194,010.

'Although he did not seek popularity, Reg Spooner was well respected by everyone, uniform and CID', Commander Terry O'Connell QPM told me. 'He was one of the shrewdest men I have ever known' – and it was O'Connell who, as a detective sergeant, features in the next case.

The story began between 29 October and 1 November 1958, when the Midland Bank, Stoke Newington High Street was entered, the strong room door was forced and a safe opened. Then £17,800 in cash was taken, fifty deed boxes were opened and a large amount of jewellery and cash was taken, of which the value was later assessed to be in the region of £60,000. At the scene, the police found a transformer which had been used to cut through the steel doors, eight burnt electrodes and a pair of 42-inch bolt cutters. It was discovered that the bolt cutters had been purchased by a certain Kenneth Shakeshaft, though when the local police arrived at his flat at Essendine Mansions, Maida Vale with a search warrant, they found nothing. But when they asked to search Shakeshaft's Ford Consul, he unlocked it before bolting and getting clean away. Inside the car's boot was a vanity case belonging to Shakeshaft's wife; it contained £8,727 in £1 notes, or almost exactly half of the cash stolen.

A year went by, then on 8 December 1959, Squad officers led by Sergeant O'Connell raided a flat in Cromwell Road; there they found a man and a woman, plus Shakeshaft, together with Henry Arthur Suttie, who was the principal reason for the raid, since they had been looking for him for three years; Shakeshaft was a bonus.

A search of Shakeshaft's bedroom revealed two cartridges of gelignite in his shoes, and in a chest of drawers some smoke canisters, a duffle coat and a pair of goggles; in a communal bathroom, two detonators were discovered.

Told he would be arrested, Suttie replied, 'You don't think it was my mad idea to keep that stuff in the flat? They must be potty', although he added, 'I suppose I'm as much to blame as anyone.'

Shakeshaft, questioned about the explosives, said, 'It looks bad, doesn't it but still, I can't be in much more trouble, can I?' When he was told he would be charged with breaking into the Midland Bank, he replied, 'Yes, I suppose I've put this day off long enough. I wish to goodness I hadn't run away that day; I would've done a year of my sentence by now. To tell you the truth, I didn't know there was all that money in the car.'

On 24 February 1960, Suttie, who had eight previous convictions, was found guilty at the Old Bailey of possessing explosives and sentenced to eighteen months' imprisonment; the following day, he appeared at the London Sessions, where he was sentenced to fifteen months' imprisonment to run consecutively to the previous day's sentence, for stealing from a shop and receiving. He was also ordered to forfeit £100 for failing to previously appear at court, or to serve an extra six months in lieu.

On the same day as Suttie, Shakeshaft was also sentenced to eighteen months' imprisonment on the explosives charge.

However, he still had to stand trial for breaking into Barclays Bank. Just over a year previously, Alan Bainbridge had been found guilty of being an accessory before the fact on that charge and had been sentenced to four years' imprisonment. He had incriminated Shakeshaft at his trial and also gave evidence for the prosecution in Shakeshaft's case.

And yet, on 4 March 1960, Shakeshaft, who told the police, 'I should think you have all the evidence you need against me', was acquitted of the break-in by a jury at the Old Bailey.

CHAPTER 6

Dog-doping and Safecracking

T hat great Flying Squad officer, Ian 'Jock' Forbes (later Deputy Assistant Commissioner Forbes QPM), who joined the Squad in 1955, once wrote, 'The CID has no place for cowards or look-before-you-leap types. They must be resolute and determined men who are ready to act upon information, no matter where it comes from.' The moral aspect of courage was exemplified by Detective Sergeant Pierce Butler, who features in the next case.

The Flying Squad, since its inception, had always retained strong links with racetracks, both for dog and horse racing, not only because of the intimidatory habits of the gangs who frequented them but also because of the possibility of interference in the sport by doping. Sergeant Butler carried out an investigation after concerns had been raised that greyhounds kennelled at Sunbury-on-Thames had been doped; but by the time four men and six women appeared at Bow Street Magistrates' Court on 29 July 1958 charged with conspiracy to contravene the Gaming Act 1845, real fears were raised that witnesses for the prosecution were being threatened. Butler successfully opposed bail for the four men, telling the Magistrate, Mr Bertram Reece, that he would be calling witnesses who had been approached by the men; and the women – all of whom were granted bail – were warned not to contact anyone who would be called as a witness.

Butler had interviewed four kennel maids in the presence of the resident manager of the kennels on 14 May. Valerie Sheen was in possession of three meatballs, three capsules containing phenobarbitone and a paper with the names of three dogs due to run at Charlton the following day. Gloria Ranger had five meatballs, five similar capsules and papers containing the names of dogs due to run at Charlton and Park Royal. She shared a room with Patricia Dalligan, and when a capsule containing 3.5 grains of phenobarbitone was found in Dalligan's jumper pocket, she said, 'I thought I'd thrown that away.' Fragments of paper were also found; when put together, they revealed the names of three dogs due to run at Wandsworth the following day.

'I should have burnt it', said Dalligan. 'They said to burn it. It was three dogs we were to do for them.'

The fourth girl, Elaine Duffy, had two capsules and the names of three dogs due to run at Charlton.

Charles Coulon, a man with seven previous convictions and adjudged by Butler to be the head of the gang, was found to be in possession of 166 tablets of phenobarbitone — 'I don't sleep very well', he told Butler. A witness named Jill Brewster told Butler that Coulon had invited her to become a kennel maid at Sunbury-on-Thames. When Daniel Swain's house was searched, an exercise book was found containing names of dogs which corresponded with those names found in the kennel maid's possession. Another kennel maid, Patricia Adamthwaite, told a witness, Barbara Baker, that she was going to dope dogs and that she should get a job at the kennels, in order to do the same.

It seemed Butler's fears regarding witness interference were well founded. Barbara Baker was a very important witness, but the day before she was due to appear at the Old Bailey to give evidence, she disappeared.

Now charged with conspiracy to cheat and defraud by means of the administration of drugs to dogs participating in racing, four men and seven women stood trial on 27 October 1958; of them, Adamthwaite and two others pleaded guilty. Two days later, due to the non-appearance of Miss Baker, the hearing was adjourned to the next session, but now all of the defendants were remanded in custody.

One month later, three more of the defendants – including Elaine Duffy and Valerie Sheen – changed their pleas to guilty. A week into the trial, so did Gloria Ranger. One male defendant was discharged on the orders of the judge. And still there was no sign of Barbara Baker.

Giving evidence, Patricia Dalligan said that although she owned the red jumper in which the phenobarbitone had been found, she had not worn it at the kennels, although Miss Ranger (who had pleaded guilty) and Miss Baker (the missing prosecution witness), both had. She knew nothing about a conspiracy to dope greyhounds and had met neither Swain nor Coulon prior to the trial.

Telling the jury that he was investigating a very serious allegation, Butler said, 'I was determined to get to the bottom of it, and to the bottom of it I got.'

In cross-examination, Pierce Butler came in for a hammering from Dalligan's barrister, Brian Leary, who said, 'Did you have any right to search either the kennel maids or their rooms at the hostel attached to Sunbury kennels?'

'Probably no right in law', replied Butler, 'but I did it.'

The Judge, Sir Carl Aarvold OBE, TD, intervened, saying, 'It may have been high-handed but you thought you were justified in the circumstances?' – to which Butler replied, 'Yes.'

Resuming his cross-examination, Leary asked, 'Is that your explanation of it?'

'It is my explanation.'

'A high-handed action?'

'I was investigating a very serious allegation.'

'You were using methods to attempt to obtain that information to which you knew you had no right whatsoever?'

'I thought I had a right to that information and evidence when I found it.'

'You were dealing with a young girl of eighteen with no experience of the police; did you think it was an honest thing to mislead her into thinking she was under arrest?'

'It never entered my head to think if it were honest or otherwise. I was satisfied she was involved in this and she knew a lot more than she would probably tell me, and I was going to find out as much as I could.'

'Whatever your thoughts were at the time, do you now think it was an honest thing to mislead a young girl into thinking she was arrested when you knew perfectly well as a police officer of twenty-one years' experience you had no right of arrest?'

'Thinking back over it, I have nothing to blame myself for.'

Summing up to the jury, the Judge said this:

> One thing is apparent in this case, namely that at the Sunbury kennels an arrangement was being operated whereby dogs were being drugged. You may think the police were in a very difficult position, because if any warning had been given to the effect that enquiries were afoot, it would have been easy for those concerned to dispose of meatballs and small capsules containing white powder. Detective Sergeant Pierce Butler knew he had no right to arrest anyone or to search anyone and he knew he had not got a warrant because he had not got, perhaps, either the information or the time at that stage, to take one out. He could have asked the kennel maids certain questions and accepted their answers, or he could, as he put it, 'take a chance'. It was a chance, because the liberty of the subject in this country is regarded very highly indeed. Sergeant Butler appreciated full well the chance he was taking and he has been criticised for taking it. You will, no doubt have

made up your minds whether that criticism is justified, or not. You will ask yourselves whether he was being an officious officer, interfering with those kennel maids as they came into that hostel, or whether he was doing his duty conscientiously as he saw it and taking such steps as he thought necessary with such speed as he considered essential. One result of his taking that chance is that seven people in this case have already pleaded guilty . . .

The remaining defendants were found guilty, and the Judge sentenced Coulon to three years' imprisonment; he later boasted to a Sunday newspaper that he had been successfully doping dogs for fourteen years. Swain, the possessor of twelve previous convictions, was sentenced to two years. It appeared that Coulon had recruited Kenneth Collishaw (eighteen months' imprisonment) and his wife, Daphne (twelve months' imprisonment) to find more kennel girls – and those girls were each sentenced to six months' imprisonment. Their shrieks and screams echoed throughout the building and could still be heard long after they were taken to the cells.

But after the dock had been cleared, it is interesting to note the words which Judge Aarvold uttered to Pierce Butler:

I appreciate that the enquiries must have been very difficult and must have caused very great anxiety and worry. No court, of course, can commend any action which interferes with the liberty of the subject, and I do not propose to mention that at all. But I want to say that you have been subjected to strong criticism in this case and the allegations have been made that your evidence was untrustworthy, unreliable and indeed, manufactured. I want to make it clear that that certainly is not my view, and I am more than pleased to be able to say to you that it is not the jury's view, either.

Many years before, Detective Len Burt was also placed in an invidious position as to the rights and wrongs of a case. Like Pierce Butler, he won in court, and like Butler, he was commended for his actions. He rose through the ranks to become Commander Burt CVO, CBE, but much later and referring to that case, Burt rather ruefully wrote, 'I have lived to learn that one is a good fellow, until things go wrong.'

★

Back now, to more conventional Squad cases, one of which was the favourite Squad ambush.

Wilhelm Frenner was a man of set habits, which in one way is a good thing but in others distinctly disadvantageous. Mr Frenner, an extremely wealthy diamond merchant, was in the habit of carrying jewellery worth anything from £10,000 to £50,000 in a briefcase strapped to his wrist, from a safe deposit in Hatton Garden, and then taking always the same route to his office, on foot: from Greville Street into Clerkenwell Road, then along Leather Lane and into Hatton Wall – on every occasion. People get to know these things.

Mr Frenner was a singularly unobservant diamond merchant; as he emerged one day from the safe depository he failed to notice a car containing two men parked immediately opposite. As he walked along Clerkenwell Road he was unaware of the car, which was keeping abreast of him, at walking pace.

But fortunately, apart from the two occupants of the car, Leslie Ray and Mehmet Hassan, there were others who were aware of Mr Frenner's movements. They included an informant and Detective Sergeant McLachlan of the Flying Squad, and before any harm could befall the diamond merchant, the Squad pounced. An unloaded revolver was found in Ray's raincoat pocket, a bag of pepper in Hassan's jacket pocket and in the car, a formidable iron bar and a map of London, showing the position of the safe depository.

They had little option other than to plead guilty to conspiracy to rob at the Old Bailey, and they received the quite merciful sentences of twenty-one months' imprisonment for Ray and fifteen months for Hassan.

Following that triumph, Sergeant McLachlan featured in the next case, after four jeweller's shops in the West End – all of the properties belonged to the Goldsmiths' and Silversmiths' Association – were entered by means of keys between 10 and 12 October 1959, and jewellery valued at £155,101 was stolen.

McLachlan, with Detective Sergeant Terry O'Connell and four other Flying Squad officers, was keeping observation outside a block of flats at Empire Court, North End Road, Wembley on 11 December, when James Whelan and Timothy McGuire emerged from the flats, both carrying bags. As they went to enter a car parked outside, so the Squad officers swooped, and although the two men did their best to escape, they were unsuccessful.

Inside Whelan's car were found six skeleton keys; in the safe at Burlington Arcade had been keys to the other three shops.

Also in the car and the bags was jewellery stolen from the shops valued at £33,242.

Prior to a remand appearance at Bow Street Court on 30 December, a plot to free the two occupants of a prison van had been thwarted by Flying Squad officers, and Colin Nicholls, appearing for McGuire, told the court, 'May I say that this has nothing to do with him and he knows nothing about it?'

Sir Laurence Dunne, the Chief Metropolitan Magistrate, drily replied, 'It would take you an awfully long time to detail the alleged crimes which have nothing to do with McGuire', but Miss Naomi Lethbridge, counsel for Whelan, not only said she wished to be associated with her associate's remarks but made a spirited, albeit unsuccessful attempt to have part of the £500 taken from her client upon his arrest released 'for the support of his wife and children'.

At the Old Bailey on 10 February 1960 their pleas of not guilty to entering the shops was accepted, but both were sentenced to twelve years' imprisonment for receiving the jewellery.

What was interesting were the remarks they made when they were arrested. McGuire said, 'This is my lot – wait until you see what's in the bags there.'

And Whelan said, 'Have a look under the seat . . . what a marvellous organization you must have at the Yard. How did you get on to us? It's fantastic!'

He must have been blessed with second sight. Within one month of Whelan's sentence, the Criminal Intelligence Bureau commenced its duties at the Yard. It would gather, collate and disseminate information regarding top criminals, deal with telephone intercepts and later be responsible for covert surveillance, both human and electronic. What became known as C11 Department would work very harmoniously with their friends at C8.

CHAPTER 7

Finding the Great Train Robbers and Forgers' Dens

T he Flying Squad's work of the 1960s was dominated by the investigation into the Great Train Robbery, which occurred at 3.00 a.m. on 8 August 1963, when the London to Glasgow mail train was stopped at Bridego Bridge, Buckinghamshire, and some fifteen determined criminals stormed the train and stole 128 mailbags containing £2,631,684.

Whatever old-time cops may say about knowing 'a big job' was going to be pulled off, forget it. No one had the slightest inkling that the robbery was going to be carried out. The Buckinghamshire Constabulary quickly realized that they had neither the resources nor the expertise to investigate such a well-planned job, so they called in the Yard, although not before removing the carriage from which the cash was stolen into some sidings, thereby negating any chance of matching scientific evidence found at the scene. The Yard sent investigators to set up an incident room, and realizing from the limited amount of evidence available that it was a London team responsible, George Hatherill (by now the Commander of the CID) asked for an input from the Flying Squad. A small team was set up to carry out the arrests under the command of Detective Inspector Frank Williams, who was in charge of 5 Squad. Formerly a South London officer, Williams was extremely well-informed; and as former Detective Chief Superintendent Charlie Snape told me, 'He had a damn good name. Highly rated.'

The biggest breakthrough came when the gang's hideout at Leatherslade Farm was discovered, and this would lead to their downfall. First, it had been legitimately purchased through the gang's crooked solicitor. Next, believing that detection of the farm was nigh, the gang had fled, leaving a huge amount of evidence in their wake – including their fingerprints.

With just seven years' service, Tommy Butler had joined the Flying Squad in 1941 and he would spend seventeen years with the Sweeney. A dark, intense man who played his cards very close to his chest, Butler was supposed to have said to his men, 'Don't place too much value in forensic evidence' – but I think that highly unlikely, because when Leatherslade Farm was discovered, he told the Yard's Forensic Science experts to take as much time as they needed, adding, 'I don't want you coming back at a later date, telling me you could have found so much more if you'd had more time.'

For all of his secrecy, Butler had tremendous energy, working 16-hour days as a matter of course, and he expected the same commitment from his staff – this at a time when overtime was not paid to the CID. He would sweep into the office in the mornings, demanding, 'Any complaints – other than financial?'

Butler had an enormous reputation as a thief-taker with very highly placed informants. They provided him with a list of names, he obtained telephone intercepts, and when fingerprints were found at the hideout, he passed his list to the Yard's fingerprint department, telling them, 'Try these first.'

Meanwhile, a great many telephone calls were coming in to the Squad office, and when information was received about 'a lot of money' being held in a four-bedroom flat on the Hornsey Lane Estate, Upper Holloway, a Flying Squad raid proved that to be the case. Unfortunately, it had not come from the train job; a printing press, four metal engraving plates bearing the impression of Bank of England £5 notes and fourteen negatives of £5 notes were seized; so was the 65-year-old housewife who occupied the flat, together with her son and another man. Her unemployed son helpfully told the officers, 'My old lady doesn't know we were making notes' – and that was just one of the 419 raids carried out by the Squad in the first three months following the robbery.

But one by one, the train robbers were brought in, and at Aylesbury Assizes on 15 April 1964 many of them received sentences of up to thirty years' imprisonment. Two of the Robbers, Ronald Biggs and Charlie Wilson, escaped from prison and others were still at large: Bruce Reynolds, Ronald 'Buster' Edwards and Jimmy White were not arrested for some considerable time.

Although the train gang were naturally slavishly hero-worshipped by other criminals, their antics also caught the imagination of the general public. As they were released from prison, there were films, television programmes and books written (allegedly by themselves), in which they were portrayed as cheerful, chirpy chappies gleefully cocking a snook at the bumbling law. The plight of the engine driver, Jack Mills, who was savagely coshed four times by the gang and never really recovered, was conveniently forgotten about by the public – and when he gave evidence in court, in the opinion of those cheerful, chirpy chappies (who denied ever being there), Mills was 'A right fuckin' actor'. The postmen on the train, who were also coshed by the gang, were seldom if ever mentioned.

Bruce Reynolds, who enjoyed the high life, was dubbed by the press, 'The Gentleman Crook'; they claimed he abhorred violence, apparently unaware of his previous conviction for grievous bodily harm and two cases of assaulting the police, for which he was sentenced to three and a half years' imprisonment.

Following the gang's release, some re-offended, one committed suicide, another was murdered and most of them have now died; but perhaps with the exception of Gordon Goody (who, with Bruce Reynolds, was thought to be the brains behind the job) most ended up on benefits, living in graffiti-ridden, urine-soaked council blocks with their wives who, thanks to the stresses endured throughout their marriages, had succumbed to mental illness. It was hardly the success story that the Train Robbers' supporters would have everyone believe.

Perhaps the most prescient comment made was when the gang heard on the radio that their hideout had been discovered and that Tommy Butler would be heading the enquiry. Roy James looked at the others and said, simply, 'We're nicked.'

They were.

*

But in spite of the time-consuming Train Robbery investigation, a tremendous amount of work, both before and after the robbery, into other aspects of crime was carried out by the Flying Squad. A large number of arrests were carried out in respect of prison escapees, either from information received or as a result of Squad officers simply keeping their eyes open. Ten prisoners broke out of Wandsworth prison on 24 June 1961, and ten days later, one of them, Charles Robson, who had been serving a four-year sentence for robbery, was nabbed after being spotted in a Paddington club by Squad officers. One month later, two more were arrested in Wallington, where they had been staying with a pensioner who described her lodgers as 'two of the nicest I ever had'. As her guests were about to be led away they were interrupted by the appearance of another of the escapees, who had decided to pay an untimely visit. He tried to escape when the Squad car arrived at Wallington police station but was pulled back. His two colleagues had disguised themselves in a fashion that one of the arresting officers described as 'pathetic'.

Raymond Jones had been serving a sentence of eight years' preventative detention when he escaped from Pentonville; Squad officers arrested him in Staines, two years later. It was considered rather more difficult to escape from the high security prison at Parkhurst on the Isle of Wight, but Ernest Taylor, who was serving a sentence of seven years' preventative detention, managed it in January 1961; fourteen months later, the Squad arrested him in Raynes Park.

Perhaps the most surprising arrest was that of John William Thackeray, who had escaped from Wandsworth. He was arrested in Paris in 1966 after he was recognized by a former Flying Squad officer, Detective Inspector Len Mountford, who by then had retired from the Force.

★

Counterfeiting continued to be an enormous problem, and a number of cases were dealt with by the Squad. A printing press, forged £5 notes and photographic equipment were found at a scrap metal dealer's premises in Willesden, and three men were arrested. Frank Williams and his team raided a flat in Paddington and under some dirty clothing found six boxes containing a total of 1,662 forged £1 notes and 9,294 forged 10 shilling notes, as well as a duplicating and a cutting machine. One of the three people arrested was a bankrupt printer, who told Williams, 'I'm not a dishonest man. It was only a hobby at first', adding, 'I just like to have a lot of money about.'

Another printer's workshop was searched and three plates bearing facsimiles of a £1 note were found in a large carton of waste material.

'Good God, fancy that!' said the printer. 'I haven't been here for a week.'

Two more similar plates were found, and when asked for an explanation he replied, 'It doesn't rain but it pours. The rubbish has been here for about six months. I don't know what to say. Can I go and ring my solicitor now?'

It appeared that he would need one, because when his lawyer applied for bail at Clerkenwell Magistrates' Court, it was refused, after Detective Sergeant Dover told the court that a number of other plates had been found and another man had been arrested in possession of a firearm.

There was a considerable find of counterfeiting equipment inside a wooden building adjoining a house in Acton, including a printing press, other equipment used in printing and, as Detective

Inspector Hoggins told Acton Magistrates' Court, 'an extremely large amount of forged National Health stamps, some completed and others in various stages of completion'. Five men were arrested, and at the Old Bailey two of them were sentenced to four and three years and two more to twelve and eighteen months' imprisonment. A fifth man was acquitted, after he alleged that 306,399 forged National Health stamps had been planted on him.

Chief Constable of the CID – Frederick Porter Wensley OBE, KPM – the creator of the Flying Squad.

Above left: DCS Ted Greeno MBE.

Above right: DCI Fred 'Nutty' Sharpe.

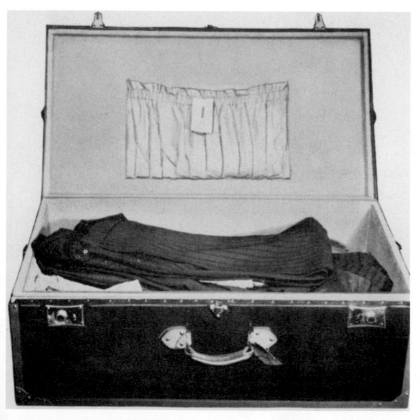

The trunk with the false bottom used in the 1934 forgery case.

Squad Leaders

Above left: D/Supt. Bob Lee.

Above right: DCS Tommy Butler MBE.

Below: DCI Walter Hambrook.

A Squad officer on top of a Crossley Tender trying to achieve an erection!

Left: A Flying Squad tender – with its aerial fully erect.

Below: Inside a Flying Squad tender. L–R: DS Bob Higgins, DC Duncan 'Jock' Careara, PC 'Jack' Frost, DCI Dan Gooch. Wireless operator PC 314 'CO' Tom Bealch.

A speedy Lea Francis Tourer . . .

. . . but not so effective when ramming bandits' heavier cars.

The 4¼ litre Invicta, in which Ockey won his KPM.

The Four Original Members of the Ghost Squad

Above left: DDI Jack Capstick.

Above right: DS John Gosling.

Below left: DS Matthew Brinnand.

Below right: DI Henry 'Nobby' Clark.

Above left: DCS Peter Henderson Beveridge MBE, who brought about the downfall of:

Above right: Billy Hill.

Below: John Charles 'Ruby' Sparks.

Villains' Kit

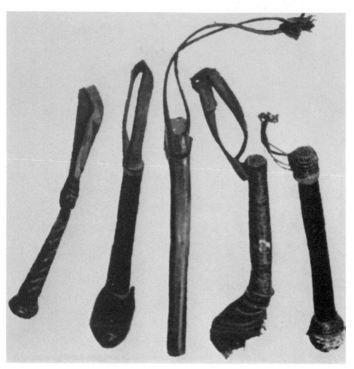 

Above left: Weapons used by the Racetrack Gangs, c. 1930.

Above right: Robbers' kit, c. 1950.

Below: Robbers' masks, c. 1960.

Above: DC Terry O'Connell showing a selection of the handiwork of 'Johnny the Boche', 1956.

Below: DCS Jim Sewell – acting on orders from on high – displaying weaponry seized from robbers following the Squad's devolvement from the Yard; since the weapons had been stripped of their protective covering prior to their production in court, the rather more experienced DS Barry Watters looks on, askance.

The Great Train Robbery

Some of the train gang at Bridego Bridge, following their release from prison. L–R: Bob Welch, Jimmy White, Roy James, Tommy Wisbey, Roger Cordrey, Gordon Goody, 'Buster' Edwards, Jim Hussey.

Leatherslade Farm, where everything started to go wrong.

In Rio. L–R: DCS Jack Slipper, Ronnie Biggs, DS Peter Jones.

Squad Officers' Line-up

Above: Squad officers in disguise, c. 1922.

Right: The Squad officers following 'The Battle of Heathrow' – L–R: Micky Dowse, Bob Acott, Donald MacMillan, Allan 'Jock' Brodie, George Draper, John Franklyn.

Squad officers at the conclusion of the trial for robbery and murder, in Glasgow. L–R, (Top): 'Nobby' Newson, Fred Snooks, Gordon Dent (Middle) Bert Barnard, Henry Poole, 'Jock' Henderson, Peter Elliott, John Batten (Front) Stuart Giblin, Ted Domachowski, Peter Jones, Jack Slipper, Peter Rimmer, Bob Robinson.

Above left: DI Edward Ockey KPM.

Above right: DS Bill Deans KPFSM.

Below left: A Squad ambush.

Below right: DI Frank Williams makes an arrest: 'Right, mister, you're nicked!'

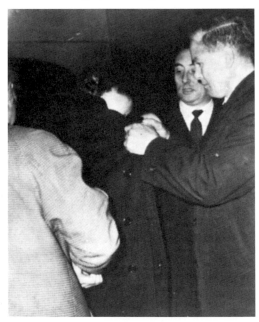

Above left: DC Phillip Williams GM, that valiant 'Four-two' with his lethal motorcycle.

Above right: DS John Wharton GM.

Below left: DS Albert Chambers GM.

Below right: DS Bob Fenton and family, following his award of the Queen's Gallantry Medal.

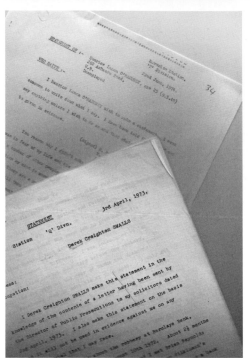

Above left: The statements of the first two supergrasses – 'Bertie' Smalls and Maurice O'Mahoney.

Above right: Weapons seized from members of 'The Wembley Mob'.

Below: Robbers' kit, c. 1980.

Arrests Made at Dewhurst's

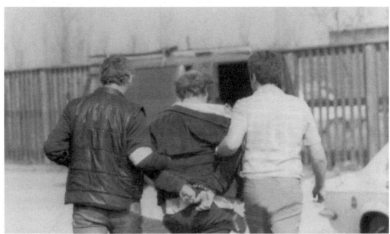

Above: Robbers go into action at Mill Hill . . .

Below: . . . only to be nabbed, seconds later, by DS Tony Yeoman.

CHAPTER 8

Armed Robberies

More normal Squad fare was arresting armed robbers, and on 15 March 1960, when a gang ambushed a Midland Bank van and robbed the occupants of £19,500, two men were arrested by Sergeant Terry O'Connell the same night. Two more arrests were made, and three weeks after the robbery, a fifth man, Frederick Wapshott, was brought in. After being left to cool off in the cells at Eltham police station (a practice now strictly forbidden), Wapshott told O'Connell, 'I've been waiting for you to come back. I'm going to tell you the absolute truth and my part in this.'

Whatever his part was, it must have been a minor one; at the Old Bailey, he received the lightest sentence of all – five years – whilst the rest of the gang received sentences of between six and twelve years' imprisonment, the trial judge telling them, '£19,000 has vanished. The duty of this court is to see that that money will not be enjoyed by any of you for some considerable time.'

It wasn't the only large sum of money to have vanished; another was £32,894 which completely disappeared, as did, apparently, the perpetrators. On the morning of 23 September 1960, security guards were taking that sum from the Handley Page factory at Cricklewood, en route to the Radlett branch of the company, when they were attacked by four or five men wielding coshes with such force that one of the guards was still too unwell to give evidence two months later.

Bertie Judd, Edward Rowlands and John Walker were arrested two weeks later and told Detective Inspector George Groombridge very conflicting stories; some agreed with others' statements, some admitting lying, others demanded £2,000 or a gang member would be shot. They had discussed carrying out the robbery, but before it could be carried out, another gang must have stepped in first and beaten them to it.

They all pleaded not guilty to the robbery at the Old Bailey; none of them gave evidence. After they were found guilty of conspiracy to rob, Walker was sentenced to two years' imprisonment and Rowlands to twenty-one months; Judd, who had previously worked at Handley Page and had told Groombridge, 'If I tell you all I know, I'd get eight years', must have been relieved to be sentenced to just eighteen months.

Arrests resulting from Flying Squad ambushes left little room for manoeuvre. On the morning of 19 July 1963 a Morris saloon was stolen in Brixton; a hired Ford van was also used to convey five men following a Securicor van containing £30,000 from the Westminster Bank, Barking Road, to Bradley & Ford, an engineering company in Forty Acre Lane, Canning Town.

A Flying Squad officer was in the back of the Securicor van, others were in cars and on foot, and as Terrence Burns waved his arms in the direction of another gang member and the gang moved in to attack, they spotted the police and were chased.

When he was stopped, Burns told Detective Sergeant Reg Lasham, 'Leave off, I'm just going for a stroll.'

Edward Wallace had a bag containing coshes, and nylon masks and stockings were found in the back of the Morris, which had been stolen very close to where another of the gang, David Deeth, lived. When he and George Sandford were stopped, and Lasham told them that they had been kept under observation for an hour, Deeth replied, 'What about it? We've just come from a factory where my mates work.'

Unfortunately, he was unable to name the factory; nor was he able to explain away the stocking he had in his pocket. Charles Devine, who had been chased through a block of flats, told his pursuers, 'I'll do the lot of you!' But when he realized the absurdity of that suggestion, he calmed down and said, 'All right, it's on us. Who put us away?'

It was suggested in mitigation that the plan had been put to them by a rogue Securicor guard for one sixth of the proceeds, but Detective Sergeant Don Neesham told the Common Serjeant at the Old Bailey that that was not the case, and four of the gang were each sentenced to four years' imprisonment, whilst Burns was sentenced to Borstal training.

A rather unconventional conspiracy to rob was uncovered after the house belonging to Marcus Marsh, a racehorse trainer, was burgled at Wickhambrook, Newmarket, and jewellery valued at £3,300 was stolen. Considerable publicity was given to this case, and as a result Francis Athoe-Harvey, a male model, and David Yoxhall, a steward, decided to capitalize on it. Neither was involved in the burglary, but Marsh was telephoned by someone calling himself 'Morgan' and told that for the sum of £500 his jewellery would be restored to him. He was told to sit in a certain row of the stalls in a cinema between 1.30 and 2.00 p.m. the following day, when the transaction would be carried out. Marsh contacted the

Yard and was given an envelope consisting of 'tops and bottoms', purporting to be the ransom.

Arriving at the cinema, Marsh sat in the wrong seat but saw Yoxhall sitting in the row where he should have been. Yoxhall said to his companion, 'He'll sit next to you in this seat and as soon as he's in, I'll move up from the end. Get him interested in the parcel but be sure to see his lot first. I'll put the frightener in on my side. You grab the bundle and run.'

Referring to a slumbering man seated behind them, Athoe-Harvey asked, 'What about the fellow behind?' to which Yoxhall replied, 'He's sound asleep.'

Unfortunately, Detective Sergeant John Keane of the Flying Squad was wide awake and had overheard every word of the conversation. He waited until Yoxhall had donned a brown wig over his blond hair before introducing himself, and was unsurprised to discover that the paper parcel which was supposed to contain Mr Marsh's stolen jewellery contained nothing more than a 2lb bag of sugar. The 'frightener' that Yoxhall referred to was a starting pistol, and this resulted in twenty-one months' imprisonment for him and fifteen months for his associate.

★

For many years, the Flying Squad had a system known as 'Early, Late and Night Provs', an abbreviation of 'Provincials'. One car for each of those shifts provided 24-hour coverage to assist provincial forces so that persons, the subject of their enquiries and living in London, could be arrested and handed over to those constabularies. Within hours of a robbery with violence at the Birmingham Small Arms company where £41,000 was stolen, a call was made to the Night Provs team at the Yard who had just come on duty, and the four men responsible were found in a house in East Dulwich, together with the loot; at Birmingham Assizes they were each sentenced to twelve years' imprisonment.

The Squad again assisted when a five-man gang armed with iron bars, Indian Clubs and chair legs blocked a road with a Land Rover in Longfield, Kent, in order to attack the crew of a bank van, throwing a brick through the windscreen and stealing £87,300. The brick-thrower and the man who hit the 67-year-old security guard so hard that he was hospitalized for several weeks was none other than Royston Shaw, who would become known as the bare-knuckle fighter, 'Pretty Boy' Shaw.

The day afterwards, Shaw, who until that time had been drawing National Assistance, purchased a white Mercedes, paying the requested price of £1,012 10s 0d entirely in £1 notes and a ten shilling note; and although he brought nine witnesses to say he was elsewhere on the day of the robbery he went down for fifteen years. So did three more of the gang.

*

John Campbell Marson had eight previous convictions, mainly for motoring offences, which included driving a car at a police officer – this gives an indication of his character – and he was serving a two-year sentence when he escaped from Lewes Prison on 4 November 1964. The reason for the escape was that his girlfriend had broken off her engagement to him while he was inside; she married on 5 December and was living in Surbiton as Mrs Cleone Castle.

Marson stole one car, then another, before purchasing a 9mm Luger and meeting up with Terrance Erasmus Williams, who was accompanied by a Miss Celia Hazel. Marson had also acquired a shotgun and ammunition, and on 22 December when they saw Cleone Castle, who had quarrelled with her husband, she was persuaded to accompany them; and in two stolen cars, a Vauxhall and an MG, they set off to London.

On the A3 they overtook Michael Young, a young man in a sports car, and Young, believing they wanted a race, sped after them. Marson and Williams forced Young's car on to the side of the road, Williams snatched the ignition key and Marson fired four shots, damaging the instrument panel, the windscreen and one of the doors, before driving off.

The next night, they drove to Chilgrove, Surrey, where there was a premises known as the Coach House; Marson and Williams had discussed fanciful plans about turning it into a club. After Marson had left, Williams and Miss Hazel were approached by the caretaker, Squadron Leader Arthur Woolnough, who told them to 'clear off'. As they walked away, Marson returned and, after a few words, fired the Luger through the car door, hitting Woolnough in the leg. In all, Marson fired four shots before driving off and joining the other two; despite his injuries, Woolnough followed them and when he was close, Williams fired the shotgun at him, the pellets narrowly missing his head.

From there, the quartet travelled to Maidenhead, where they stole a two-seater Mercedes belonging to the racing driver Roy Salvatore. Now fully aware that a police hunt was underway for them, they decided to split up; Williams and Miss Hazel went to

Dublin, and Marson and Mrs Castle drove to Shrewsbury and York before returning to London on 6 January.

Marson met a friend and ordered him to get into the Mercedes; with Cleone on his friend's lap, he drove off, but in Millbank he was spotted by Police Constable Michael Wheelhouse, a police motorcyclist, who commenced a chase. The Mercedes tore down the Embankment, reaching speeds of 90mph; other police motorcyclists and two police cars joined in the pursuit. Nobody was in any doubt that Marson was equipped with two firearms and was more than ready to use them.

Police Sergeant Arthur Porter was in charge of a 'Q' Car with an aid to CID, Roger Oliver. He told me, 'Roger appeared to have a few contacts and a couple of addresses Marson was known to visit. We decided to visit an address in Chelsea and on our way we picked up a message from Information Room saying that Marson was driving a stolen car.'

Marson's driving had already knocked a Mini on to the pavement, and he had hit two Rolls-Royces. The radio message to the police was, 'Suspect in Beaufort Street', and as the 'Q' Car containing Porter and Oliver was approaching that location, so was a Flying Squad car driven by Police Constable Geoffrey Bocking and crewed by Detective Sergeant David Wilson and Detective Sergeant Peter Woodmore, as were a number of other police officers and vehicles.

The first to reach the crashed Mercedes was PC Wheelhouse; dismounting from his motorcycle, he wrenched open the door of the stolen car, whereupon Marson shot him in the arm.

'Look out, he's got a gun!' shouted Wheelhouse, but by now Marson was out of the car and running, gun in hand. Police were in hot pursuit, and as Manson ran towards Earls Court Road he fired another shot before taking deliberate aim at Police Constable Derek Birkhead and firing; the shot missed and hit a parked car.

'On reaching Bramham Gardens, I saw him standing by the railings of the gardens', Arthur Porter told me. 'I called, "Stop, police!" and with that, he fired a couple of shots at me and Roger, who had by then caught up with me.'

Marson climbed into the basement area of a hostel at the corner of Collingham Road, and Police Constable David Cadogan slipped the leash of police dog 'Simon', who darted forward, before Manson shot him dead.

Sergeant Wilson of the Squad shouted 'Come out!', and Marson fired a shot which shattered the wing mirror of a car a foot away. Wilson scooped up an armful of milk bottles and flung them down at the gunman. Other officers also threw milk bottles, and Marson started to climb out of the basement.

'A uniformed police officer leant out of a window and hit him on the head with his truncheon', said Wilson. 'With other officers, I ran to the point where he was climbing. He fired two shots into the group of officers, and one, Police Constable Cross, called out.'

Now Sergeant Woodmore climbed on to the railings, shouting, 'Throw away the gun and give yourself up!'

Marson stood up, faced the officer and pointed the gun at him. With that, Woodmore dived off the railings on top of Marson, 10ft below, grabbed his right arm which held the gun, and they fell to the ground. As they struggled, and Marson was relieved of the gun, he repeatedly shouted, 'I will kill you all!'

Three live rounds remained in the gun, which could hold nine; Marson had an additional fifteen rounds in his pocket.

He seemed overcome by events, and he was taken, as Arthur Porter told me, 'semi-conscious' to Chelsea police station.

At the Old Bailey on 8 April 1965 Marson pleaded guilty to a collection of serious offences, including possessing a Luger pistol with intent to endanger life, stealing four cars, wounding Wheelhouse, Cross and Squadron Leader Woolnough and shooting at Porter and Wilson with intent to resist arrest.

John Hazan QC said in mitigation that his client saw himself not only as a rejected suitor but also 'as a latter day Sir Galahad, who wanted to rescue a maiden from the clutches of someone he considered undesirable'. Disregarding the fact that Sir Galahad was a monastic knight, more interested in finding the Holy Grail than rescuing miscellaneous totty, Dr Francis Brisbey, the medical officer at Brixton Prison, chimed in, saying that Marson was of below average intelligence and was suffering from 'impaired development'. The judge sentenced him to fourteen years' imprisonment and disqualified him from driving for twenty years.

His associate, Williams, who had seven previous convictions, appeared at the Old Bailey three weeks later and, for using a shotgun with intent to resist Marson's arrest, maliciously damaging Michael Young's sports car and assaulting him and taking and driving away two cars, he was fortunate to be sentenced to three years' imprisonment.

Wheelhouse and Woodmore were both awarded the George Medal. There were three awards of the British Empire Medal for Gallantry, two of which went to Porter and Oliver, plus three awards of the Queen's Commendation for Brave Conduct, as well as commendations for many other officers.

Apart from the other officers' gallantry, the Flying Squad input came from the Squad driver, Geoffrey Bocking, who had won a George Medal eleven years previously and who drove on this occasion at perilously high speeds to get the officers to where they should be, as well as from the ingenuity of Sergeant Wilson who utilized milk bottles as weapons and the raw courage of Woodmore with his daring 10 ft dive to subdue and disarm a near-lunatic gunman.

★

It has previously been mentioned that the Criminal Intelligence Department (C11) worked harmoniously with the Squad; apart from disseminating pertinent information to the Squad, they had their own surveillance team, faceless men and women who carried out observations and passed what the criminals were doing on to the Squad by means of concealed radio transmitters, before noiselessly slipping away. Their surveillance was carried out on foot and from a variety of vehicles. But in addition, unmarked powerful motorcycles were used and these were known as 'Four-twos'.[1] They were perfect for following suspects in busy London traffic; and their riders, like their counterparts, reported what they had seen to the Squad before disappearing. They were certainly not expected to carry out arrests; however, there are always exceptions to every rule . . .

The activities of Peter Rose had been of interest to C11 for some time; when information was received that he and his associates, Michael Morris and Michael Engelfield, were plotting to rob a bank, a joint operation was set up by C11 and the Squad. Detective Inspector (later Detective Chief Superintendent) Jim Marshall was in charge of a deployment of officers from 4 squad, and Rose's gang were followed for four weeks. The location where the robbery was to occur was not precisely known, but it was clear that it was likely to be in the Streatham area of South London, so it was at that police station that the Squad secreted themselves whilst the watchers from C11 carried out their surveillance. Three cars were stolen and put down at locations to facilitate the robbers' getaway; one of the Four-twos, Detective Constable Reg Jenkins, saw three men get out of a stolen car wearing caps and carrying holdalls and walk towards the District Bank. The Squad

[1] The 'four' referred to the four Metropolitan Police districts from where the officers had been seconded; the 'two' denoted that the vehicles possessed two wheels.

were alerted, their vehicles roared north along the southbound carriageway of the High Road, and as they screeched to a halt, a shot was fired at Detective Constable (later Commander) Ray Adams and Detective Inspector Marshall. Two of the gang – Morris and Engelfield – were armed with sawn-off shotguns, Rose with a revolver.

Detective Sergeant Pat O'Brien ran after Engelfield, who threatened to shoot him, but O'Brien nevertheless continued his pursuit. Jenkins tried to run down Engelfield but missed him; he tried again but was knocked from his machine by a passing car. He then saw Morris coming towards him pointing a shotgun, but when he confronted him, Morris turned and ran off.

Engelfield, meanwhile, was chased into a block of flats by Detective Sergeant John Wharton, who found him on the top floor; he went for his sawn-off, which was lying on the floor, and there was a terrific struggle before he was finally subdued.

Detective Constable Phillip Williams was the second Four-two; when he initially saw the three armed men coming towards him, he drove straight at one of them but missed him; as he went to turn his motorcycle around, a shot was fired, aimed at his back, which missed. Rose hid behind a parked car and, as Williams accelerated towards him, he pointed his revolver – a .357 Magnum – at the officer, who rammed his 500cc BSA straight into him, lifting Rose on to the handlebars before both men crashed to the ground. Rose scrambled to his feet and at a distance of 2–3 ft pointed his revolver at Williams, who leapt at him; a shot was discharged and a fierce struggle ensued, until O'Brien drew his truncheon and 'sticked' Rose so fiercely that it brought matters to a swift conclusion.

Morris was now dashing through crowds of shoppers, pointing his shotgun at them; Marshall and Adams were in hot pursuit. When he ran into a front garden Morris pointed his shotgun at the officers, telling them he would shoot; Marshall and Adams approached him from different wide angles before pouncing on him, and Adams grabbed the sawn-off while Marshall whacked him with his truncheon.

Rose was convicted of attempting to murder Williams and that, plus using a firearm with intent to resist arrest, resulted in his being sentenced to fourteen years' imprisonment; Morris and Engelfield were each sentenced to ten years.

The gang's actions also resulted in the award of George Medals to Williams (whose actions, many believed, would result in an award of the George Cross) and Wharton, with British Empire Medals for Gallantry for Marshall, Adams, O'Brien and Jenkins.

Phill Williams was much admired and a good friend to the Flying Squad for many years. Now aged eighty-two, he has lost none of his enthusiasm; when he telephones me he announces himself by quoting his Metropolitan Police warrant number – 'It's 143516, here!' – and he tells me, 'If I was nineteen again, I'd be first in the queue.'

*

The Squad had been in existence for half a century and it was riding the crest of a wave. Tommy Butler's insistence that he be allowed to extend his service by five years paid off when he arrested the elusive Great Train robber Bruce Reynolds, after he'd spent six years on the run. Detective Chief Inspector Tom Morrison DCM had given the Flying Squad the insignia it deserved – a swooping eagle – after he pinched the concept from the Eagle Star Insurance Company. As the decade came to a close, in 1969 the Squad had made 1,548 arrests and recovered property valued at £700,000; and during that year, a George Medal, two British Empire Medals and a Queen's Commendation for bravery were awarded to members of the Squad, who had also received fifty commendations from the commissioner.

The press portrayed the Sweeney as tough, granite-jawed, incorruptible if rather unorthodox detectives, who could be pretty well relied upon to get their man and if the reporters injected a healthy dose of hyperbole into their columns, it was essentially a correct picture.

But now, storm clouds were gathering for the Flying Squad.

CHAPTER 9

Ronnie Biggs in Rio

During the 1960s, four members of the Squad stood trial on charges of demanding money with menaces, corruption and conspiracy to pervert the course of justice. After a week's trial, the jury found them not guilty and the judge awarded them costs.

Two other Squad officers stood trial on charges of corruption, and after juries failed to agree after two trials, the prosecution decided not to seek a third and the men were discharged. But a rather disquieting matter arose during the trial; one of the officers, a detective sergeant, admitted that he had told a magistrate lies on oath, when he was requesting a search warrant.

In fact, it appeared that this was not an isolated incident and that such things were done to protect the identity of an informant. For example, if the disgruntled wife of an armed robber reported to police that the previous day she had seen him secrete firearms in the loft, and if police secured a warrant under the Firearms Act and went to retrieve the guns and arrested the husband, he would know that his wife had been the only person present when he hid the weapons and that he had mentioned this to nobody else; consequently, he would instantly know that she was the grass.

Therefore it was often thought expedient to obtain a search warrant under the Theft Act and stipulate that it was 'divers goods' that the officers were looking for. This was not too far from the truth, for if a shotgun was found, it was bound to have been stolen. Consequently, when that search extended to the loft and, bingo, the gun was found, it would appear to be just the robber's bad luck. It was not always as cut and dried as that, of course. Sometimes the informant would have to be arrested as well. They would be questioned and, denying all knowledge, would be released due to lack of evidence; on occasion it might be necessary (with the informant's consent) to administer a public punch in the face to provide verisimilitude to the proceedings.

Often, in the case of a wife being the informant, she would be advised beforehand to greet the officers with screeching verbal abuse; although on one occasion these histrionics got rather out of hand, when the arresting officer told the suspect, 'Tell that silly cow to shut her fucking mouth!' and the husband, who had no idea that it was his wife who had precipitated his downfall, took umbrage, and it was the officer who wound up with a black eye. So that was the type of situation that some Squad officers considered to be part of their bread-and-butter workload; it was part of the Squad's unconventional way of 'getting things done'.

But matters changed dramatically in 1972, when Ken Drury, the Flying Squad commander, was accused of corrupt practices; following an investigation which took years to complete, Drury and others were sent to prison.

Former Detective Sergeant Mike Bucknole succinctly explains the situation:

> A blinkered culture became the norm and symptomatic of senior uniform officers and politicians attitude to crime fighting. They simply didn't understand the rules of engagement with the enemy. The enemy wasn't within, but outside of the police ranks amongst the thugs and villains who thought they were untouchable. There were 'black sheep' within, but this wasn't institutionalised corruption on the level that Sir Robert Mark and his following of untrained investigators perceived. What ensued was the most respected and admired detective force in the world at Scotland Yard being disseminated by incompetent 'senior' decisions, and it has never been allowed to recover since.
>
> We understood the nature of the beast, because we got very close to them without them suspecting the oncoming hit! However, we were betrayed by a minority who gave the media ammunition to throw at the majority. This culminated in the rules for meeting informants and frequenting meeting places of known villains to be changed by senior officers as a 'safeguard'. The working detective questioned, who was this safeguard for? Was it to protect the senior officer's job, those who had never done a day's work as a detective investigator in their life, or the villain who grasped at any straw to save his own back?
>
> In my experience as a career detective at New Scotland Yard (1964–93) the science of the use of informants had fallen away rapidly since it was demonised by senior uniform officers in the 1970s. Some of those officers like Deputy Assistant Commissioner David Powis, also known as 'Crazy Horse', were more a hindrance than

a help, with their petty directive memoranda. Senior officers were clueless about crime investigation because they'd never done it. They'd never been amongst the violent 'muck and bullets' but they tried to lay down guidelines for something they knew very little about. Powis wrote two 'comic-cuts' books about crime in 1971 and 1977 that were dated when he wrote them because of his inexperience in criminal investigation techniques. They were more suited to the quite pleasant fictional policing of *Dixon of Dock Green*. Powis acknowledged his Victorian attitudes and standards, but never his outdated incompetence that was alien to the skill required for late twentieth century villain-busting. It is obvious from the presentation in the books, his so-called 'manuals', that he was sadly lacking in detective ability and certainly in the Victorian ingenuity of a pragmatic genius like the fictional Sherlock Holmes.

He and some of his colleagues were frightened by the use of informants from the perspective of the consequences that might come from their use. He and others like him were an embarrassment when meeting and paying reward money to informants for their positive information leading to charges being proffered. The directive was that they had to be present and personally give the reward to the informant. Their perverse use of language was 'foreign' to the snout, and the directions given to them by senior police officers of D.A.C. rank, in the Metropolitan Police, were irrelevant to the informant's way of life. The informant's trust often had to be recovered by the handler after such an encounter if they were ever to be of use again in the future.

The lack of training from experienced detectives to younger contemporaries today has been compounded over the years by the fact that there have been very few practical investigatory skills handed down. In my view this is because the system has changed: no career detectives, no Detective Training School and the mockery of hiring detectives direct from the public sector without any previous practical knowledge. It is coupled with the over-regulation of allowable investigatory techniques that are available to the investigating officer. This is to the detriment of successful investigation of crime. The proper use of informants was one of the greatest tools available to assist efficacious conclusions to cases.

Sadly, the skill has been lost through neglect and misdirection. This was the stock in trade of the Flying Squad, coupled with the skill of organizing 'pavement ambushes' of armed robbers in the act of committing their heinous crimes with sawn-off shotguns. Flying Squad officers also had the ability to blend in with their surroundings, coupled with a keen sense of humour and the utmost regard for their colleagues' requirements.

Added to that, following accusations of corruption in the City of London Police, further allegations were made against Metropolitan officers, and the ill-fated Operation Countryman was formed to investigate those claims. Eight Flying Squad officers stood trial; all were acquitted. During the 1970s, newspaper reportage of the excellent work carried out by the Flying Squad appeared to dry up, and in that atmosphere of demoralization it was surprising that any work at all was carried out by the Squad.[1]

★

But of course, work did continue. In November 1971 seven men were charged with conspiracy to dispose of stolen goods after a combined operation by the Squad and the Federal Bureau of Investigation, who raided a house in Park Street, Mayfair. Bearer bonds and stock certificates valued at £30 million had been stolen from an office in Chicago three months previously; bonds worth $12 million were recovered. The team were extradited to the United States and the Squad were called to give evidence – not including Charlie Snape, who had played a prominent part in the investigation, since he was in the middle of a trial at the Old Bailey; salt was rubbed into his wounds when he discovered that the rest of the team were receiving $50 per day expenses.

In an ambush led by Frank Williams, Squad officers were dressed in Security Express uniforms and as a result surprised a gang of Irishmen, one of whom, James Farrell, threw his sawn-off shotgun into a canal, threw himself in after it and swam to the other side (as did Charlie Snape); following a spirited punch-up, Farrell was sentenced to thirteen years' imprisonment for robbery, conspiracy to rob and possession of firearms. On 5 May 1971 he escaped from Chelmsford Prison, and when a house in Kilburn

---

[1] For a more detailed account of this imbecile venture, see *Operation Countryman: The Flawed Enquiry into London Police Corruption*, Pen & Sword True Crime, 2018.

Lane was raided four months later, he dived out of the first-floor window. This time, there was no water to cushion his impact and he had to be scraped off the pavement. Not that that curtailed his antics; in 1978, for another robbery, he was jailed for seventeen years.

★

It's now time to return to the Great Train Robbery investigation. Following the thirty-year sentences, Charlie Wilson had been sprung from Winson Green Prison, Birmingham, and his escape lasted 3½ years before he was arrested by Tommy Butler, in Canada. 'Buster' Edwards gave himself up, and Jimmy White was arrested at a seaside town in Kent. That left Ronnie Biggs.

In the week following Biggs' escape from Wandsworth Prison on 8 July 1965, the Yard received 371 messages from people who believed they knew of his whereabouts. Each alleged sighting had to be examined. It was not until August 1969 that information was received that Biggs was in Melbourne, Australia with Eric Flower, one of the people with whom he'd escaped. Flower was arrested, but Biggs was missed by two minutes. On 25 November 1972 the Commonwealth State Police informed the Yard that Biggs, using the name Michael John Haynes, had travelled from Melbourne to Panama in February 1970. Enquiries to trace him were made without success, and by the time 24 January 1974 arrived there were twenty-seven box files containing sightings of Biggs.

It was on that date that Detective Sergeant Peter Jones – a member of the Flying Squad but not one who had been involved in the Great Train Robbery investigation – was told by the Squad's commander to report to the office of Deputy Assistant Commissioner Ernie Bond OBE, QPM, a highly respected and experienced officer who had previously served two tours with the Flying Squad.

Also present in Bond's office were Assistant Commissioner (Crime) Colin Woods and Commander Peter Walton, head of CID Administration at the Yard, as well as Detective Chief Superintendent Jack Slipper, operational head of the Flying Squad. Joining as a detective constable, Slipper would spend a total of nine years with the Flying Squad, being involved in some of its most important cases, including the Great Train Robbery.

Agreeing to be involved in an enquiry which required the utmost secrecy, Jones was told that he would be going to Brazil with Slipper, with a view to returning with Ronnie Biggs. The information which had led up to this challenge was as follows.

A *Daily Express* reporter named Colin Mackenzie had conducted a telephone conversation with Biggs and was also in possession of a photograph bearing his fingerprints. Mackenzie had not disclosed Biggs' telephone number, nor was he willing to part with the photograph, since he intended to carry out an interview with Biggs, apparently and if necessary, against the newspaper's wishes. Because of Mackenzie's attitude and without the reporter's knowledge, Ian McColl, the editor of the *Daily Express*, had informed the police.

Brian Hitchin, the newspaper's news editor, needed to confirm that it was indeed Biggs to whom Mackenzie had spoken and he therefore told Mackenzie to telephone Biggs again; only when contact had been made would Hitchin supply Mackenzie with a list of questions which could only be correctly answered by Biggs himself. What followed was recounted by Peter Jones:

> On Friday 25 January there was a meeting with Brian Hitchin, Jack Slipper and me at the Pillbox pub at Westminster Bridge. Hitchin informed us that contact had been made with Ronnie Biggs at 11.00 pm on 24 January and the conversation had lasted nineteen minutes. Hitchin also stated that he had stood alongside Colin Mackenzie, who did the talking, whilst the relevant questions were put to Biggs. Hitchin wrote down the answers.
>
> Q Describe the position of the front door of your house in Redhill and the garden.
> A It's a small garden of roses. It had a wall along the left-hand side with a red wooden gate. There was a small wooden coal shed at the left-hand corner in the back garden. (*This was correct*)
> Q What is your wife's birthday?
> A 17.5.39. (*17.5.38 was the correct answer*)
> Q What are your sons' birthdays?
> A (*The names Christopher and Nicholas were given correctly but their dates of birth were not completely accurate*)
> Q Your birthday?
> A 8.8.1929 (*Correct*)
>
> In view of these questions and answers, Jack Slipper was quite clear that the person must be Biggs. When we returned to Scotland Yard, he contacted the Post Office security division, and as a result of enquiries made by that division, he received a call stating that the telephone call made by Mackenzie to Rio was Rio 2569377 and that the premises in question referred to 33 Avenida

Prado, Apartment 1207. Making this enquiry was only a precaution, in case Mackenzie failed to cooperate with the *Daily Express* or the CID.

Later that day, there was a meeting in Ernie Bond's office with Mackenzie, Hitchin, Andrew Edwards (the lawyer for the *Daily Express*) and Jack Slipper. Mackenzie was furious that the police had become involved, and the discussions became very heated. The newspaper wanted to have initial access to Biggs, after which they would hand over the information to the police. Bond refused, as he did when Mackenzie suggested that he would get Biggs' story, then persuade him to return to the United Kingdom. Bond pointed out that refusal to hand over such information as he possessed about Biggs was an offence for which he could be prosecuted. Mackenzie then handed over a photograph of a railway engine and carriage and the sun; it was allegedly signed by Biggs and it certainly bore one of his fingerprints.

Mackenzie gave an account of meeting a young man named Constantine Benckendorff, who told him that he had met Ronnie Biggs in Rio; he had been the conduit between Biggs and Mackenzie. The decision was made to go along with the *Daily Express* and permit them to have some time with Biggs to get their story, before making the arrest. This was because the Yard was extremely concerned that without that agreement, Mackenzie might telephone Biggs and tip him off regarding the Squad's involvement. Apparently, years later, Mackenzie admitted that he had thought of doing just that.

Peter Jones now takes up the tale again:

On Monday 28 January 1974 Jack Slipper, Ernie Bond and I discussed the following alternatives, as there could be considerable difficulties in telling the Foreign Office or the Home Office about the decision to arrest Ronnie Biggs:

1. That the *Express* could make contact with Biggs and work alone.
2. That we could work through Interpol.
3. That a formal approach could be made with the Brazilian Government.
4. That an approach could be made through the Foreign Office.
5. That we should go to Brazil unannounced and contact the local police on our arrival.

Ernie Bond decided that No. 5 was the best option.

There had already been a number of leaks from Interpol and British Government departments – in fact, Ernie Bond was currently investigating those matters – hence the decision for the officers to go straight to Rio. At a meeting with Mackenzie and Hitchin it was decided that Mackenzie and Bill Lovelace, the photographer for the *Daily Express*, would go to Rio on Wednesday, 30 January, that Slipper and Jones would follow on Friday, 1 February, and that the arrest would take place on 3 February, allowing Mackenzie to file his copy with the newspaper for publication on Monday, 4 February. At least, that was the plan.

But when Slipper received a telephone call from a member of the Yard's Press Bureau asking if it was true that Biggs had been arrested in Australia for being drunk and disorderly, and asking where Biggs had last been seen, Slipper thought – with some justification – that there *had* been a leak. It was decided to go to Rio that very day and, informing the *Express* personnel that the arrest date would be Friday, not Sunday, Jones was dispatched to buy airline tickets at a travel agent and to a bank to acquire Brazilian cruzeiros. Brian Hitchin was told the officers would be catching the 7.15 pm flight from Terminal 3 at Heathrow, and to avoid Slipper being recognized at the airport he arranged for all the airport press reporters to be in the bar at Terminal 1, where he would buy them a drink and thank them for their services.

Pausing only for Jones to submit a request for urgent annual leave for seven days to visit his ailing mother (who was in excellent health), he and Slipper boarded the flight to Rio and landed at 6.00 am local time the following day. Booking into the Excelsior Hotel and giving their professions as Met officers – not entirely untrue – they met Brian Vine, senior reporter for the *Express*, who had flown down from Canada. Bill Lovelace, the photographer, joined them, leaving Mackenzie to get his story from Ronnie Biggs at the Trocadero Hotel. Some angry words were exchanged regarding the change of plan, but as senior man, Vine stipulated that Mackenzie and Lovelace could have until 12.30 pm the following day to complete both the interview and the photographs.

When Lovelace later saw Biggs, in company with his girlfriend Lucia that evening, Biggs suddenly said, 'You haven't told Old Bill . . . and they're down the road, waiting for me?'

This remark was laughed off by Lovelace and Mackenzie, although later that evening, as Slipper and Jones were returning to their hotel after a meal, they happened to see Biggs and Lucia.

As Jones said, 'It was as well we were on different sides of the road.'

On Friday, 1 February the officers met the local Commissioner of Police, Dr Ivo Reposo Jr., at Copacabana police station. The British Consul and Vice Consul, Henry Neill and Francisco Costas, were also present, the Yard's documentation was produced and the Commissioner expressed great interest in the case.

He suggested that Biggs should be picked up with the assistance of the local Federal Police and taken to their headquarters for processing. Henry Neill agreed, saying that he knew the head of the police, Carlos Alberto Garcia, and that he anticipated no problems at all. He did stress that the only difficulty that might arise was that Brazil had no extradition treaty or reciprocal agreement with the United Kingdom, so it would be helpful if Biggs would sign a document agreeing to return to England with the officers. It was agreed that the signal to move in for the arrest would be when Bill Lovelace came out on to the balcony of Room 909 of the Trocadero Hotel and purported to take photos of the scenery; that would be confirmation that Biggs was in the room.

Joined by the Commissioner, the officers made their way up to the hotel's ninth floor. When Benckendorff answered the knock on the door, they walked straight in to see the *Express* personnel, Lucia lying naked on the bed and, wearing a pair of red swimming trunks, Ronnie Biggs himself.

'Fancy seeing you here, Ronnie', said Slipper to the stunned prison escapee, who could only stutter, 'Fuck me!' before recovering his wits and turning to Lovelace and Mackenzie, saying, 'I knew I should never have trusted the fucking *Daily Express!*'

With one side accusing the other, and Jones taking the names of everybody in the room, Slipper took Biggs to one side and told him he would be taken to his own flat to pick up any of his possessions; Biggs said that he would prefer to return to England as soon as possible, rather than rot in a Brazilian jail. At that point, the first cracks began to appear. Biggs asked that he should not be handcuffed upon leaving the hotel; it was a small concession to make, and since there were sufficient officers there to quell a small riot, Slipper mentioned the request to the Commissioner, saying that this was fine with him as long as the Brazilian police didn't mind.

Unlike Slipper, the Commissioner had not worked his way up the promotional ladder from walking the beat. His appointment had been a political one, and in fact he was a doctor of law. He was therefore unused to dealing with international gangsters and, seeing what he assumed to be a criminal attempting to lay down the law, he decided to flex his law-enforcement muscles. Opening his jacket, he tapped the butt of his revolver and told Biggs, 'No trouble – or else!'

That – plus, perhaps, the realization that he was en route to resume the twenty-nine years of his interrupted sentence – caused Biggs to blow a gasket; he screamed threats at the Commissioner which only resulted in the revolver butt being tapped meaningfully again. Slipper managed to defuse the situation by tell Biggs that if he did run he would certainly be shot, and that given Brazil's record on human rights, that would probably be a merciful release.

Having visited Biggs' sparsely furnished apartment, prisoner and escort arrived at *Policia Federal Pacacio Do Catete* to meet Inspector Garcia. Apart from the obligatory pistol-butt-tapping (which Biggs now seemed to recognize as the norm), there were no problems. Garcia agreed that if Biggs was not wanted for an offence in Brazil he would be released to the Squad officers at 6.00 pm, enabling the three of them to catch the 7.00 pm flight to England. In the meantime, Biggs signed a short statement saying that not only did he wish to return to England, he wanted to do so that very day, and his signature was witnessed by the Vice Consul.

Marion Jones told me, 'I knew Peter was going somewhere, but I didn't know where. The first I knew of it was when neighbours told me, "Quick, put the 10 o'clock news on – Peter's on there!"'

But having packed their bags and settled their bills at the Excelsior, the officers returned to police headquarters to discover that Biggs had allegedly told Garcia that with two Americans he had been smuggling drugs into the country from Miami. Garcia stated that he would be unable to complete the necessary enquiries before 6.00 pm and therefore Biggs would have to be detained until 6.00 pm on Monday, 4 February, when he was sure Biggs could be released into the Yard officers' custody; in the meantime, Garcia suggested that Slipper and Jones should book into a hotel and enjoy the weekend.

The Vice Consul, Francisco Costas, was quite optimistic that Biggs would be released on Monday, although with the Brazilian police taking forty-five sets of Biggs' fingerprints, one for each of Brazil's districts, this seemed to be less and less likely; it was also possible that the Brazilian authorities were miffed at the way the British police had entered their country to conduct their enquiries. Matters were certainly not helped by the British Consul, Henry Neill, losing his temper with Garcia and banging his fist on the table in a very undiplomatic manner, demanding that Biggs should be released immediately.

On Monday Garcia proposed a deal; he would release Biggs at 6.00 pm that day, in time for the trio to board the 7.00 pm plane to London, providing that the Yard issued a statement saying that it had been the Brazilians who had found Biggs in the first place and that they had called London over to bring him back. Was it worth eating a large slice of humble pie in order to get Biggs back? Probably, but it was never put to the test, because at 6.20 pm that evening Garcia told the officers that Biggs was not going to be released and that the British authorities had sixty days to apply for his extradition. Since no extradition treaty existed between the two countries, this appeared to be a non-starter.

So the officers returned home empty-handed, to a barrage of criticism from the press and the public. A photograph taken by the *Daily Express* showed Slipper sitting alone, next to a vacant seat, the inference being that the seat had been reserved for Biggs, but as Peter Jones told me, 'It was my seat – I'd just gone to the toilet!'

Could the matter have been handled any differently – should Slipper and Jones have gone at all? The answers are, no, it couldn't, and yes, they should. Quite simply, there was no other way that the situation could have been handled, and the duo came so close to bringing Biggs back.

Biggs capitalized on that fact that another of his Brazilian girlfriends, Raimunda de Castro (an 'exotic dancer') was pregnant. Since there was a Brazilian law which prohibited the deportation of the father of a child born in that country, Lucia was dumped. So, just as quickly, was Biggs' wife Charmian, who had stuck steadfastly by him.

Few of the train gang were as charismatic as Ronnie Biggs, living it up in Rio, being photographed wearing a policeman's toy helmet and gleefully sticking up two rude fingers for the camera – before, thirty-eight years after his escape from prison, he returned voluntarily to England, suffering from ill-health and a large dose of self-pity.

★

Jack Slipper once wrote that Peter Jones 'could always be relied upon for his ice-cool logic and lightning reaction if the going got tough'. That was exemplified shortly after their return from Rio when they went to Glasgow High Court to give evidence in a case of armed robbery.

Prior to the Rio expedition, on 21 December 1973, there had been an armed robbery at the British Rail Engineering Company in Charles Street, Glasgow in which £9,854 was stolen. A security guard had been shot at point-blank range and had died instantly, and two more British Rail security guards were shot and seriously injured. The Scottish police had the name of one of the suspects who lived in London and requested help from the Yard, which the Squad was only too happy to provide. With the Squad and the Scottish officers working together, the suspect was arrested and named everybody else responsible, taking the officers all over London, pointing out the addresses where the suspects lived.

Peter Rimmer told me, '"Uncle Jack" [Slipper] got eight Squad and others together and late at night/early morning of Xmas Eve, we hit a flat in Holloway and recovered some of the cash hidden as presents under the Xmas tree. A strong bond was established with the visitors and all spent Xmas with the Squad families.'

It was quick work indeed; as a result, four of the robbers appeared at Glasgow Sheriff Court on 27 December, and later, two more robbers were added to the other four.

Peter Jones had carried out the arrest of Sidney Draper at Warden Road, Hampstead. Draper was in bed at the time; his hands were concealed by the bedclothes, and Jones, pointing his service revolver at a spot right between Draper's eyes, told him to show his hands or he'd shoot.

This was the evidence which Jones gave at the High Court in Glasgow on 25 March 1974 which prompted the trial judge, Lord Kissen, to ask what would have happened had Draper not shown his hands.

'I'd have shot him, my Lord', replied Jones. There was a collective gasp in the crowded courtroom and Jones continued, saying, 'One man had already been murdered and I wasn't planning on being the next.' It was precisely that type of resoluteness which had prompted Jack Slipper's comments about Peter Jones' capabilities.

On 10 April six men were sentenced to life imprisonment and with recommended minimum sentences of 119 years, in what was then the longest trial with the heaviest sentences in the history of Scotland's legal system.

Peter Rimmer's enduring memory of the case was that of the old court sergeant telling him, 'I wish all of the young coppers in Glasgow could have seen you Squad officers give evidence; it was the best I'd ever seen.'

CHAPTER 10

Balcombe Street

After Peter Barnes and James Richards were hanged on 7 February 1940, the Irish Republican Army's war against, as Buchan put it, 'a dull, mercantile England', temporarily fizzled out. It had been all very well (and enormous fun) setting off explosions, causing a huge amount of damage and injury to Londoners, but although ninety-four members of the IRA were sentenced to between ten and twenty years' penal servitude, their reasoning was that it wasn't worth getting hanged for.

By the time 'The Troubles' resurrected themselves in 1969, and a mainland offensive was launched in 1973, there was one important difference: capital punishment had been abolished.

It commenced on 8 March 1973, when four crude bombs were deposited outside the BBC's armed forces radio station, New Scotland Yard, the Old Bailey and the Ministry of Agriculture. The first two were defused, the others detonated. During that year, ten more bombs were planted; all except two exploded, and over seventy people were injured.

By the time Detective Constable Bob Fenton joined the Flying Squad on 26 November 1975, there had been four shootings since 1973 and a further 42 explosions, resulting in another 310 injuries, with thirteen dead. The day following Fenton's appointment, Ross McWhirter, the co-founder of the *Guinness Book of Records*, who had offered a £50,000 reward for information leading to the arrest of those responsible for these outrages, was shot dead by the IRA.

'Operation Combo' had been set up by the police in order to capture an IRA cell; some 700 officers, both uniform and CID, were deployed on foot and in vehicles in central London. The concept was that there would be a central ring of officers on foot tasked with detecting IRA activity, plus an outer ring of vehicles ready to come in and make the arrests. Only uniformed officers were armed, to prevent a 'blue-on-blue' incident. The Flying Squad was deployed to form part of that outer circle and they, like all of the other officers, were issued with hand-held radios, all tuned in to the same frequency.

Fenton was in the rear offside passenger seat of a Flying Squad car – a bright yellow Ford Granada Mark II, understandably nicknamed 'The Yellow Canary' – driven by Police Constable Peter Wilson and crewed by Detective Inspector Henry Dowswell and Detective Sergeant Phil Mansfield. On the evening of 6 December 1975 at 9.15, they were about to leave the Yard. Bob Fenton takes up the story:

> We heard on the radio that shots had been fired into Scott's restaurant in Mount Street, Mayfair, the scene of a previous incident when a bomb had been thrown into the restaurant, killing one person. The shout was put up by two uniform colleagues on the operation who witnessed the drive-by shooting. It later transpired that two shots had been discharged but an automatic weapon they had tried to use had jammed without firing. The front nearside passenger had fired two shots (later confirmed as from a .30 Carbine rifle), and they noticed that the rear offside passenger had a handgun.
>
> The officers said that the vehicle contained four males and they put up the make, colour and registration mark of the vehicle, a dark blue Ford Cortina, CBY 140H, which had been stolen earlier from the W14 area, and it set off east, along Mount Street. The occupants later transpired to be Martin Joseph O'Connell, Henry 'Harry' Duggan, Hugh Docherty and Edward Butler. We then left the Yard to hopefully join the chase, and the skill of Peter Wilson as our driver came fully into play.
>
> We made our way at speed, with blues and twos, following the commentary over the radio given by officers at certain locations, following the vehicle. The Cortina crossed Oxford Street, into Portman Street, then into Gloucester Place, and left into Park Road. At this point we were close, travelling up Park Road from the south. Just after Rossmore Road, the Cortina stopped by Alpha Close and the four men decamped on foot with their arsenal of weapons, south, back down Park Road and turned into Rossmore Road.
>
> Apparently, an SPG [Special Patrol Group] carrier had overtaken the fleeing suspects in Rossmore Road who fired at them, and the carrier had stopped and returned fire, with the result that the suspects had turned and run back towards us since we had turned into Rossmore Road and had driven towards the obvious direction of

the shots. We had stopped just past some steps which led down from the railway bridge to Taunton Place, still on the blues and twos.

As they approached us, they all had handguns and fired several times at us whilst we were still in the car; they split into two, with two coming down our offside and two, our nearside.

Henry, Phil and myself left the vehicle and gave chase. The four men ran to the steps and the last turned and fired at us, more towards Henry, who ducked down. The last man then disappeared down the steps. Henry saw an armed SPG officer, and together they went down the stairs in pursuit. The suspects now split up, two going into Balcombe Street and the other two into Boston Place. By pure chance they met up with the other two and then they all entered a flat at 22B Balcombe Street, where they took Mr and Mrs Mathews hostage; the rest is history.

What Fenton fails to mention is that of the three shots which punctured 'The Yellow Canary', two hit the front of the car, the third hit the rear; that was the shot which passed between Fenton and Dowswell as they chased the terrorists on foot. It was the gun which fired that shot that was later proved by ballistic tests to have been the one used in the murder of Ross McWhirter.

The heroic, holed-up terrorists demanded a car to take them to the airport and an aeroplane to fly them and their middle-aged hostages to Ireland. In response to this, DAC Ernie Bond stated, 'They're not going anywhere and they're not getting a flight to Ireland. We're not going to make any deals at all.'

The tense stand-off lasted for six days until the terrorists received what Donald Trump would refer to as a 'misspeak', to the effect that the Special Air Service Regiment was on its way. Shooting, bombing and murdering innocent members of the public were all quite acceptable to this craven bunch, but the thought of being ever-so-slightly riddled with bullets by members of the SAS was stretching their resolution a bit too far, and they couldn't wait to surrender.

Convicted of seven murders, conspiracy to cause explosions and falsely imprisoning John and Sheila Matthews, the terrorists were handed down a large number of life sentences; in 1998 they were transferred to Portlaoise Prison, Dublin, before being released the following year under the provisions of the Good Friday Agreement.

Henry Dowswell was awarded the George Medal, as were Inspector (later Commander) John Purnell and Police Sergeant

Phillip McVeigh; the last two had commandeered a passing taxi, which followed the car containing the suspects. After the suspects' car stopped, Purnell and McVeigh got out and gave chase while being constantly shot at. The taxi driver, James William Hackett, later said, 'I've always wanted someone to jump in my cab and say, "Follow that vehicle!"'; he was awarded the Queen's Commendation for Brave Conduct, as was the Squad driver, Peter Wilson, plus two other officers. Bob Fenton and Phil Mansfield were two of the five officers to be awarded the Queen's Gallantry Medal.

Fenton, Mansfield and Dowswell later collected their cheques for £25 from the Bow Street Reward Fund which, as Fenton told me, 'The rest of the Squad helped us spend, and more, at the local pub!'

A tie with an interesting motif was struck to mark the event. The design showed an orange circle with a broken green 'Z' inside it and a white link chain around the outside. The letter 'Z' represented the code name which had been given to one of the terrorists by the police. The chain depicted the police action at the siege and the other two colours denoted the Irish national flag.[1]

---

[1] For a further account of the IRA's mainland atrocities, see *Death on the Beat: Police Officers Killed in the Line of Duty*, Wharncliffe Local History, 2012.

CHAPTER 11

A Likeable Rogue

The robbery at the Bank of America, Davies Street, Mayfair was sophisticated, exceptionally well planned and carried out by professional criminals; on 24 April 1975, ninety-eight safety deposit boxes were opened and valuables, including cash, krugerrands, gold bars and jewellery, valued at anything between £8 and £12 million, were stolen. That much is widely known; less well known is that a raid had been previously attempted at the same branch of the bank on 25 October 1974.

Stuart Buckley had been released from prison in May 1974 and started working for the bank as an electrician. He met up with an old friend, Frank Maple, and after he mentioned his new employment, Maple allegedly said to him, 'That bank has a lot of money in it and soon it's going to lose some of it.'

With the exception of the vaults, Buckley had access to all areas of the bank, and amongst others, Leonard Wilde – also known as Leonard Minchingdon and, because he was said to resemble a German, 'Johnny the Boche' – was taken into the bank by Buckley to study the locks and vault doors. Wilde was a legendary 'key-man', able, it was said, to cut an excellent facsimile of a key from memory.

Detective Inspector Tony Stevens describes what happened on that first, abortive occasion:

> They drilled the door with a large drill that attached to the door, held in place with electric magnets. The job was done overnight when some Bank of America staff were working on the top floor. One of the team was posted to the stairway to warn them if the staff came down. The watcher thought he heard something and tried to warn the driller, but he didn't hear, so the watcher turned off the electric switch. The large drill fell off the door and the drill bit snapped off in the door. They tried new drill bits but they overheated, they tried to cool them by breaking into a Coca-Cola machine, but in the end they gave up.

However, some of the same gang participated in both raids, and the way the case was cracked was due, once again, to an amalgamation of C11 and Flying Squad expertise. Observations had been carried out by C11 on a criminal named Jimmy O'Loughlin, who had met up with Wilde; interest deepened when Buckley was introduced into their circle. They had been followed to the City branch of the Bank of America and, believing it was there that a raid would take place, C11 kept observation on that branch for a couple of weekends, but nothing happened.

Meanwhile, Buckley had discovered the combination of the vaults by hiding in the ceiling space above the vault's door; poking a tiny telescope through the polystyrene tiles, he recorded the numbers as the bank's managers opened the vaults. These were passed on to the gang. Buckley was not present on 24 April 1975, the night of the raid, but when access to the vaults had been gained, as the gang drilled into the safety deposit boxes, they were unaware that bank employees were still in the building; when they came down to investigate they were threatened and tied up.

The following day, when the balloon went up, C11 knew at least some of the persons who must have been involved; they gave Jack Slipper the names, and the Squad went to work. O'Loughlin was the first to be arrested as he left his house carrying suitcases; they were found to contain jewellery from the bank valued at £¼ million, plus a large amount of cash.

Buckley was next and soon provided the Squad with a blueprint for both jobs; he led the police to his share of the loot, £68,000, hidden in a wood in Surrey. Leonard Wilde was an accomplished key-man, no doubt about that, but he had a great deal to learn about being circumspect. On the morning following the robbery he and his wife Vivienne went shopping for kitchen units at a furniture store in Hendon. Wilde ostentatiously pulled out a large wad of notes, peeled off £1,085 for payment and returned the wad, which apparently contained as much again as he had paid out, to his pocket. A search of his home at Devonshire Road, Palmers Green revealed tools for cutting precision-made keys.

Billy Gear left his wife's car parked on double yellow lines on the day of the robbery and received a parking ticket. He paid the fine, 'hoping no one would notice' – but they did, and he made a full confession, taking the officers to a safe deposit in Hatton Garden, where he had secreted his share of the loot. Gear was a prankster; Trevor Binnington recalls that they recovered four hundred more krugerrands than Gear thought he'd stolen. 'Go on, have some!' he kept saying on the return journey.

Peter Colson who, it was said, had planned the job with Wilde at the Oasis swimming pool, Holborn, proved more difficult to find, but he was eventually nabbed in a telephone kiosk making an injudicious phone call to one of his paramours.

One by one, the conspirators came in, but only a fraction of the loot was recovered, about £500,000. Buckley was given supergrass status; sentenced to seven years' imprisonment for his part in the job, he was ready to give evidence against his co-accused when the trial commenced at the Old Bailey on 11 June 1976.

That morning, John O'Connell, one of the defendants who was on bail, left his home at Church Vale, East Finchley, en route to the Old Bailey; one minute later, he was shot in the back of the legs with a sawn-off shotgun; his left leg later had to be amputated. It appeared that he was in a position to say something disadvantageous about one or more of the other defendants; so was Buckley, but he was in protective custody and O'Connell was not.

If this was a plan which had been hatched by any of the defendants, it backfired badly, because it pretty well guaranteed police protection for the jurors. Of the hundred potential jurors who filed into court, thirty-nine were exempted because of the anticipated length of the trial – between six and ten weeks. In fact, it would take double that time.

The trial of seven men and one woman got underway. Wilde's defence was that on the night of the robbery he was at home watching television with his wife and daughter. Seeing as how his wife was one of the defendants, charged with three counts of receiving stolen property, her word alone might not have carried too much weight as an alibi witness. So it was said that a Mrs Susan Hilliard was also present during the television-watching. But that lady had written to the police saying that she feared for her safety, and when Mrs Vivienne Rosaline Wilde was acquitted of all charges and collapsed, sobbing, into the arms of her husband, the trial Judge, Alan King-Hamilton, took an almost unprecedented step of calling her back into court. He said:

> I just want to say this to you, and please regard it as a solemn warning. If anything happens to Mrs Hilliard as a result of what you do or what you cause others to do as a result of the evidence she has given in this court, then you can expect no mercy at all.

Another defendant was acquitted, the rest were convicted, and on 16 November 1976, to the usual, predictable accompaniment of screams from ladies in the public gallery, some of whom struggled with the attendants and one of whom collapsed and had to be carried from the court, sentences were handed down.

Wilde and Coulson were sentenced to twenty-three and twenty-one years' imprisonment respectively, and both had bankruptcy orders in the sum of £485,000 made against them. Billy Gear and Jimmy O'Loughlin, both convicted of the robbery, received eighteen and seventeen years respectively, and there were also convictions for receiving part of the proceeds: Henry Jeffrey, twelve years, Henry Taylor, three years and Edward Gerty, two years. Micky Gervaise, who had participated in the first conspiracy at the bank, received eighteen months' imprisonment.

Trevor Binnington recalls, 'I took a part in the downfall of "Johnny the Boche" with the recovery of new, numbered Bank of England notes traced to the Bank of America, two days before they hit it. This was courtesy of a sneering comment of his wife about "not having found the rainy-day money" in three searches. I'd love to have been a fly on the wall the first time they met after that.'

Wilde was no stranger to making unfounded allegations against the police. When he had appeared at Tottenham Magistrates' Court on the morning of 9 July 1956, after being arrested following a violent struggle by Detective Constable Terry O'Connell of the Flying Squad, he bellowed, 'Tell them how you punched me!'

To this, O'Connell, who at 6ft 1½ inches had been a former member of the wartime 45 Commando, smoothly replied, 'He was one of the most violent prisoners I have ever had to deal with.'

Gelignite, detonators, over 700 gadgets for opening locks, plus bundles of skeleton keys and celluloid for slipping locks, were seized – 'It was the finest set of housebreaking implements I ever saw', O'Connell told me, and although Wilde did his best to put the blame for possession of those items on a dupe, he was convicted.

He had ten previous convictions for housebreaking, burglary, assault on police and possessing a firearm; he had only been released from a five-year sentence for officebreaking the previous year. Now, he was sentenced to ten years' preventative detention.

If Wilde was a stranger to the truth, it was a trait shared by his wife; screaming, 'My husband is innocent!' at the judge when Wilde was sentenced, she went on to allege that 'a senior police officer' had accepted £9,500 in bribes to permit prisoners to escape; and although this caught the imagination of Jack Straw, then MP for Blackburn, and was passed to Operation Countryman (who believed there were fairies at the bottom of the garden), it then went to Scotland Yard's CIB2 Department (who didn't).

Wilde got a result when the Court of Appeal reduced his sentence to twenty years; so did John O'Connell who, one year after the other defendants had been weighed off, limped into the Old Bailey to plead guilty to conspiracy. His barrister told the court that he had wished to say certain things which might have incriminated someone else; some days before his attendance at court, several men had tried to persuade him not to stand trial – hence the shooting. His sentence of imprisonment was suspended.

That left Frank Maple. Tony Stevens traced him to Spain, where it was explained to the police chief in Málaga that Maple had two convictions for three offences. Deciding that three offences (rather than two convictions) made Maple undesirable in Spain, the police chief ordered his arrest. It appeared a very civilized arrangement; the officers simply strolled out of the police station with Maple across the road to a café, where the interviews took place. When Stevens questioned the lack of restraint on Maple, the Spanish officer (who incidentally owned the café) mentioned that he carried two handguns, one at his waist, the other on his calf. He said that Maple was well aware of this, as he was that if he tried to run, the Spanish cop would have no compunction in shooting him down.

Tony Stevens, who spent eleven days in Torremolinos, takes up the tale:

> With some partial admissions by Frank and the evidence of Stuart Buckley there was enough to seek his extradition from Spain. The papers were prepared by us and sent to the Director of Public Prosecutions Office. They cocked it up and it was out of time. At this stage, Frank was released from prison and went to Morocco.

It was suggested that the release was achieved with a payment of £25,000, which eventually led to an investigation of local governmental officials and some sackings.

From Morocco, Maple moved on, and by the time the defendants in the bank case had been sentenced, he was serving a seven-month sentence for illegally entering Greece under an assumed name. The British Consul, Mr John Forbes-Meyler, formally requested Maple's extradition on 23 June 1977, not only for the Bank of America job, but also for a £250,000 jewellery fraud at Christie's.

Maple was in great demand; at the same time, Austria requested his extradition for an armed robbery in February 1977. Living under the name of William Nichol, he had participated with two other men in binding and gagging the night porter of a hotel at

Kitzbühel ski resort and rifling safes containing jewellery and valuables belonging to the guests valued at 3.5 million schillings (£135,000).

Austria won. The jury of six men and two women at the court in Innsbruck took three hours to unanimously find Maple guilty of the robbery, rejecting his defence that he had been blackmailed into participating in it, and on 25 April 1978 Judge Walther Murr sentenced him to nine years' imprisonment.

Although the Tirol Provincial Court had approved Maple's extradition to England, Judge Murr stated that he would have to serve his sentence before being handed over to the British authorities.

'Seems rather a long time, doesn't it?' murmured Maple, but not, perhaps as long as all that, because three and a half years later, Tony Stevens brought him back.

Having spent some time in solitary confinement, 'He was extremely pleased to see me', recalled Stevens. 'As the plane descended, he raised his glass of red wine, with a tear in his eye.'

On 2 November 1981, he appeared at Bow Street Magistrates' Court, where he was charged with seven offences.

'Back in the UK, I went to see Stuart Buckley, now living under a new identity', Stevens told me. 'He strongly refused to return to London to give evidence against Frank, and eventually no evidence was offered and he was released. Frank was a likeable rogue — I seem to recall he did surface somewhere.'

That wouldn't surprise me in the least.

CHAPTER 12

Supergrasses

Stuart Buckley had become a supergrass when that valuable commodity was still in its infancy. In time, proper accommodation would be designed for these people to serve their sentences; in Buckley's time no such accommodation existed, and to be segregated from other prisoners for his own safety, he was detained in what was known as 'The Nonces' Wing' at Reading prison, where the most depraved sex killers and child molesters served their sentences. This environment so revolted Buckley that it really was touch and go whether he would give evidence, and it was only as a result of considerable tact and assistance by the prison staff that he was persuaded to do so.

But about a year prior to Buckley being released from his prison sentence, before getting involved in the Bank of America robbery, another criminal was starting to dictate to police a statement which commenced:

> I, Derek Creighton Smalls, make this statement in the knowledge of the contents of a letter having been sent by the Director of Public Prosecutions to my solicitors, dated 2nd April 1973. I also make this statement on the basis that it will not be used in evidence against me on any criminal trial that I may face.

This astonishing document, beginning in a way which had never been seen before (and never would be again) was dated 3 April 1973 and written at Wembley police station by Detective Sergeant Terence O'Regan, who in his thirty-second year of service had deferred his retirement to be part of a remarkable investigation. The statement ran to 29 pages, outlining 21 armed robberies which had netted £1,288,031 and naming 22 names. A shorter, two-page statement was taken on 10 April, to clear up any ambiguities.

A gang of armed robbers known as 'The Wembley Mob' had carried out this series of robberies, starting on 2 October 1968 at the National Provincial Bank, Brighton, where £72,000 was stolen, and ending in August 1972, when a Security Express van was hit in Totty Street, Bow, netting the gang £40,760.

It was clear that the same team had participated in these robberies, and a special task force was set up at Wembley police station. Detective Inspector Vic Wilding was in charge; he had previously served on the Flying Squad, and other former and serving Squad officers – Mick McAdam, Reg Dixon and others – were brought in, to firm up the team. The investigators had their first big break following a raid at the Palmers Green branch of the National Westminster Bank which occurred on 22 May 1972 and at which £10,729 was stolen. A woman witness saw a man whom she described as 'Italian-looking' sitting in a red Cortina near the bank before the robbery; it was used as a getaway car. Looking through the albums at the Yard, she picked out the man as Smalls – known to his friends as 'Bertie'.

His previous convictions were not particularly impressive; they included living off immoral earnings and possessing a loaded gun. However, he was of interest to C11; his name had been mentioned previously when he had been pulled in for armed robberies, but there had been insufficient evidence to support charges.

But what was interesting was that an off-duty detective constable had been in the vicinity of the bank three days prior to the robbery. He had noticed a red Jaguar containing three men which had stopped outside the bank. One of the men had pointed at the bank, and two of them had got out and walked into the premises before returning to the car, which then drove off. He noted the registration number – KUR 7G – and the Jaguar was traced to a garage forecourt near Tower Bridge in which Derek Smalls had an interest. Now, another woman, who had been tied up at a robbery at Ralli Brothers, a private bank in Hatton Garden, on 26 March 1969 when £296,451 was stolen, also identified Smalls as one of the raiders.

Finding Smalls became a priority, but it was not until 22 December 1972 that he was located at an address in the market town of Rushden, Northamptonshire. The following day, when the front door was opened by Smalls, police rushed in and he was arrested.

Right from the start, Smalls talked of 'doing deals', although he gave little away. However, the evidence was mounting up, and after the committal papers were served on him he realized he could be staring twenty years' imprisonment in the face. It was not until he told Wilding, 'I can give you every top robber in London', that a deal was struck. With the consent of the Director of Public Prosecutions, a written agreement was reached between Smalls and his solicitor that he would make a statement naming all of his co-conspirators and give evidence against them – in return, he wanted his freedom and all charges to be dropped.

On 3 April Smalls was bailed from Harrow Magistrates' Court into police custody and commenced his statement. Many of those he named were already under suspicion; there were others about whom the investigators knew nothing.

By 6 April the Flying Squad had been called in to carry out the arrests under the command of Jack Slipper, and over a hundred officers received their briefings. Eleven inspectors were in charge of the teams, to which two police marksmen were allocated, and the round-up commenced. The prisoners were brought in, weapons and other evidence were seized. It was the beginning of the end of the Wembley Mob; their sentences would total 308 years.

When the Court of Appeal dealt with the prisoners' appeals they upheld – perhaps grudgingly – most of the convictions but reduced practically all of the sentences. Lord Justice Lawton remarked:

> The spectacle of the Director of Public Prosecutions recording in writing, at the behest of a criminal like Smalls, his undertaking to give immunity from further prosecution is one which we find distasteful. Nothing of a similar kind must ever happen again. Undertakings of immunity from prosecution may have to be given in the public interest. They should never be given by the police. The Director should give them most sparingly and, in cases involving grave crimes, it would be prudent of him to consult the law officers before making any promises.

This was the acerbic response of Lord Dilhorne – he had been both Solicitor General and Attorney General – to those comments:

> I am wondering to what extent it is right for any court to give directions to the Director as to how he should conduct his business. The Director of Public Prosecutions works under the Attorney General. He does not work under any judges at all and any directions he receives as to the way in which he does his work surely must come from the Attorney General. I would have thought it quite wrong for it to come from any judicial authority at all. He may be condemned for what he has done but he must not be told what he has to do in the future.

The police were, of course, delighted with the outcome of Smalls' endeavours. Previously, there had been cases of criminals turning

Queen's Evidence – leaving the dock to enter the witness box and give evidence against their co-accused, before returning to the dock, hopefully to receive a lesser punishment. But this was unprecedented, and the view of the police was that it must continue.

However, the Attorney General and the Director of Public Prosecutions both felt that there would be a great deal of public disquiet if career criminals were allowed to walk away scot-free. But what would happen if the next supergrass – their official name was 'Resident Informant' – who like Smalls was expecting a twenty-year sentence, was to receive a substantially reduced sentence, spend that sentence in relative safety and then be relocated with a new identity?

There had never been a better way to split up gangs than to ensure that robbers who had worked together for years could no long trust each other. It not only extended to 'best mates', to men who had been godfather to each others' children or best men at their weddings; it went far, far deeper than that. The desire to get a greatly reduced sentence could lead to brother grassing brother, father and, on one auspicious occasion, mother. It would ultimately lead to a whole team of robbers being arrested and queuing-up to become supergrasses, only for the latecomers to be told, 'Sorry, you were too slow; we've got enough, now.'

Even before the trials of 'The Wembley Mob' were completed, the guinea pig who would ascertain whether a substantially reduced sentence could be viable was put to the test.

*

When George de Buriatte was sent down for ten years in January 1965 for attempted armed robbery, Judge Edward Clarke QC commented that he 'had a bad record' – and he was right. In 1972 de Buriatte was acquitted of a series of Post Office robberies; Detective Inspector Bob Connor who was running 4 Squad paid him a visit, and de Buriatte commenced a prolonged career as a 'snout'.

Maurice Lanca O'Mahoney was a 25-year-old exceptionally violent career criminal and part of a team – it included John Thorne, Joseph Stevens and Angus Smith – who invited de Buriatte (described as being 'as sound as a bell') to be included in the robbery of a Securicor van. It appeared that de Buriatte was not quite as trustworthy as the gang might have wished; they were kept under observation for six consecutive Saturdays by C11 and the Squad; but in the belief that the job had blown out, on the seventh Saturday, 1 June 1974, the observation was not covered.

It was then, at 6.00 pm at Phoenix Way, Heston, Middlesex, that the Securicor van was attacked, and the gang were well-equipped to do so; their robbers' paraphernalia included an axe, a sledgehammer, two sawn-off double-barrelled 12-bore shotguns together with eight cartridges, two loaded revolvers, a Beretta and a Luger 9mm automatic, as well as an assortment of woollen hats, balaclavas and nylon overalls.

The van was rammed by a stolen low-loader, the windows were smashed in with the axe and sledgehammer, shots were fired and one of the guards was smashed over the head with a hammer. The gang were hoping to net a prize of £150,000; in fact, they got £13,152.43p.

On the morning of 11 June the gang was rounded up, with the exception of O'Mahoney, who escaped; he was arrested at the address of his girlfriend, Susan Norville, on 12 June. She was arrested as well, as were her parents, who lived in Fulham; at their address O'Mahoney had left his share of the robbery, £1,200, one of the shotguns, a pistol and clothing which had been worn during the robbery. Susan made a full statement to the police in which she described in detail the planning of the raid; this was pretty authentic, because she had been present when the robbery had been discussed.

But O'Mahoney refused to say anything – until, on remand at Brixton prison, the word went around that he and Susan had grassed up the rest of the team. When O'Mahoney was attacked and threatened with having his eyes gouged out with a toothbrush, he decided to 'roll over'. He was remanded into police custody at Chiswick police station, and former Detective Sergeant Trevor Binnington takes up the tale:

> He made a number of statements with loads of detail about the Phoenix Way job. When eventually he came to give evidence at the trial, his recall was remarkable; he admitted hundreds of burglaries. From memory, he navigated us around parts of London to identify the offences. In some cases, years after the crime, he was very often able to describe the point of entry, method and layout, as well as what was stolen and how it was disposed of. I can't recall him being wrong about any of it and I put it down to the effect on memory of adrenalin flow, as well as natural ability. The work generated by Mo's other revelations of his involvement in robberies, burglaries etc. kept C8 teams busy for a sustained period. When I was called to the witness box by Mo's defence, I declared seeing more of him in 90 days than my family.

On 19 September 1974 O'Mahoney pleaded guilty at the Old Bailey to one case of robbery, one of attempted robbery and one case of burglary. He asked for ninety-nine other offences to be taken into consideration and was sentenced to five years' imprisonment.

Detective Superintendent John Swain who had been directing the day-to-day operations was told by His Honour Judge Aarvold OBE, TD:

> I would like to commend you and the officers involved in this case. All too rarely do I feel obliged to offer commendation but in this case in particular it is most unusual to hear the accused thank the police for the way he has been treated and dealt with and I would like to thank you for the excellent work done by you and your officers.

Although O'Mahoney was put into the prison system, much of his sentence was spent at Chiswick police station and in all he made seventy-three statements comprising 249 pages. His output was enormous. Of course, he mentioned numerous robberies, attempted robberies and conspiracies to rob, as well as burglaries, but there was much more. There were cases involving thefts of lorry-loads, counterfeit money, handling stolen goods, firearms offences, insurance frauds, long-firm frauds, jury tampering, murder, attempted murder and conspiracy to murder.

As a result, 277 people were detained, and of those, 159 were charged with serious offences where in excess of £2 million had been obtained. Weapons and the proceeds of crime were also recovered.

One of the first cases in which O'Mahoney gave evidence was also the longest trial ever held at the Old Bailey at that time – 111 days – before Judge Bernard Gillis QC. This concluded on 11 December 1975 and resulted in convictions in respect of Thorne (fifteen years), Smith (fourteen years), Stevens (twelve years) for conspiracy to rob and for the Phoenix Way robbery and others, plus Ronald Cook (fourteen years) and Eric Gibson (six years). Terence Marks and Ozer Arif were both given two-year suspended sentences. The same suspended sentences were imposed on Stevens' wife Sandra and his mother, Mrs Emily Bloomfield, for conspiracy to pervert the course of justice, and Thorne's mother Eileen was convicted of obtaining stolen money for the benefit of her son and was conditionally discharged.

O'Mahoney gave compelling evidence in a number of trials, as a result of which quite a number of criminals were convicted, although others were not.

On 2 March 1976 five men were jailed for terms of between seven and fourteen years for robbery and attempted robbery as a result of O'Mahoney's testimony at the Old Bailey. However, Judge Griffith-Jones commented that if Judge Aarvold had known more about the robberies when sentencing O'Mahoney he would probably have imposed a longer term, and he accepted that O'Mahoney's behaviour was worse than that of the defendants.

It was the last time that he would give evidence. Released from custody thirteen days later, he stated that because of threats and other pressures, he would no longer assist police and confirmed this in a letter to John Swain dated 7 June 1976. Three cases which relied on O'Mahoney's testimony were called at the Old Bailey on 1 July 1976; no evidence was offered.

Moral? Defer the supergrass's sentencing until all the cases against the defendants have been dealt with.

★

On 10 August 1978 an enquiry was set up by Detective Sergeant Mike Bucknole and the late Detective Constable Ray Wood OBE. Information had been received from two separate sources that Ray Fowles and Norman Jones were responsible for a large number of robberies in South London, but what Bucknole describes as 'the demoralisation and divide between working detectives and administrators' is described in his own words about speaking to the operational head of the Flying Squad:

> Initially, a verbal struggle on the telephone had occurred between me and Detective Chief Superintendent Sewell, who was reluctant to allow us to travel out of the Metropolitan Police District to substantiate the information obtained. I surmised this senior officer was one of the 'cautious' ones. I explained that I was convinced that all the information supplied and the enquiries made to substantiate the robbery offences would lead to the biggest breakthrough into South London robbery teams that the Flying Squad had effected. Sewell defended his wary position and said, 'That's an extravagant claim, Bucknole. I'm not so sure, we'll have to see, you and Wood keep out of trouble!'

But Bucknole and Wood went right ahead with their enquiry; the arrest of Fowles and Jones led to their becoming supergrasses, together with Peter Rose, released only a year before from his fourteen-year sentence for Phill Williams' attempted murder. Between them, they confessed to a total of 315 offences and named 198 criminals who had committed 640 major offences.

Fowles and Jones were each sentenced to five years' imprisonment, with Rose receiving seven; Detective Superintendent Phillip Corbett spelt out 'the damage to big crime' at the sentencing of former seaman Norman Jones, who joined Raymond Fowles and Peter Rose in telling all at the Old Bailey on 23 July 1979.

★

Gordon Reynolds was a Squad driver at Finchley; he told me that they had been looking at a team of blaggers, including John Hammond and John Kennedy – when on the morning of 12 May 1980 they vanished. Reynolds recounts what happened:

> At 9.30 that morning, there was a call to a robbery at East Finchley; a guard had been shot. It was obviously down to this team, so we searched the area for them and – I think it was the C11 surveillance team – found them at the Guinness Trust Buildings at Stoke Newington. We got over there and there was only one way in and out, so the entrance was blocked with a Squad cab. I got in there and chased the cars until I rammed the Mercedes into a dustcart. John Kennedy, who had got the guns, jumped out and on to the railway lines. We chased him, got him down and then all of a sudden, a train pulled up with two of our blokes on board – having heard what was going on, they'd gone straight to Stamford Hill Railway Station and commandeered a passing train!

It was a good haul, which included Christopher Wren, who turned supergrass. On 2 March 1981 at the Old Bailey, Hammond admitted shooting the guard – he said the gun went off by accident, but then they always do, don't they? – as well as eight robberies and asked for twelve other offences to be taken into consideration. John Kennedy pleaded guilty to seven robberies and asked for thirty-three other offences to be taken into consideration, while Ronald Johnson (said to be 'the brains of the outfit') admitted six robberies and asked for another 119 other robberies and burglaries to be taken into consideration; all were jailed for fifteen years.

★

More and more criminals rolled over and became supergrasses. One of the most unusual was Donald Walter Barrett, whose criminal career had commenced in 1954. A serial robber, he had been a close associate of Bertie Smalls until that worthy denounced him in the witness box and saw him sentenced to seventeen years' imprisonment. The Court of Appeal reduced that to twelve years, and upon his release, Barrett immediately started robbing, again. He was caught, and now he, too, decided to reap the rewards of becoming a supergrass and enthusiastically named everyone he had ever worked with. Sadly for him, the once almost mandatory five-year sentence was not now the norm; Barrett was sentenced to fourteen years' imprisonment, later reduced to seven.

Released into society once more, he tried and rejected work as a £200-per-week scaffolder, and even though he had been a supergrass, other robbers still worked with him. This was because (a) he was a first division robber and, having spent a considerable time with the police, would be aware of their tactics and thus able to apprise his associates on how to avoid detection, and (b) he could never be a supergrass again. Not all of the robberies he tried were successful, but those that were brought in a total of £1,177,133.80p. Barrett and his team used disguises, carried firearms, strapped proxy bombs to security guards which, they informed them, would be detonated by remote control if they failed to comply with their demands. They also kidnapped a custodian's family at gunpoint and kept them tied up overnight before gaining access to a depository containing £480,000 in cash.

Following a long investigation, the main contenders were identified, and after a rolling surveillance consisting of C11 Personnel, the Force helicopter, the Police Firearms Unit and the Flying Squad, Barrett and his close associate, David Croke, were arrested on 11 August 1986 on the M1 motorway after they left the Newport Pagnell service station, having hi-jacked a van containing gold bullion valued at £283,500. Both men were in possession of loaded handguns and radio scanners.

Barrett initially had nothing to say; neither had Croke, who in fact made no admissions whatsoever. But Barrett didn't know that; he believed that Croke, who had just one conviction for shoplifting (and therefore was unused to the persuasive ways of police interrogators), was singing like a bird; if that were the case, Barrett, with his huge number of serious convictions, would be looking at a sentence of life imprisonment. At fifty years of age, when could he expect to be released? He had been a recalcitrant Category 'A' prisoner in the past, had lost privileges and remission and had been sent to 'The Block'. Now, with a reputation as a former supergrass, he would be sent to a mainstream prison, where everyone would know who he was and what he'd done. He could be dead in a month; possibly even in week or so. The thought of 'going behind the door' with the nonces, the sex offenders, (which had happened in Stuart Buckley's case), was a grim proposition.

There was a possible solution: to volunteer to become a supergrass for a second time. That was what happened. Barrett gave brief details about who he could name and what property could be recovered, and for the first (and last) time, the Director of Public Prosecutions gave his approval for someone to become a double-supergrass.

Barrett gave his testimony in a most convincing fashion, and Croke, given the weight of evidence against him, pleaded guilty to a number of serious offences and was sentenced to twenty-three years' imprisonment and made criminally bankrupt to the tune of £528,352. Other defendants were sentenced to a total of thirty years' imprisonment, whilst Barrett was told by His Honour Judge Michael Coombe QC, 'Nobody could be permitted for a second time the leniency you were given' and was sentenced to sixteen years' imprisonment and made criminally bankrupt in the sum of £840,519.

Barrett appealed the sentence, which was reduced to twelve years, but when he was released he robbed a supermarket, and although he tried quite persuasively to become a third-time supergrass, the general feeling was that he had too little to offer.

Croke, too, appealed, and his sentence was reduced to twenty-one years, but after his release he was convicted in July 2002 of the contract murder of a businessman and died while serving a life sentence.[1]

★

Supergrasses slowly vanished from the police armoury for a variety of reasons: sometimes poor handling (inexperienced officers thought the supergrasses had become their friends and treated them as such, taking them out to pubs, police sports grounds and even taking them home for Sunday lunch with their families), but mainly because of their increasing lack of credibility.

A classic example, former Detective Superintendent Tony Lundy told me, of one who should never have been given supergrass

---

[1] For a full account of Barrett's and Croke's behaviour, see *The Real Sweeney*, Robinson Books, 2005

status was Micky 'Skinny' Gervaise, who had been convicted for his part in the Bank of America case. He brought the old homily of 'running with the hares and hunting with the hounds' to an art form; this was an opinion shared by His Honour Judge Peter Slot. After Gervaise had given evidence at the Old Bailey, the judge asked the jury, 'You would not honestly hang a dog on his evidence, would you? You would not dream of finding a man guilty on his evidence alone, would you?' In case any doubt lingered in the jurors' minds, the judge emphatically added, 'Well, I would not!' – and it was obviously a view shared by the jury, who hurriedly acquitted the man in the dock.

Errol Walker was not the only black supergrass but he was certainly the first. Roy Herridge QPM had originally dealt with him compassionately during a drugs case, and when Walker was arrested in April 1982 in Ealing for a robbery he wanted to talk – but only to Herridge, who at that time was a detective inspector on the Squad. Given the status of Resident Informant, Walker was debriefed at Feltham police station, named names and, admitting twenty-six other robberies, was sentenced to five years' imprisonment.

Herridge told me, 'I was spending Christmas 1985 with relatives in Devon when I received a telephone call from the Assistant Commissioner telling me that Walker had murdered his sister-in-law and was holding her daughter Karlene captive. Walker wanted to speak to me.'

A car was sent and Herridge was taken to Poynter Court, Gallery Gardens, Northolt, where Walker had already tied the child to a chair with flex, slashed at her arms and legs (severing several tendons), placed a plastic bag over her head and threatened to cut off her right hand. It was one of those unhappy situations when negotiations simply don't work. Screaming, 'She dies, she dies!' Walker plunged a kitchen knife into the little girl and he was shot twice. Mercifully, the child survived; so did Walker, who was sentenced to life imprisonment in December 1986 for murder and attempted murder.

Supergrasses were expected to tell the full, unblemished truth in court; to be caught out telling just one lie could ruin their integrity and would compromise all the cases in which they gave evidence. Unfortunately, thanks to the clumsy, almost bovine efforts of the constabulary officers who made up the personnel of the ill-fated 'Operation Countryman' to investigate police corruption, that was what happened. They told supergrasses (plus any other criminal they met) that they could secure them reduced sentences, offer no evidence against them, even engineer free pardons, and a number of the supergrasses made up the most mendacious stories about innocent officers which the simple, gullible souls of 'Countryman' with little or no experience of dealing with cunning, manipulative career criminals, hungrily lapped up.

Four years later, at a cost of £4 million, those officers who had been referred to as 'The Swedey' or 'Malice in Blunderland' and had been given the title of 'detective' to precede their over-promoted ranks, wandered off back home to their various constabularies, as unaware of how to apply the criminal law and conduct investigations as they had been when they started. They left behind demoralized officers with their reputations in tatters, criminals smirking at the impossibly easy way they'd duped the yokels and truthful supergrasses wondering why they'd suddenly been dumped.

Feelings about the demise of the supergrasses were mixed. Working detectives bemoaned the fact that one of their most valuable tools had been denied them. Senior CID officers, transported from the ranks of the uniform department (where at least they had been reasonably competent), sighed with relief at not being asked to authorize matters about which they knew nothing. Serial criminals must have felt like cheering from the rooftops.

One supergrass tired of his new identity and relocation and returned to South London, where he was well known. Sitting in his local pub, he asked the clientele what they would have done had they been in his position? Noting the sawn-off shotgun hung from a lanyard around his neck, the customers had no hesitation in chorusing, 'The same as you, mate!'

What of Bertie Smalls, who kicked off the whole concept of supergrassing? He kept a reasonably low profile and died of natural causes, aged seventy-two, in January 2008. But as Don Barrett told me, 'They should have put a bullet in his nut; that would have stopped it in its tracks.'

CHAPTER 13

Undercover Work

U
ndercover (or UC) work is one of the more dangerous pastimes in policing. It involves an officer – male or female – entering a hostile environment, posing as a criminal. Irrespective of whether that officer is purporting to be an armed robber, an art dealer, an arms supplier or a paedophile, he or she has got to be completely convincing and has got to know his or her stuff. They have to be utterly resolute, to be able to think on their feet and above all, if the wheels come off – and that's a common occurrence – to be ready with some quick, believable answers, because usually, they're on their own, with no chance of back-up. One classic example was when an undercover officer using the alias of 'Charlie' had infiltrated a gang of Yardies. Several meetings had gone by without difficulties; the next did not. The gangsters' mood had changed dramatically (and not for the better), due quite possibly to their all being out of their skulls on crack cocaine. In a dingy Harlesden flat, 'Charlie' was invited to sit down on a lavatory, before a Browning Hi-Power pistol was stuck in his ear and he was told, 'Know what, Charlie? We fink you da Bill.'

Since 'Charlie' is today alive and well and living the life of a country gentleman, it's clear that he survived that really tricky situation; however, I can say without reservation that if I had been in 'Charlie's' shoes at that time, I would have made full and prolonged use of his seating arrangements!

Nowadays, there's a specialist department set up to train undercover officers, with all sorts of technology to help them out, plus wardrobes, fast cars and personal jewellery to add authenticity to their roles. It's not a part that would suit everyone, but in the days when UC work was traditionally carried out by the Flying Squad, it suited Detective Sergeant John Grieve. No training for UC work existed in those days and Grieve didn't have access to an expensive wardrobe, so he borrowed an expensive watch, a costly leather jacket and some jewellery. This was done to impress a very violent, dangerous gang of Triads, to inspire confidence so that they would supply half a pound of Chinese heroin to him for the sum of £45,000. It succeeded.

It began in 1976; a criminal informed police that he wished to impart information regarding organized crime, and this led to him being introduced to John Grieve. Over the period of a month, encounters were set up in various coffee bars in the Soho area; as Grieve told me, 'They were confidence-building meetings.' Grieve was the 'buyer'; the man referred to as 'Mr Big' and the brains behind the operation was Detective Chief Inspector Mick O'Leary.

With both officers certainly looking the part, the deal was supposed to go down at the Bull Ring in Chelsea. They were in possession of the money, drawn from the Yard's Finance Department, to prove to the Chinese that they had sufficient funds for the deal. But with the area filled with surveillance officers and the whole of 7 Squad, the sellers had a sudden change of heart; they wanted another meet – immediately – with people higher up the chain.

The undercover officers and some of the gang set off; Grieve, through his covert radio, was able to inform Detective Chief Superintendent Jack Slipper that they were on their way to the Liverpool area. They were followed by the Squad and surveillance officers, and Slipper overtook their vehicle, in order to get to Liverpool first, inform the local police of what was happening and procure extra assistance.

It was the first of two trips to Liverpool. At one stage the gang leaders suggested exchanging female hostages to ensure there was no betrayal until the money and drugs were exchanged. They even brought their own woman to be swapped, but Grieve managed to persuade them that such a course of action was totally unacceptable to his boss – Mick O'Leary.

At a local warehouse the drugs were handed over, and when they returned to a hotel, Grieve signalled to the surveillance team that the drugs were in the car. One of the gang accompanied Grieve to a room in the hotel where O'Leary was waiting with the money; he was being minded by another gang member who rather unnervingly passed the time practising martial art moves. (At the trial, the *Evening Standard* reported this, with typical Fleet Street hyperbole, as 'The Deadly Kung Fu Gamble of Mr Big'.)

As the money was being counted, the arrests went down; Grieve and O'Leary 'escaped', although Grieve later revealed his identity, interviewed all of the prisoners and at the Old Bailey gave evidence under his right name.

At the trial it was, of course, never intended to call the informant. Grieve got the shock of his life when a prison officer quietly told him that his informant was in the Old Bailey cells and had asked him to pass on the message 'Don't worry'.

Grieve was at court as an undercover officer, informant handler, exhibits officer and officer in charge of the case – 'Don't worry', indeed!

What was the informant going to say? Grieve didn't know, the prosecution counsel didn't know, but the defence thought they did. They had been told that he could undermine the prosecution's case – that's what they had told the judge – but hadn't had time to take a statement; therefore they were unaware of what precisely he could say in their favour.

The trial Judge, Alexander Karmel QC, took hold of the situation. Calling the informant into the witness box, he asked a few questions and elicited the man's name and criminal career, confirmed that he was here of his own volition, that he was a serving prisoner and that, wishing to give evidence of criminality, he had been introduced to Grieve. It was now the turn of the defence, but the informant turned out to be a model prosecution witness and described in detail the defendants' criminality. In desperation, it was suggested that he had manipulated the defendants – 'That's impossible' replied the informant. 'John always found a reason to exclude me and when the operation had gone down, he had me locked up in a police cell.'

It was quite true. As Grieve told me, 'I had the source detained in "protective custody" at Cannon Row, called in to see him periodically, purchased refreshments for him and on one occasion, took him out for a drink. The judge did not think this was worthy of criticism . . . this was precisely to avoid the suggestions made at the trial of criminal manipulation and conspiracy.'

On 15 December 1976, two of the gang members, Shik Man-chan and Kuan Wah-tang, who denied telling the police that they were members of a Triad secret society, were each jailed for six years; Ali Dhalai of Liverpool was sentenced to eight years' imprisonment and Kun Lam-ng, also from Liverpool, was jailed for five years.

The judge commended Grieve and O'Leary and thanked the informant for his evidence; the latter happily went back to his prison cell. And his reason for purporting to give evidence for the defence and then transforming himself into a prosecution witness? Simple. It was because his girlfriend had died from an overdose of drugs, supplied to her in London.

Grieve had studied other trials involving informants and under-cover work and subsequently, as a detective chief inspector, was involved in writing the rules and drawing up training methods for participation in criminal cases. He told me, 'A defence lawyer told someone else I knew that every line they thought up to attack us or our evidence, we had blocked off. This aspect of foreknowledge I consider was part of the Flying Squad professionalism I so admired.'

John Grieve ended his career as Deputy Assistant Commissioner Grieve CBE, QPM, BA (Hons), MPhil, HonDL, Professor Emeritus – and with a large clutch of police commendations for inspired criminal investigations which included a commissioner's high commendation for courage plus a monetary award from the Chief Metropolitan Magistrate at Bow Street.

It was a far cry from the days when he returned to the Met from university, having obtained a degree in philosophy and psychology. 'As much use as a degree in flower arranging to a detective!' caustically remarked a senior officer.

Little did he know!

CHAPTER 14

Four Area Offices

When Detective Inspector Tony Lundy of the Flying Squad flew to Montreal in March 1977 to collect a prisoner, he was hugely impressed by the fact that the police of that city had a dedicated robbery unit who dealt with the investigation of all robberies committed in the area. Every piece of evidence – descriptions of suspects, weapons and vehicles used, forensic evidence – was collated, and this led to many of the capital's robberies being solved.

Without doubt, Lundy was a highly successful detective who would go on to run a series of successful supergrasses, but now he pestered his senior officers to adopt Montreal's premise in London. It paid off.

On 10 July 1978, 80 per cent of the Squad's workforce was deployed from the Yard to four area offices: Chiswick (later Barnes), Walthamstow (later Rigg Approach, Leyton), Rotherhithe (later Tower Bridge) and Finchley. They were to investigate all robberies and attempted robberies at banks, Post Offices, cash-in-transit vehicles, building societies, jewellers and betting offices, and were tasked to target and arrest those responsible. Prisoners arrested for those offences by uniform or divisional officers were to be handed over to those offices, to be dealt with by them.

That left just four squads at the Yard; 9 and 11 (who were used for special and often secret enquiries) and 10 and 12 Squads. Unlike the four area offices, they had no crime book to work from; as far as they were concerned, it was business as usual, using their informants to put up work. They had some excellent successes.

★

As a young detective, Mick Geraghty had the good fortune to be mentored by that highly successful detective, Peter Holman MBE, QPM, who knew a thing or two about running informants. Geraghty quickly discovered that a kind word said at court on behalf of a prisoner could pay dividends, but the information which resulted often came from unexpected quarters. In early 1982 Geraghty took a phone call in the Flying Squad office from an East End receiver who, thanks to Geraghty informing a magistrate that the wife of the prisoner in the dock was expecting their third child and that he had a good job to go to, had received a conditional discharge instead of the expected (and well deserved) 'half a stretch'.[1]

'I won't forget you, Mick' were the receiver's words as he left court, and it appeared he hadn't.

Now, his information was that a man named Phelps who lived in South-East London was getting a team together to rob a security van when it delivered wages on a Friday to a factory named Dewhurst. It was sparse enough information but it was all there was, so Geraghty got to work.

> My first job was to identify the premises. I did this and found that the target premises was a meat processing factory, part of the Dewhurst Butchers Group, situated between Yarnton Way and Hailey Road, SE2 at the eastern end of Thamesmead, near Belvedere. The offices were at one corner of the factory but I noticed it was all glass and that the offices were all on the first floor; you could, in fact see everyone who worked in the offices. I carried out surveillance on a Friday to verify that the information was correct about the security van attending. As I watched, a security van arrived and entered the grounds. I saw two guards enter the reception area carrying the cash, they went to an office on the first floor where there were two women and a man working, and the guards handed over the cash. The door was locked behind them and I saw the staff sorting out the wage packets, so the information appeared correct.
>
> I identified Phelps and surveillance was carried out to identify his associates; he was seen to be in the vicinity of Dewhurst, especially on Fridays, to see the delivery of the cash.

Weeks now went by; although it was clear that the robbery was going to take place on a Friday, Geraghty had no idea which one. He similarly had no idea if the team was going to attack the guards as they took the cash from the vehicle. If they did, the alarm could be raised, either by the driver of the security van or by any staff looking out of the windows. Or would they wait until the wages had

---

[1] A 'stretch' was a year's imprisonment; therefore, 'half a stretch' was six months.

been delivered and the van had gone, before attacking the wages staff? This would entail taking more time, going up and down the stairs. And if they did and they were surprised, might they take hostages?

As the weeks went by, surveillance was set up using C11 personnel and officers from 10 and 12 Squads. On one week Phelps and two associates were followed to the factory in their getaway car before leaving the scene and going to a house which one of them entered. In the meantime, the security van arrived, made its delivery and left. Then, inexplicably, the team returned to their original spot by the factory. After a while, Phelps got out of the car and walked along Hailey Road, where he was able to see the wage packets being paid out to the staff – it was obvious they had missed the van, so he left. So did the surveillance team.

On the next occasion, 16 April 1982 – this was the twelfth consecutive Friday – the C11 team picked up the suspects in their car and followed them to the same spot. The security van arrived, made its delivery and left. The gang's car drove up Hailey Road and they got out. Two were carrying something. From an observation van, Woman Detective Constable Julia Pearce relayed the information over the radio that six feet away from her, all of them had donned white coats and hats as worn by the Dewhurst personnel and had climbed through a gap in the fence. Now there was no doubt about it – the staff in the wages office, now in possession of £18,000, were going to be attacked.

The tension was palpable. One of the observation vehicles was seen to be moving slightly, and the occupants were sharply told over the radio to remain still. The agitation was due to flatulence in the van; understandable, in the circumstances!

'We were doing surveillance in a gown van', Detective Sergeant Tony Yeoman told me, 'although the only aperture was being used by a C7 officer[2] who was filming the whole thing. When the order to "attack" came, we had to adjust to the sunlight after the darkness in the van. We were all shouting probably contradictory things at the blaggers and told them to lie down.'

The robbers were in possession of two sawn-off shotguns and a cosh; the police had their .36 Smith & Wesson revolvers and staves, one of which was wielded by Detective Sergeant Gerry Gallagher.

'One of the suspects had a sawn-off shotgun tied to his leg with what looked like an old piece of skipping rope,' he told me. 'He

---

[2] An officer from the Yard's Technical Support Unit.

made a move towards the shotgun but didn't level it or attempt to use it as he was set upon and brought to the ground.'

'I remember running towards a man in white starting to kneel on one knee as though he was going to sing a song', recalled Geraghty. 'I was screaming, "Get down, get down!" and pointing my gun at him. I jumped on him and laid him flat. He was armed with a double-barrelled shotgun, tied to his arm with twine. As he lay on the ground, I took a look round and saw Phelps on the ground with a wooden cosh and the third man lying with a single-barrel shotgun.'

During the robbers' interviews admissions were made regarding an armed robbery at Lloyds Bank, Woolwich when, armed with a sawn-off shotgun and a knife, they had stolen £9,000. During the searches which followed, Geraghty found the remains of the shotgun barrels which had been sawn off and the hacksaw responsible.

At the Old Bailey, sentences of up to fourteen years' imprisonment were imposed; a fourth man who was arrested was cleared of all charges. His Honour Judge Francis Petre told Geraghty, Yeoman and Gallagher:

> Let me say at the very outset that in my view, the officers of the Flying Squad performed with extraordinary efficiency and I think on the observation, arrest and interviews, they should be commended. A straightforward and in my view, excellent piece of work, so far as you three were concerned.

The officers had various recollections of the incident, most of them quirky.

Gordon Harrison from 10 Squad summed the matter up perfectly. 'This was what the Flying Squad was all about', he told me. 'Why the hell would you join the police to work as a staff officer or in policy, when this real policing was available?'

Flying Squad driver Mick Gray had been in the back of the observation van with Julia Pearce for a considerable time until, inevitably, he felt the call of nature, which was catered for by a small trap door in the floor of the van. As he told me, 'I said, "Julie, you'll have to look out of the window". Later at the nick, somebody said, "How did it go in the van?" and Julie, deadpan, replied, "Well, Mick got his willy out on me!"'

Julia Pearce recalled that as she leapt from the back of the van the drop was higher than she realized, and she landed on her knees. By the time she reached the suspects they were all handcuffed, and it was then that she realized that blood was pouring from the torn holes in her jeans. Given a couple of handkerchiefs to staunch the flow, she carried on with the searches and all the other administrative work, as well as being appointed exhibits officer. She told me, 'I'm convinced I started the 'holey jeans' fashion!'

Perhaps Tony Yeoman's memory was the most idiosyncratic of all the recollections. As he raced towards the suspects in the bright morning sunshine, the leader sank to his knees, took off his hat and told him, 'You've got to admit it, Guv'nor, it's a nice day for it!'

★

The next case also involved Tony Yeoman, a video of the crime and a robbery; but the information was even sparser than in the Dewhurst job. At least then, the venue of the robbery was known – all that was known in this case was that Richard Bernard was intending to commit a robbery. That was all. Who the victim was going to be, and where, when and with whom the robbery was going to be carried out, was a mystery.

It was not too difficult to trace, identify and carry out surveillance on Bernard; nor, within a short space of time, to discover that he and his associates Terrence Willard and Andrew Fraser had control of five vehicles, of which four were stolen and plated.

Officers from 10 and 12 Squad were utilized, and on Saturday, 12 March 1983 the three men were followed in a vehicle, first to Northway Crescent, then Mill Hill Broadway; they arrived at 4.20 pm and there they remained until 4.31 pm, when they drove off.

Was this where the robbery would take place? It was a possibility but who was to be the victim? Would it be a premises, a cash-in-transit van or a person?

With this paucity of information, it was reasonable to assume that the robbery – whatever form it might take – would be on a Saturday afternoon, between 4.00 pm and 4.30 pm in Mill Hill Broadway. Would a changeover vehicle be put down in Northway Crescent? That was a possibility as well.

The following week, Saturday, 19 March saw observation points set up opposite to where the men had sat in their car the previous week, plus one in Northway Crescent. Flying Squad cars were parked around the periphery to drive in as and when necessary. At 2.05 pm two stolen Rover saloons drove into Northway Crescent, and the driver of one of them got out and into the other vehicle, which then drove off. At 4.06 pm the second Rover drove into Millway and stopped; Fraser was driving and he remained at the wheel, while Bernard and Willard, both wearing gloves and what appeared to be woollen hats, got out at 4.21 pm and walked around the corner into Mill Hill Broadway.

About 15 yards from the junction was a telephone kiosk, which both men entered. Their arrival had been covertly filmed and, what was more, a surveillance team was mingling on foot with the shoppers in that busy thoroughfare. At 4.36 pm Bernard and Willard suddenly tensed, then pulled down the woolly hats which were transformed into balaclavas and ran out of the kiosk, both clutching staves. Their target was the assistant manager of Budgens supermarket who was carrying the day's takings – £8,885.48 – in a carrier bag to the night safe at the nearby National Westminster Bank. He was repeatedly cracked across the arm holding the bag – one of the blows fractured a bone in his hand – then Bernard grabbed the bag and both men ran off, still carrying their staves.

Tony Yeoman, in charge of the surveillance team, who had been on the opposite side of the road, had started to run across the road as soon as he saw the two robbers dash out of the telephone kiosk; but by the time he reached the pavement, the robbery had taken place. He grabbed Bernard around the waist, pushed him towards Willard and, seizing him at the same time, rammed both of them into a shop window.

To those who were there – or those who viewed it on the video afterwards – it was a terrifying sight. As the three bodies hit the window, it bowed inwards – it seemed inevitable that the glass would break in the middle, which would cause the upper part to come crashing down on them like the blade of a guillotine. Then, in what was a split-second (but which seemed much longer) the glass sprang back into place – it was as though a combined weight of some 40 stone had never been imposed on it – and the three men crashed to the pavement.

Within seconds, more Squad personnel arrived and the prisoners were handcuffed, as was Fraser, around the corner.

At Acton Crown Court on 8 July the three men pleaded guilty, and Bernard and Willard were each sentenced to five years' imprisonment and Fraser to four and a half years. At the conclusion of the case, the Assistant Recorder, Mr Stuart Moore, QC said:

> This is an unusual case in the sense, not of the thoroughness of the police work, but in the unusual way the police have been able to get this result by what is obviously the most skilful of operations. The photographs were of first-class, excellent quality, the video shows what a shocking crime

this was. I have nothing but praise for the team who conducted the enquiry.

So it might be thought that Yeoman would have received high praise from the commissioner. Not a bit of it. The senior officer who penned the initial report mentioned nothing of Yeoman's heroics; all that was said was, 'Both men ran off but as they did so, they were immediately arrested.'

When the report written by the court sergeant which contained the Assistant Recorder's fulsome comments reached the Squad's Acting Commander, who unlike the Assistant Recorder (and the rest of everyone on 10 and 12 Squads) had not seen the video, he, knowing no different, therefore wrote:

> The police work in this case, however good, was basically routine and I am of the opinion it is not suitable for recommendation for further commendation.

And that was how, thanks to the bone-idleness of a senior officer who could not be bothered to write a half-hour report (which was how long it took me to write this account), Yeoman was denied the approbation he richly deserved.

Much the same thing happened when two highly dangerous criminals who were later sentenced to eighteen and twelve years' imprisonment respectively were arrested for conspiracy to rob and possessing a loaded firearm. They were tackled by Detective Sergeants Alan Branch and John Redgrave ('as tough as woodpecker's lips') and Detective Constables Mick Geraghty and Mark Bryant (later Colonel Bryant MBE, DL) who, knowing the men were in possession of a firearm and about to rob the occupants of a security van and although being unarmed themselves, wrestled the two to the ground. It should have resulted in gallantry awards for all of them, but the thought of compiling a gallantry report within fourteen days of the men being committed for trial was one that was obviously far too overwhelming for the senior officer concerned.

But that, alas, has been the fate of so many brave, talented Metropolitan Police officers, over so many years.

★.

The Squad teams at the Yard had many more successes: a stolen £2½ million Rembrandt had been recovered, but no one knew the identity of the thief until he was tracked down over a matter of months and sentenced to three years' imprisonment. Similarly, nobody knew the identity of one of a gang of burglars, the rest of whom were caught in the act of breaking into a warehouse; he escaped completely, leaving Detective Sergeant Alan Branch with a black eye – he *was* cross!

Officers from 10 Squad were handed a letter forwarded to them from the commissioner's office which read: 'Dear Commishoner, the guys in this flat are doin' robbin' and got guns.' An address for these supposed miscreants was provided and, since a positive result was thought unlikely, the case was put on the back burner until, with nothing else to do, officers knocked politely on the door of the flat. The occupiers, three brothers, were in possession of shotguns, a revolver and ammunition. They and a fourth member of the team admitted carrying out twenty-seven armed robberies. The incriminating letter was not revealed in court; nor was the fact that ten of those robberies had been committed after the letter had been received!

Two armed robbers who stole £11,000 from a security van were each jailed for ten years – however, there were spin-offs in which various gangs had conspired to rob the same van, and they were jailed for between four and seven years. But when Steven Waldorf was shot and severely wounded by police after being mistaken for a dangerous criminal named David Martin, the Squad was called in to lead the hunt for Martin. He was captured ten days later, without shots being fired, having been chased along a London Underground live railway track by Squad officers. They received no commendations, either; it was thought politically incorrect to praise the gallantry of those officers because of the stigma attached to the case, even though it had not been Flying Squad officers who had shot Waldorf. In that case, praise was denied through snivelling gutlessness, although it's quite possible that bone-idleness was a contributory factor as well.

CHAPTER 15

The Squad Shoot Back

D etective Sergeant David Kelly was actually on annual leave on 13 July 1982 when he received a telephone call from the Flying Squad's Walthamstow office asking if he wanted to be part of a long-running case in which, since a stolen car had been put down the previous night, action appeared to be fairly imminent.

The gang was comprised of Terry Edwards (on the run from a ten-year prison sentence), 'Titch' Pomeroy and Jamie Salmon. Their plan was to rob the Co-op bank in Hackney High Street and make their getaway in a stolen Mini. The Mini was selected because the gang intended to escape through Victoria Park, and it was small enough to go through the bollards that would obstruct larger pursuing vehicles. As Kelly told me, 'You have to remember that this case took place in the days of when C11 provided the surveillance; C7 provided the technical; and the Squad provided the armed muscle!'

Kelly was armed and in an old-style Granada driven by PC Keith Banks; in position since around 6.00 am, by 11.35 they were thoroughly bored with watching a Mark 4 Cortina in Gore Road which was thought to be the gang's last 'changeover' vehicle. In addition, Kelly was annoyed, believing he had been assigned to a 'longstop' position and that in consequence, if there was any action, he would miss out on it. But he was wrong.

A transmission from the officer keeping the Mini under observation stated that everything was quiet; but within seconds, Keith Banks turned to Kelly and said, 'Look, the villains' plan could have worked, as there's a Mini coming through the park now!'

He was right – and the officer in the OP was wrong; the Mini which had been kept under observation was not the robbers' car; that vehicle, containing the three robbers, complete with guns and stolen money, pulled up and the gang started to transfer to the Cortina. Kelly immediately informed the other Squad men that the wrong Mini had been kept under observation and called for back-up.

Telling Banks to try and block them off from escaping, Kelly wound down his window as per his firearms training; as they pulled alongside, Terry Edwards who was in the back of the Cortina pointed a gun at the officers. Before Edwards could shoot, Kelly fired his gun and saw the Cortina's rear passenger window shatter.

The two cars were shunting back and forth, with the Squad car trying to block the Cortina in, but the robbers managed to pull away. Kelly fired another shot as they did so, then they gave chase until the gang's car was baulked in traffic. As Kelly told me:

> Having seen three of them enter the vehicle and being convinced that my shot had at least killed one of them if not more, we were amazed to see all three decamp from it. Edwards and Pomeroy ran off together, while Jamie Salmon, the third member of the gang, ran off in a different direction. Keith and I ran after Edwards and Pomeroy and arrested them both. Salmon was arrested sometime after.
>
> When we examined the Cortina later, we found that my first shot fired from all of about two feet away had shattered the glass but had not entered the vehicle, and neither had my second shot. In retrospect I would have been better off to try and club Edwards with the butt [of my gun]!

The gang appeared at the Old Bailey on 18 April 1983 and pleaded guilty to robbery; Edwards received the longest sentence, of fourteen years, to run concurrently with the interrupted sentence he was already serving.

'Keith and I were awarded High Commendations and the Bow Street rewards,' said Kelly, adding, 'In addition, I received words of advice that shooting guns in built up areas could be dangerous!'

★

These were prescient words; as mentioned in the previous chapter, on Friday, 14 January 1983 police had opened fire in a crowded London street at a car believed to contain a dangerous armed criminal named David Martin. In fact, one of the occupants, an innocent young man named Steven Waldorf, had been shot and seriously injured, and now the whole of 10 and 12 Squads at the Yard were searching for Martin. Consequently, when the Squad at Walthamstow received good information that the security van due to collect the day's taking from one of the shops in Chapel Market was to be robbed on 22 January, the Squad's personnel were very thin on the ground.

Kelly now takes up the tale:

We believed that one of the suspects was a man called James Daly, who was wanted by the Squad at Tower Bridge for armed robbery, having shot a security guard. He was also wanted in Ireland for armed robbery using a machine gun!

I was armed in the back of the observation van together with four unarmed colleagues who cheerfully reminded me that you could get into a lot of trouble as the man with the gun, referring to the Waldorf incident!

Daly was spotted on the plot and the attack was given by Peter Wilton, our DCI. We were first to engage and I jumped out of the van screaming, 'Armed police!' expecting Daly to either confront me or to surrender. He did neither but turned and ran, and I followed. I was about six feet behind him when he half turned and fired a sawn-off shotgun at me that he had concealed down the front of his trousers. Fortunately, the blast hit the pavement beside me and I only sustained a couple of ricocheted pellets to my face. He immediately threw the gun down in the crowded market, so I held my fire and managed to catch him and crash him into a shop doorway and arrested him. It was then that my unarmed colleagues joined me and one of them pointed out that I had been hit, which I had not realized until then.

Apparently the Commissioner's first words on being told about the job were 'Did we shoot anyone?' and he was most relieved with the answer. Needless to say, the Met unashamedly used my case to counter the adverse publicity of the Waldorf incident. Frank Cater, the Squad Commander at the time was like my press agent and I was promised every award from the VC downwards!

When we did a walk-through reconstruction on the Monday morning with David Pryor, our gun lab expert, he told me that if I had been standing a foot to my left when Daly shot the gun, we would not have been having the conversation!

Daly was convicted on a number of charges at the Old Bailey and received a total of seventeen years.

I was awarded the High Commendation and another Bow Street award and then the Queen's Commendation for Bravery.

Counselling was then unknown; going to the pub served as guidance and support following stressful situations. So Kelly was surprised when the senior officer, Peter Wilton, put his arm around his shoulders and explained that when they had seen Daly fire the gun from their OP they had at first feared the worst as Kelly had stumbled forward. Kelly was not aware of this and was a bit taken aback by Wilton's show of affection, until Wilton explained that his overriding thought at the time was this could have jeopardized his chances on a selection board for promotion.

'There goes another fucking board!' was his comment, and Kelly's angry response was couched in words not really suitable or sensible for a chief inspector's ears.

'But', Kelly told me, 'when I later reflected on it, I realized that it was a shrewd piece of man-management designed to bring me back down to earth gently.'

Kelly's career continued with another posting to the Squad as a detective inspector; more commendations for bravery followed, and after serving for five years as Assistant Chief Constable of Kent Constabulary he was awarded the Queen's Police Medal, before serving as Chief Constable of the Sovereign Base Area's Police in Cyprus for nine years, finally retiring on New Year's Eve 2012.

Not many police services can boast senior officers of David Kelly's calibre who have repeatedly displayed courage and detective ability. More's the pity.

★

The Area offices were working hard at investigating their reported robberies, with some spectacular successes, plus some which came purely by chance.

There had been a series of 'Lone Ranger' attacks, all on branches of the Leeds Permanent Building Society, all over London, Hertfordshire and Essex. The gunman had carried out something in the region of twenty successful armed robberies, and following a weekly meeting at the Yard, Detective Chief Inspector Peter 'Pee Wee' Wilton of the Walthamstow office returned to that office to tell Detective Sergeants Terry Mills and the late Charlie Collins that the 'powers-that-be' were hopping mad that so many robberies had been carried out at the same building society; and with that, they were dispatched to solve this crime wave.

There was not a great deal to go on. Just one branch office had managed to capture a picture of the gunman on CCTV; it was a rather blurred image and it appeared to show a workman, perhaps a builder, wearing a hat and working clothes. There was also a witness who, the previous week, had seen a van driving off at high speed. She had not even been aware that there had been a robbery, since the van had been parked some distance away from the branch where the robbery had occurred. The woman had not noted the registration number of the van but had noticed part of a telephone number on the side of the vehicle – '508', which was the telephone exchange for the Loughton area.

So the witness was not aware if that van could be connected with the robbery, which she hadn't witnessed, and neither could the officers. But that, plus a blurred photo, was all they had, so they set off to Loughton police station and showed the photo to the collator, who was unable to identify the suspect. It was then a matter of the officers picking up a copy of 'Yellow Pages' to trawl through all the builders in that area. But before they started compiling a list they noticed that directly at the back of Loughton police station there was a scaffolding-cum-builders firm, so that was their starting point. They showed the photograph to the young girl in the reception area who looked at it without interest before remarking, 'He'll be back around five.'

A quick phone call was made to DCI Wilton for some armed back-up, and when the suspect, Frederick Newman, arrived at the office he was greeted by Mills and Collins. Their accusations were met with denials, but when he accompanied the officers to his van, a search under the driver's seat revealed a handgun and a bag containing cheques from the Hoddesdon branch of the Leeds Permanent Building Society. Just a bare two hours after being sent out on a seemingly impossible task, as Mills told me, the situation had been transformed: 'From zero to heroes!'

There were a number of coincidences in that case. Newman had attended the same school as Mills, albeit Newman was four years senior to him.

Newman had just been released from prison for a series of robberies, colloquially known as 'wrap-ups'; on the pretext of delivering a parcel to elderly householders – the youngest was seventy-four, the oldest, eighty-three – the victims would be pushed inside their homes and tied – or wrapped – up before their property was stolen. Sickening and quite unnecessary violence had been used by Newman and his associate who had used hired vans during the robberies. They had been arrested, one hour after the officers had been dispatched to stop these robberies, just by chance – very much as in Mills' case – as they returned the hired vehicle to the depot.

'Do you think I'd be stupid enough to hire a van with my own driving licence if I was going to do robberies?' Newman asked scornfully when he was arrested; but he was and he did, and after a lot of stolen property and a loaded revolver were found, he received an extremely lenient sentence of four years' imprisonment after a trial in which very serious allegations of impropriety were made against the arresting officer.

Since that officer was me, I was especially delighted when for the series of Building Society robberies Newman was sentenced to ten years' imprisonment.

That was a straightforward case for Terry Mills; the next case in which he (and many others) participated was anything but run-of-the-mill.

CHAPTER 16

The Security Express Robbery

S ecurity Express was a cash-in-transit company with a depot at 38–54 Curtain Road, EC2. In 1983 they had secured the contract to collect from the Ideal Home Exhibition, and this meant that the collections would be seven days a week, with the cash stored in their vaults.

On Easter Monday, 4 April 1983, several masked men armed with a handgun and a sawn-off shotgun grabbed hold of one of the staff who had opened the gates to permit entry to the premises to seven of his colleagues, and forced their way in. As the other staff members arrived they were seized, tied up and blindfolded. To obtain the keys to the vaults, one of the employees had petrol poured over his trousers and a box of matches rattled against his ear, to encourage compliance. During the raid the men spoke with pseudo-Irish accents, although the name 'Ron' was mentioned. After five hours the gang left, taking with them £5,961,097 in cash.

With a reward of £500,000 on offer from Security Express, the investigation from the Walthamstow office, led by DCI Wilton (and supplemented by officers from 10 and 12 Squads at the Yard) got underway, and an incident room was set up at City Road police station.

There was little to go on. None of the staff was able to describe the attackers, and despite a lengthy scientific forensic examination of the scene, there was nothing to identify any person as being present. It was the beginning of an investigation which would continue for over fifteen years.

But one month prior to the robbery, on 2 March 1983, police had visited the premises of J.W. Knight & Sons (Metals), Ridley Road, E8. They were eventually admitted by James Knight, and in an upstairs office they found his brother, John Knight; a third brother, Ronnie Knight, then married to actress Barbara Windsor, was not present. But four other men were: in an adjoining office were Terrence George Perkins, William John Hickson, Ronald Everett and John Mason. All appeared extremely apprehensive and most reluctant to discuss their reasons for being at the metal yard. The officers formed the opinion that they had been discussing something, but there was a complete absence of papers that would have indicated a business transaction. All had criminal records, one of them stretching back to 1944, so details of this meeting were recorded.

Now, following the robbery, three men came under Flying Squad scrutiny: two were Perkins and Hickson, the third was John Horsley, and they were seen to be meeting in Dalston; but although leads were followed up, observations were carried out and addresses were searched, the months went by without success.

In the meantime, a robbery occurred at the Brink's-Mat warehouse on 26 November 1983. Gold bullion valued at £26 million had been stolen – and now Flying Squad resources were really stretched, with the Barnes Squad office leading the investigation, plus anybody else who might be able to assist. A car linked to the robbery was found abandoned in Malvern Road, just west of London Fields. Cross-checking of indices revealed that the Walthamstow officers had an interest in John Horsley, who had a garage in Malvern Road. Working on the assumption that when adding two and two together, the result would *have* to be four, on 20 January 1984 the bullion enquiry officers steamed into Horsley and accused him, point-blank, of being involved in Britain's biggest ever robbery. Horsley denied any involvement in the Brink's-Mat job, but staggered the officers by admitting full knowledge of the Security Express robbery. He pointed the Squad men in the direction of the house of his father-in-law, who like Horsley lived in Waltham Cross, and they recovered £279,326 of the stolen money.

The car which prompted Horsley's arrest? Neither that nor the Brink's-Mat robbery had anything to do with him or the rest of the gang. The decision to abandon the vehicle so close to Horsley's garage had been pure coincidence. There we can leave the Brink's-Mat investigation; it will soon return to be examined in detail, never fear.

The day after Horsley's arrest, Hickson and Perkins were arrested; the following day, John Knight. On 8 February 1984, Alan Stanley Opiola, who had a garage in Enfield where he had helped count the money, was arrested. He was 'turned' by Detective Inspector Reed McGeorge, as was his wife Linda by Julia Pearce, and on 14 May 1984 he pleaded guilty at the Old Bailey to receiving some of the proceeds of the robbery and was sentenced to three years and three months' imprisonment; he would later give evidence against other members of the gang, including James Knight, who had been arrested on 19 March 1984.

There were a number of people in the Costa del Sol region of Spain to whom police wished to speak. They were Ronnie Knight, Ronnie Everett, John Mason, Clifford Saxe and George Foreman. The latter, who had been convicted with the Kray brothers in 1969, was regarded as a very active criminal with fingers in a number of very lucrative illicit pies. Following the arrests in the UK, they were reported to be keeping a rather low profile. The shutters on the luxurious new homes belonging to Saxe and Knight were kept tightly closed, although work still continued on constructing John Knight's mountainside mansion, reputedly at a cost of 70 million pesetas. Perhaps he cherished a forlorn hope that there had been a terrible mistake and he would be released from prison in order to enjoy it. Since, within days of the robbery, John Knight had paid £251,000 into several Building Society offices in his local High Street in his own name, this did seem unlikely.

The first trial was held at the Old Bailey before Judge Richard Lowry QC between 18 February and 7 June 1985. Three were convicted of the robbery: John Knight and Terence Perkins (both received twenty-two years' imprisonment and had criminal bankruptcy orders imposed) and John Horsley (eight years' imprisonment and a restitution order in the sum of £283,025.31p made); two more were acquitted of the robbery but convicted of handling stolen goods: James Knight, for receiving £247,750, got eight years' imprisonment, and William Hickson, for receiving £36,000, six years.

Four other people accused of receiving some of the stolen money were acquitted, and the cases of two more, accused of conspiracy to pervert the course of public justice were not proceeded with.

Detective Inspector McGeorge was given the day-to-day running of the enquiry. At the conclusion of that case, he wrote:

> Part of the information received about these persons who had committed this robbery alleged that they were an old team, coming out of mothballs for one last big job to pay for their retirement. When you consider that in 1983, the average age of this gang was 48 years, this has proved to be true. In respect of those in Spain, it has turned out to be an excellent pension fund enabling them to have a luxurious retirement.

Officers had conducted enquiries in Spain, Paris, Switzerland and Australia. Detective Sergeant Neil Wraith came to the Flying Squad at Rigg Approach in 1987; he had not been part of the original investigation, but Detective Sergeant George Moncrieff had. The two now worked together, and Wraith recalls:

> Ronnie Knight was living in the villa that was originally owned by himself and Barbara Windsor, El Limonar, and was co-habiting with Susan Haylock, much to Barbara's disgust. They decided to tie the knot, and to assist proving association of the five, George and myself went to Spain and attended the area where they married, a posh 'do' on the Costa. We couldn't get into the celebrations but, assisted by the local police, were able to see the guests arriving, and sure enough, all members were present. After that trip, except for a short trip to the Channel Islands with Reed for some more background and financial statements, the papers were 'put to bed'.

Then came the arrest of Foreman.

> I was by then the only person dealing with the papers, as George and Reed had been transferred, and in late July 1988 he had been arrested in Spain, had become extremely violent and a doctor was called and Foreman was seriously sedated to board the Iberia flight to Heathrow. With other officers from Rigg, I went to the airport, arrested Foreman and he was taken to Leman Street police station. I remember Foreman saying to Reed, 'I don't want to be verballed during any interview as I'll be saying nothing!'
> Reed just said, 'We've enough evidence to charge you already and you will not be interviewed except to confirm your name.'
> Reed was referring to a massive amount of circumstantial evidence already in place concerning Foreman.
> The late Simon Webber was on the Squad at Rigg at this time, and as he had been on the enquiry at the time of the original offence he was seconded to help Reed and me with the necessary further investigation, as was Julia Pearce, and the four of us were given an office at Woodford police station to put together the necessary court papers. Simon and I were sent to Spain.

Before leaving, the officers had to be in possession of a Commission Rogatoire (known colloquially as a 'Com Rog') – an official document signed by a representative of the Crown Prosecution

Service, written both in English and the language of the foreign country concerned. This had to be presented to the judge of the area where the enquiries were to be made. If the judge agreed, local police would accompany the English officers, but only matters specifically referred to in the Com Rog could be investigated. If the judge and the police were of a helpful persuasion, matters could be successfully disposed of in no time at all. However, that was not always the case, as Wraith explains:

> Our enquiries began with the assistance of the two local officers assigned to us. Slow was not the word. Each day after that, arrangements were made to deal with one enquiry per day, but arrangements were not made until the morning of the enquiry, and if the person was not available, then no enquiries could be made; Simon and I had a lot of spare time on our hands.
>
> One enquiry that did come to fruition was at the local branch of Banco de Bilbao, and a statement was obtained from the manager regarding an account in the name of Foreman.
>
> During the taking of the statement, the manager asked Simon and me if we were going to open a safety deposit box being held at that branch in the names of Foreman, Everett and Mason. We were somewhat surprised as we knew nothing of the box, but of course, said, 'Yes.'
>
> Before we could proceed, one of the inspectors said, 'You cannot do it as it is not on the Commission Rogatoire and permission will be required from the judge, who will not be sitting for two days.'
>
> This was on a Friday, and we needed to wait until Monday. On the Monday we were delayed at court until late afternoon, when the judge finally decided that we could open the box. He had, until then, been apparently deliberating as to whether to allow us the opening. We eventually returned to the bank the following day, and after a locksmith was called, the box was opened. It contained an elastic band and nothing else. On the way out of the bank, the manager called me over out of hearing of the police officers and stated that the owners of the box (Mason and Everett) had appeared on Monday and emptied the box of its contents. He was not aware of the contents. Judge, police or bank manager? One of them spilled the beans to the baddies – I think, not the bank manager.

After that, matters went from bad to worse. Wraith and Webber discovered their telephone calls to London were being intercepted, there was a furious argument with one of the Spanish inspectors which caused him, worryingly, to place a hand on his gun, and both officers were observed at a bar by the heavily-built occupants of a large saloon with a Spanish registration plate which drove slowly past them. When they provided the registration number to the police the following day, they were told they had noted it incorrectly. It was time to go home.

Between 12 March 1990 and 5 April 1990, Freddie Foreman stood trial at the Old Bailey. It was proved that on 1 April 1983 his bank account contained £72.69p; by August that year, £358,000 reposed in new accounts. The jurors were given police protection, but when a juror was relieving himself at a public urinal and was told, 'On that Freddie Foreman trial, are you? Well, you'd better find him not guilty or you'd better emigrate to Australia!' – that was absolutely nothing to do with Foreman or any of his associates, good gracious, no. The Old Bill were responsible, that's who. It's the sort of thing they do all the time. At least, that's the explanation gangsters give when they pen their memoirs.

Foreman was acquitted of the robbery but found guilty of receiving £363,280 of the stolen money and was sentenced to nine years' imprisonment.

Ronnie Knight deposited a total of £264,225 cash with his accountant between 15 April 1983 and 14 December 1983. Six weeks later, on 23 January 1984, that amount had increased to £314,813. In August 1983 he had purchased two apartments in Marbella at a cost of £70,000; one month later, a further property was purchased near Marbella at a cost of £33,000.

After John Knight was arrested at 2.00 am on 22 January 1984, his brother Ronnie fled to Spain later the same day.

His girlfriend (later his wife) Susan Haylock followed him to Spain the next day. By an amazing coincidence, who should she see at the airport but Freddie Forman, who astonishingly just happened to be flying to the same destination. According to Foreman, she was carrying a huge holdall, stuffed, as he said, 'full of used banknotes' which she was taking to Ronnie. It was too big for the overhead locker, so Foreman had to push it under his seat – blimey, wot a larf!

Ms Haylock was overdrawn at her bank on the day after the robbery to the tune of £1.87p. However, between 6 April and 31 December 1983, her finances improved dramatically after she deposited a total of £24,094.80p, including a cheque for £15,000, later transferred to Ronnie Knight's account. In addition, on

14 April she found it necessary to hire a security box. A great many transactions were carried out in different currencies and different countries; several flats were purchased in Spain, as well as an Indian restaurant and a nightclub, and Ms Haylock purchased a new Mercedes-Benz with bundles of notes in £1,000 wads – she was questioned, but never prosecuted.

Ronnie Knight returned to this country on 2 May 1994, when he was arrested. I said to Reed McGeorge at the time, 'What happens when you question him and he makes no reply to any of your questions?'

He replied, 'I don't want him to answer any questions. I've got enough evidence to sink him, on paper.'

It looked as though he had. On 4 January 1995 it was Ronnie Knight's turn to climb the steps at the Old Bailey, where he pleaded not guilty to the robbery but guilty to receiving £314,813 from the robbery, and that was accepted by the prosecution. Judge Gerald Gordon told him:

> Clearly, I do not know what precise role you played. But professional robbers such as those involved are not going to hand over the sort of sums you got unless the person to whom they give it is very deeply involved himself.

Knight apparently had no assets, so no compensation order could be awarded to Security Express, and he was sentenced to seven years' imprisonment.

'After Ronnie's trial, Mac and I started on Everett and Mason', Julia Pearce (by then a detective sergeant) told me. 'Through a source, we found that they were importing drugs into the country. The information was passed on to Customs & Excise while we continued on the financial side.'

Turning now to Everett, at the time of the robbery his National Westminster Bank account at Forest Gate was overdrawn. His cheques were being returned 'Refer to drawer', and the issue of a new chequebook was delayed until such time as he brought his account into credit. He also had an account at Barclays Bank, Bedford Row, and this, too, was briefly overdrawn during that period, until it was suddenly refreshed with the deposit of £4,000, all in £1 notes. Between 24 May and 29 November 1983 he suddenly paid £323,200 into two fresh bank accounts, money which was later disseminated to ten banks in London, the Channel Islands, the United States and Spain. He acquired a false British passport in the name of Ronald Page on 14 June 1983.

On the same date, a false British passport in the name of John O'Donnell was issued to John Mason, who between 24 May 1983 and 13 March 1984 deposited £417,700 cash into two bank accounts, funds later dispersed to accounts in the Channel Islands, the United States, Switzerland and Spain. By preparing a schedule of all the bank transactions, Simon Webber was able show that Mason's share of the robbery was £420,680; Mason is still adrift.

In 2005 Everett was sentenced to eight years' imprisonment for conspiracy to import cannabis and had to pay a confiscation order of £120,402.

On 1 April 1983 Clifford Saxe's bank account was overdrawn by £133. By November 1983 it was proved that he had access to over £287,000 in cash.

'Clifford Saxe died some years ago', Peter Wilton told me. 'He was a very lonely man because he had already lost his wife.'

Reed McGeorge and Julia Pearce were told that they had a week to pack up the office at Woodford and return to Rigg Approach, but by now McGeorge had had enough. He had joined the police in 1960, so he had more than enough time in to claim his pension, which in 1999 he did. He and Julia Pearce had worked on the Security Express enquiry for sixteen years. Both of them, plus Neil Wraith and Simon Webber, were amongst those commended by the commissioner for their work in that very protracted case.

Julia Pearce never returned to Rigg Approach, either; she was posted elsewhere and later retired, after thirty years' service; but not for long. After cutting her teeth as exhibits officer on the Dewhurst job and progressing to deal with the exhibits on the Security Express job, her expertise was thought too good to lose.

'I was asked to re-write the exhibits officers' course and then deliver it for a year', she told me. '*Then*, I retired!'

DC 'Gentleman John' Fordham – one of the seriously good guys . . .

... and some of the less seriously good guys.

Above left: Kenneth Noye.

Above right: Freddie Foreman.

Below left: Dennis Arif, arrested during Operation Yamato.

Below right: Terry Smith.

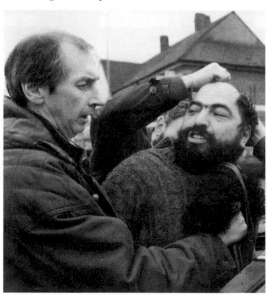

Above: Steven Charalambous in police uniform.

Right: Charalambous with false moustache and black tie which was partially severed by a police bullet.

Below: Loukas Menikou – arrested.

"YOU KNOW I'VE CLEAN FORGOTTEN WHAT I CAME IN FOR!"

JAK's cartoon of the East Acton Post Office shoot-out.

DS Alan Knapp, having been awarded the George Medal.

Knapp's silver laurel leaf for the Queen's Commendation for Brave Conduct, plus his George Medal.

The staff at Rigg Approach

Above: L–R: DI Reed McGeorge, DS Fred May, DCI Mick Newstead, DI Bob Brown, DI George Raison, DS Gordon Livingstone.

Below: The Rigg Approach surveillance team.

The Knightsbridge Safety Deposit Box Centre robbery

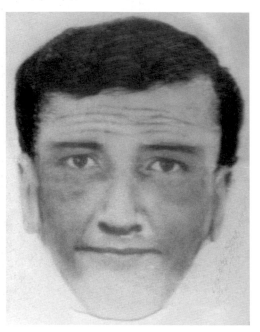 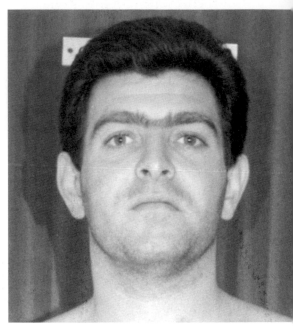

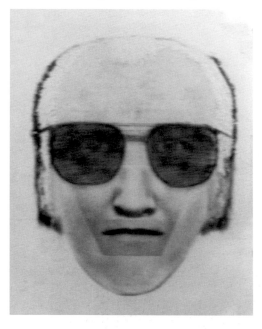 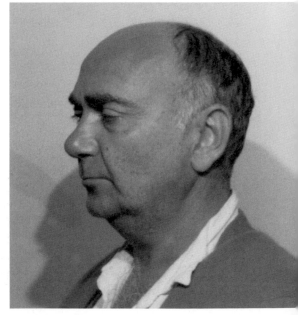

Above left: Photofit of Valerio Viccei . . .

Above right: . . . and the genuine article.

Below left: Photofit of David Poole . . .

Below right: . . . and the genuine article.

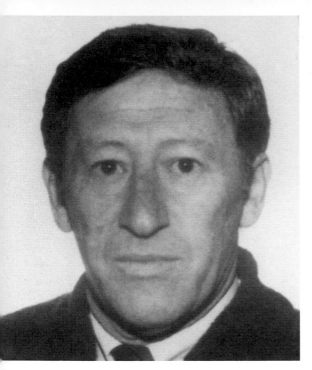

Above left: Eric Rubin.

Above right: DI Dick Leach.

Below: A photograph of Viccei and his girlfriend Helle Skoubon taken at Parkhurst top security prison with a cheeky message for Dick Leach.

Above: A selection of recovered loot from Knightsbridge.

Below: A selection of the Knightsbridge loot taken from the boot of Viccei's Ferrari.

Right: D/Supt. Tony Lundy – expert handler of supergrasses.

Below: John Grieve – undercover.

'Operation Cockburn'

Above: The arrest of Robert Patrick Stubbs.

Below: The arrest of Arthur Gary Edney.

Above: The arrest of James Albert Hampton.

Below: The arrest of William Robert Griffiths.

Left: Edney giving his eyes a treat in Norwich.

Below: Operation Cockburn's robbery equipment.

Above: The burglars' entry to the Hatton Garden vaults.

Below: (Top row, L–R) John Henry Collins, Daniel Jones, Terry Perkins. (Bottom row, L–R) Carl Wood, William Lincoln, Hugh Doyle.

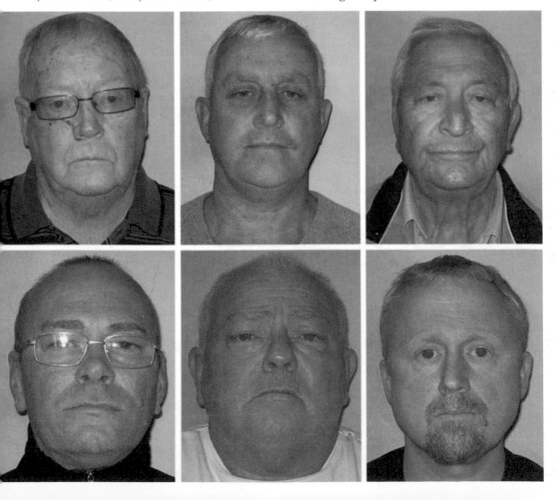

Above: The digger used
to gain entry to the
Millennium Dome.

Left: The De Beers diamond.

Above: Following the automatic weapon attack on the Flying Squad car, L–R: Swinfield (kneeling in a blue shirt), Redford, Stubbs and Macaskill (standing in a blue shirt).

Right: Back row, L–R: DS John Swinfield, DC Peter Redford. Front row, L–R: PC John Macaskill, DS Michael Stubbs.

Michael Stuart Moore QC (left), to whom the Flying Squad owes a huge debt of gratitude, together with the author in a Suffolk garden, June 2018.

CHAPTER 17

Brink's-Mat

The story of Britain's biggest gold robbery is pretty well known. On 26 November 1983 at 7.00 am a number of armed robbers viciously attacked the staff of the Brink's-Mat warehouse at Unit 7, on the Heathrow International Trading Estate, Hounslow; employing the technique – just as had been used at the Security Express robbery, some eight months earlier – of pouring petrol over the legs of one of the custodians, the vaults were opened and three tons of gold, valued at £26 million, was stolen. The Flying Squad were called in and a number of arrests were made. On 3 December 1984 Brian Robinson (his brother-in-law, Tony Black, had been one of the guards at the warehouse and gave evidence for the prosecution) and Micky McAvoy were each sentenced to twenty-five years' imprisonment for the robbery.

But the gold was not immediately recovered; and while painstaking enquiries were carried out to discover the whereabouts of the bullion and those responsible for its dispersal – enquiries that carried on for years – the purpose of this narrative is to pinpoint one man and the police officer he killed.

Detective Constable John Fordham had been a highly respected member of C11 Department since February 1976; in 1981 he had volunteered to become one of the surveillance officers known as 'Rurals' – trained by members of the Special Air Service Regiment and the Royal Ulster Constabulary surveillance unit known as 'E4A' – who could provide intelligence after being infiltrated into inhospitable countryside locations in conditions of extreme physical hardship. On one occasion Fordham had remained up to his neck in water for 48 hours in order to carry out surveillance.

Suspicion had fallen on Kenneth Noye (described as a building contractor) as being someone who had assisted in the distribution of the gold, and observation was kept on Noye's house, Hollywood Cottage, set in 20 acres of grounds at West Kingsdown, Kent. The property was surrounded by high walls topped with barbed wire, and its gates were electronically controlled. It was known that extremely large, powerful Rottweiler guard dogs patrolled the area, but they had been observed via a covert camera by dog handlers who had come to the conclusion that they were harmless domestic pets; should the need arise, the animals would be manageable if they were fed the yeast tablets which Fordham and his partner, Detective Constable Neil Murphy, had in their possession. On 26 January 1985 the two officers, dressed in camouflage clothing and balaclavas, took over from two other C11 operatives – 'I was delighted when I knew it was John, because he was so good', Detective Sergeant Tony Yeoman told me. Yeoman was one of a number of Flying Squad officers posted around the perimeter; search warrants had been obtained because it was thought that Noye's associate Brian Reader was going to carry out an illicit transaction with him. The C11 officers were in place in case the occupants of the house tried to escape or dispose of evidence.

However, three minutes after Reader arrived at the house at 6.15 pm and as soon as the officers entered the grounds, the dogs sensed their presence. Noye would later agree with the dog handlers' opinion that they were gambolling, playful pets, but in fact, nothing could have been further from the truth.

Murphy threw the yeast tablets to the highly aggressive, snapping, snarling animals, but they had no effect at all in placating them. Their frenzied barking would be certain to attract the attention of those in the house, so he transmitted the message on his covert radio, 'Dogs – hostile' and signalled to Fordham to retreat, because it was C11 policy to withdraw ('Blow out, rather than show out') if an operative's position was compromised.

At 6.26 pm he radioed, ' Neil out, towards fence' and, believing that Fordham would follow him, was surprised to hear Fordham's transmission, one minute later: 'Somebody out, halfway down drive, calling dogs.'

Murphy climbed a tree, to see someone with a torch searching the area where the dogs had last been seen, so he dropped to the other side of the fence and, hammering on it, shouted, 'Keep those dogs quiet!' – hoping that the occupant would think he was an irate neighbour.

But at that moment, the householder – Noye, who was armed with a kitchen knife – shone his torch on a man dressed in a balaclava, four or five feet away. No one but Noye knows precisely that happened thereafter, but this is the account he later gave to an Old Bailey jury.

> I just froze with horror. I thought that was my lot, I was going to be a dead man. The man didn't say a word. Immediately I shone my torch and caught his face, he caught me straight across the face with what I thought

was a weapon. I didn't see anything. I think I might have imagined it at the time as you usually relate a masked man with a gun. I received a swinging blow across the eye and the front of my face. I immediately put my hand up to his face, grabbed his head and started striking with the knife as fast as I could, with all my strength. He came at me – I struck at his front all of five times. I was frightened for my life. I had struck him but it seemed to have no effect he was overwhelmingly on top of me. I was fighting for my life, I wanted to wound him.

Noye said he left the scene and met Reader coming down the drive carrying a shotgun. Taking it from him, Noye and Reader returned to where Fordham was lying.

'Who are you?' asked Noye. 'If you don't take that mask off and tell me who you are, I'll blow your head off.'

'SAS', groaned Fordham, taking his mask off and adding, 'on manoeuvres.'

Murphy could hear the 'blow your head off' remark, plus a woman screaming, and looking over the wall he saw two men and a woman standing around Fordham's body; one of the men – he said it was the one not holding the shotgun – kicked Fordham. Both Noye and Reader later denied that that had happened.

But that was not the explanation that Noye gave to the police that night.

The first officer to arrive was Detective Constable David Manning, who shouted, 'I'm a police officer', to which Noye, lifting the shotgun, replied, 'Fuck off, or I'll do you as well.'

He then backed off, walking back towards the house, still pointing the shotgun at Manning, who knelt down besides Fordham, who groaned, 'He's done me . . . he's stabbed me.'

Manning attempted first aid, but Fordham's life was draining away.

Tony Yeoman is one of the most equable of men; in the fifty years I've known him, never once have I known him lose his composure. He was one of the officers at the house where Noye had been detained, and it was Noye who discovered that Yeoman did possess a temper.

'Do you realize that the police officer you stabbed is dying?' he asked Noye, who replied, 'He shouldn't have been on my property', adding rather unwisely, 'I hope he fucking dies.'

'What sort of animal are you?' shouted Yeoman, shoving Noye against a wall. 'I really lost it because of what he'd said about John and I punched him in the eye', he told me, over thirty years later.

Yeoman described exactly what had happened in his statement during the court case.

'What else could I do? It happened, so I had to say so', he told me. 'I was expecting a really rough time in court, but not a word was said about it.'

Noye had little to say about it, either – at that time. A different complexion was put on matters during Noye's testimony at the Old Bailey, the inference being that his black eye had been sustained minutes earlier, courtesy of Fordham.

The post mortem the following day revealed that Fordham had sustained ten wounds – five in the front of his body, three in his back, one in his armpit and one in his head – made by a knife 1cm wide and 7cm long. The victim of a knife attack will often sustain 'defence wounds' – that is, cuts on their arms or hands with which they have attempted to ward off the blows. But there were none in Fordham's case; and after the first blow to the heart had been struck, the four that followed were given when Fordham was immobile, giving rise to the belief that Reader had held him while Noye carried out the stabbing, then reached behind to continue stabbing him in the back. Furthermore, there was a bruise to Fordham's chest consistent with a kick, which Murphy swore he had seen delivered. Lastly, had Fordham punched Noye in the eye, one would have thought that there would have been abrasions on his knuckles – but there weren't.

Noye's wife Brenda was charged (the case against her was later dismissed) with her husband with Fordham's murder, as was Brian Reader, who was found trotting down the road to the A20 and imprudently accepted a lift from the occupants of a car who turned out to be police officers.

At his trial, Noye challenged practically all of the police evidence, including that he had offered a £1 million bribe to the enquiry's senior officer ('In a bank anywhere in the world that you tell me . . . I just want you to ensure I do not go to prison'). There was no denying that he had stabbed Fordham – but he claimed it was in self-defence.

On 12 December 1985 the jury of seven men and five women at the Old Bailey took 12 hours and 37 minutes to unanimously deliver verdicts of not guilty to Fordham's murder in respect of both Noye and Reader.

However, they were not released; incriminating evidence had been found at Noye's house, including eleven gold bars weighing 13kg and worth £100,000. They were lying in a shallow gully by the garage, wrapped in a piece of material, underneath an old tin of paint and covered by a rubber mat. Additionally, £2,500 in new £50 notes was found in Noye's safe. The notes all bore the same prefix – A24. The same prefix was found on notes at Reader's house, as it was on the £50 notes totalling £50,000 which Mrs Rosemary Ford discovered in a Marks & Spencer's carrier bag poked underneath her back garden fence. She handed them in to the police but truthfully told them she had no idea as to their provenance. Neither did her neighbours, who were Noye's parents. Nor did Noye's sister, who lived nearby with her husband.

The trial of Noye, Reader and five other defendants on charges of receiving stolen goods and conspiracy to evade VAT got underway at the Old Bailey in May 1986. The police had gathered together important evidence, and by July, Noye, Reader plus two of the other defendants were found guilty of both charges.

And now something interesting happened. During the murder trial, Noye's legal representative had told the jury that the Kenny Noye he knew 'was a jovial sort of fellow – gregarious. I know he abhors violence . . . I have never seen him lose his temper on any occasion or show the slightest signs of violence at all.'

And when he had been acquitted of murder, Noye did as most gangsters do in those circumstances. Fawningly, he told the jury, 'Thank you very much. God bless you. Thank you for proving my innocence because that's what I am, not guilty.'

It's true the effect was slightly marred when he turned, grinning, to the Flying Squad officers at the back of the court and mouthed obscenities at them.

But now, having been found guilty on the gold charges, his demeanour towards jurors changed.

'I hope you all die of cancer!' he screamed at them, and just to ram the point home, Reader, pointing at the jurors, shouted, 'You have made one terrible mistake. You have got to live with that for the rest of your lives.'

Not to be outdone, Brenda Noye shrieked from the public gallery, 'Never has such an injustice been done – there's no fucking justice in this trial!' – which rather reflected the thoughts of the Flying Squad officers regarding the first trial.

I was present at court the following day. The mood of my contemporaries was one of relief, now that Noye had been found guilty of something. Judge Richard Lowry QC sentenced him to thirteen years' imprisonment for receiving the gold and fined him £250,000. For a VAT offence he received another twelve months' imprisonment and was again fined £250,000. He was ordered to pay £200,000 towards the cost of the prosecution and was sentenced to an additional two years' imprisonment in lieu of failing to pay the fines; since his assets had been frozen, that seemed unlikely. Reader was sentenced to a total of nine years' imprisonment.

Noye later pleaded guilty to receiving some Meissen porcelain valued at £3,000 which had been stolen from the home of Lord Darnley, two years before his arrest; he was sentenced to four years' imprisonment, to run concurrently with his existing sentence.

In 1994 Noye was released on licence and the following year, he handed back almost £3 million of the robbery's proceeds to the underwriters. However, on 19 May 1996, in a road-rage attack on an M25 slip-road, he first punched a complete stranger, Stephen Cameron, in the eye, then stabbed him with a knife twice – and as Cameron lay dying, Noye drove off smiling, before vanishing. He was arrested in Spain over two years later, extradited and, on 14 April 2000 after 8 hours and 21 minutes of deliberations, a jury found him guilty by a majority of 11–1. He was sentenced to life imprisonment; a recommendation was later imposed that he should serve a minimum of sixteen years. On Friday, 6 April 2018 he was released for the first time on limited day-release, to acclimatize him to the outside world.

By the time you're reading this, the 71-year-old convicted murderer should be freely walking amongst you.

*

I attended the unveiling of the memorial to John Fordham on Tuesday, 1 September 1987 at the junction of the A20 and School Lane, West Kingsdown. I occupied seat 35 in stand 'B', and all members of the Fordham family were present at that emotional ceremony, together with Neil Murphy, to lay flowers; speeches were made by the Rt Hon. Lord Denning PC, DL, the Commissioner, Peter Imbert QPM and Michael Winner.

The area was packed. Everyone who knew 'Gentleman John' Fordham wanted to be there. Many – those who were there on that terrible night of 26 January 1985 – bore mental scars which will probably last forever.

CHAPTER 18

Scenes of Crime Officers

I n 1969, civilian Scenes of Crime Officers (SOCOs) were introduced to the Metropolitan Police. Like their CID counterparts, some were good, others were bad and there were one or two who could be labelled 'tragic'. They had to examine scenes of crime, gather the evidence and submit samples to the laboratory for detailed examination. Their paperwork had to be immaculate. They – and the detective in charge of a case – had to work together to achieve a result. That did not always happen.

I worked on one investigation where the SOCO refused to discuss the case with me. I was waiting to give evidence outside Court No. 12 at the Old Bailey when I saw the SOCO being carried out, having fainted in the witness box.

'You've got a right one 'ere, Guv!' muttered a court usher to me.

After the Squad had been devolved from the Yard to four area offices, SOCOs were posted to each office. Without doubt, the finest was Paul Millen, who was sent to Rigg Approach. He was every bit as much a detective as the rest of the staff and utterly tireless in his quest for evidence. Time and again, his search for fibres, blood, head hair and paint samples at a crime scene would result in exact matches being made with the samples taken from suspects and with further evidence obtained from vehicles, discarded clothing and premises known to have been frequented by them. His work in one such case brought high praise from the Forensic Science Laboratory at Cambridge; it was followed by a DAC's commendation.

In another case, Millen decided that indentations on a key fob left in a getaway car used in a robbery might well be teeth marks. They were – and after a suspect was arrested and persuaded to give impressions of his teeth to a forensic odontologist, they matched, exactly. In the same case, a jacket abandoned at the scene was discovered to contain a key which was found to fit the front door of one of the suspects – but not before Millen insisted on having the key photographed, to prevent allegations being later made that the key had been taken from the suspect and planted. The same applied to the bitten key fob, in order to obviate similar allegations that the suspect, once in custody, had been forced to bite it.

But the name of one of the suspects plagued Millen. He felt sure he had heard it before; and after searching through hundreds of case notes, he discovered that he had. The jacket's owner had been previously arrested on suspicion of armed robbery. His jacket had been submitted to the police laboratory to determine if it could be matched to fibres from the seat of the getaway car. It couldn't, and the jacket was restored to its owner; but not before a small segment had been snipped out by the laboratory staff. Millen re-examined the jacket; there was the hole – and the laboratory had retained the cut-out section, which fitted perfectly. It led to the robbers' convictions, plus the rare award of a commissioner's commendation for Millen.

Never was it a case of 'us and them' with Millen; he had a perfect partnership with the Squad officers, and on the occasions – very rare, indeed – that he said that nothing could be done, his word was accepted without reservation. The officers knew that Millen had explored every possible avenue to obtain a result. Like Flying Squad officers, SOCOs often were on the end of hostile cross-examination in the witness box – some stuttered, some faltered and, as already mentioned, some fainted, but Millen revelled in it. He simply would not give up – if a defence barrister tried to talk over him, Millen went straight back at him: 'Excuse me – I just need to say . . . I have to make this point quite clear . . . the point I'm making is this . . .' It was a joy to watch.

A case which led to an interesting development was one in which a robbery had been carried out and the Squad officers were convinced they knew the identity of those concerned.

'One man had showered and the other was showering when the police burst in', Millen told me. 'There was no sign of the proceeds of the crime, but the men were arrested and clothing recovered.'

The getaway car had not then been found, neither had the stolen money, the guns or balaclavas; but Millen knew that when they were, forensic samples taken from the suspects would be of paramount importance and the most obvious would be hair samples, to try to match any which might be found in the balaclavas. But since both suspects had showered, surely any residue on their hair from the balaclavas would have been washed away?

This was where Millen was on top of his game. He remembered reading a piece in a forensic science journal which concluded that even after washing, some fibres could remain. He took a combing sample from one of the suspects, carefully combing backwards and forwards using a comb within a kit primed with moistened lint and then combed over a sheet of paper, which he placed within an exhibit bag which was sealed and labelled.

To avoid allegations of contamination, Millen had asked a police doctor to carry out the same procedure with the second suspect, but the doctor had taken umbrage at Millen's instructions and the comb and paper were not well presented, although the bag had been sealed and labelled. The two items were immediately dispatched to the laboratory, even though the getaway car had yet to be found; Millen was well aware of allegations of impropriety that could be made.

The car, proceeds of crime, guns and balaclavas were discovered some days later; a SOCO other than Millen carried out the examination.

Examination revealed that the hair samples taken by Millen matched fibres from one of the balaclavas; none were found in those taken by the doctor. A shoe mark was found linking a suspect to the scene, so that, plus the hair samples, formed an integral part of the prosecution's case.

The defence case was this: the evidence was planted and Millen was part of a Flying Squad conspiracy to frame their clients. The second SOCO who examined the vehicle and other evidence was also said to be part of the conspiracy – it mattered not that this was impossible, since the head hair samples had been submitted to the laboratory days before the finding of the car and the other items.

Millen was furious – all the more so when both defendants were acquitted. He set up an independent professional accreditation to protect professional individuals through the Forensic Science Society. Its members included many scientists, lawyers and academics, and it led to the establishment of the society's Diploma in Crime Scene Investigation. By 1989 this was a reality, the first of its kind in the world, and holders of the diploma were present in four continents. Millen later went on to become the society's vice-president and later, a fellow of the society.

Years later, Paul Millen, by now in retirement told me:

> I saw that part of my role on the Squad was to install discipline into its investigations, not only in the examina-tion of scenes but that of suspects. When new aspects of science were applied, the Squad officers needed protection from their own enthusiasm so as to ensure evidence was not compromised or contaminated. It was when a suspect was detained following an armed robbery

that a small finite time window opened that needed to be fully used. The modern Flying Squad officer learnt a lot of best practice and good conduct which had its success in future covert operations.

'Don't place too much value in forensic evidence.' Did Tommy Butler really say that, over fifty years ago? I doubt it, but if he did, he was wrong.

CHAPTER 19

The Knightsbridge Robbery

T he robbery, opposite Harrods Department Store, of Security Deposits PLC, 146 Brompton Road, SW3, also known as the Knightsbridge Safety Deposit Box Centre, took place on 12 July 1987. It was an audacious job which involved the loss of anything between £30 and £60 million, an impenitent Italian playboy, a number of international characters and police agencies, a sprinkling of beautiful women (several of whom had much to say to the newspapers, if not the police) – and the Flying Squad. The investigation would take eight years to complete.

On that Sunday afternoon at 3.15 two men approached the company posing as prospective customers. One was Eric Rubin, a Russian émigré living in Brooklyn, New York with his wife and granddaughter, and the other was Valerio Viccei. Born in Ascoli Piceno near the Adriatic coast on 22 January 1955, Viccei, the son of wealthy parents, joined the extreme right-wing group *Fronte della Gioventù*, and it is highly likely that the robberies he carried out were to boost their funds. He was wanted in his native Italy for absconding from bail for a number of armed robberies and he was appealing an eight-year sentence in respect of them. The Italian authorities suspected him of fifty-six other robberies, and although he had been cleared of attempting to blow up a crowded Italian passenger train in 1974, he had also been suspected of (but not charged with) blowing up a train in which twelve passengers had been killed, the same year.

Leaving behind his wife, Noemi, née Bambini ('He was the worst of the worst. I curse the day I met him'), he had not been entirely idle since his arrival in England on New Year's Day 1986. Between 14 April 1986 and 22 May 1987 he had carried out armed robberies at the Crédit Lyonnais, two branches of Coutts & Co, the Midland Bank and the American Express, all of which had made him and an accomplice £286,551 richer. In the light of what was to follow, he would no doubt have regarded that as 'chicken-feed'.

On that Sunday afternoon the two men were met by the owner of the premises, Parvez Latif, who took them to the vault area to show them the facilities as prospective customers. There the two men produced a handgun and a sawn-off shotgun from their briefcases, and Latif and two guards were handcuffed to a pillar in an anteroom to the vault. However, at this point it was not two but three men who were concerned in the robbery; Latif was involved in it, up to his armpits. Whilst on the run in London, Viccei had opened security box No. 1086 at the Knightsbridge Centre as a legitimate customer, although using a false identity. In it he was able to store firearms, forged documents and money stolen in his bank raids. He and Latif became friends, partying in the clubs and taking cocaine. But Latif was in impossible financial straits; desperate for money and an inveterate cocaine-user, he had cut the minimum rates for box rental from £200 per year to £99 and the maximum rate from £980 to £800. When Viccei proposed an audacious plan to rob the vault, with Latif's share to be one third of the proceeds and the other participants to receive £100,000 each, this seemed the answer to all of Latif's problems; deeply in debt, he willingly entered into the conspiracy.

Now that Viccei had control of the building and the vault, Peter O'Donoghue and David Poole were let into the rear access, bringing the total number of miscreants up to five. The newcomers were petty criminals who had socialized with Viccei in coffee bars of St John's Wood and Hampstead – but this robbery was out of their league. Poole's role was to stand outside the main entrance dressed as a security officer, with a radio link to Viccei, while during the next hour and a half, using a sledgehammer and an industrial drill, Viccei, Rubin and O'Donoghue broke open 121 of the 800 operative safety deposit boxes containing gold, jewellery, cash, sovereigns, stamp and coin collections, securities, valuable documents, foreign currencies and in one case, two kilos of cocaine. At 5.15 pm another guard entered the premises; he, too, was attacked and handcuffed.

A quarter of an hour later, the five men left the centre; they left 'Closed' signs on the front and back doors apologising to customers for the inconvenience, saying the closure was due to 'security improvements'. CCTV cameras had been installed but were not functioning and therefore did not record the robbery; similarly, no central alarm was activated when the boxes were smashed open.

Eight Japanese-made 'Bos' bags (each measuring 6ft by 4ft) were used to transport the loot in a van which headed towards the Hampstead area. En route, Poole and O'Donoghue were dropped off – almost immediately, they left the country. Rubin went to a flat in Primrose Gardens, Belsize Park and there he stayed for a few days, before flying to New York.

Viccei then drove to a private garage at the rear of Brownlow Court, Lyttleton Road, Hampstead which belonged to Stephen Mann, a man without a criminal background who worked in insurance; he and Viccei repacked the stolen property, then drove to a rented flat at 6 Reddington Road, Hampstead, where the cash and valuables were sorted out by Viccei and his elderly father, who had arrived from Italy. During the following month Viccei travelled to Colombia, Tel Aviv, Paris, Antwerp, Switzerland and Luxembourg, using five different passports, trading in stolen gems and paying vast amounts of cash into various bank accounts.

Meanwhile, the Flying Squad based at the Barnes office got to work. For a total of eight days the vault area was sealed off, and exhibits, fingerprint and scenes of crime officers worked tirelessly to unravel the mystery of who had done what. After three days, blood was found on a number of the boxes and discarded articles; on the fourth day a bloodstained fingerprint was found on box No. 2722. The fingerprint was Viccei's – but he was not on file in the Yard's Fingerprint Bureau. However, the Italian police believed that Viccei had fled to England and were monitoring his parents' telephone calls and correspondence. They had been able to identify Israel Pinkus, an Israeli, and Tino Vallorani, an Italian national and boyhood friend of Viccei as being his associates and living in North London. Accordingly, Viccei's fingerprints had been forwarded to the Yard, in case he was arrested.

So now the Squad knew one man who was involved; intensive surveillance was carried out on Vallorani, although not, initially, on Pinkus, who had accompanied Viccei to Israel, where stolen diamonds were sold to an Israeli business syndicate. But it was a problem finding out who the victims of the robbery were.

Safety deposit box centres were not regulated by government licence but run by private individuals, and their vetting of customers varied considerably. Many of the box holders did not reside in the United Kingdom, and Latif had permitted his clients to use company names, pseudonyms and nicknames. Consequently, any person who wished to stash stolen money, drugs or firearms could do so without fear of detection; and because of this, the police were unable to identify many of the owners of the stolen property. Initially, property was identified from thirteen of the 121 losers, either found on the floor of the vaults, or in Viccei's possession or at other premises – 'flops' or addresses belonging to criminal associates, banks and other deposit centres. Meanwhile, London's gangsters applauded the coup; 'Buster' Edwards of Great Train Robbery notoriety commented, 'I would love to have been in on this one.'

During the surveillance, a black Ferrari Testarossa sports car was seen parked outside White's Hotel, Bayswater. It had been purchased by Viccei for £87,000 following the robbery and he was awaiting an export licence to ship it to Colombia. It was of particular interest because at about the same time a vehicle registered to Israel Pinkus had also been parked outside the same hotel and had received a parking ticket. On 11 August 1987 Detective Inspector Dick Leach of the Squad approached the manager of the hotel and showed him a photograph of Viccei.

Leach told me, 'I said, "Do you know this man?" and was mightily surprised when I received the answer "Why, yes – that's Mr Raiman, a guest at the hotel. You've just missed him – he left wearing a red blazer!"'

The vehicles of three different surveillance teams operating in London were now directed to the Bayswater Road, where the Ferrari was seen approaching Marble Arch.

A Testarossa is capable of 190 mph but not when it's hemmed in by Flying Squad cars at Marble Arch. Flying Squad driver Graham 'Chalky' White takes up the tale:

> I was driving the observation van that day and I drove into the Bayswater Road. The Ferrari was stopped in traffic and the driver's window was open. I got out of the van and reached in to grab the ignition keys, but Viccei put his foot down and I was dragged for about 20 yards. Luckily, someone with a baseball bat smashed the windscreen.

The moral of this particular escapade is, never take liberties with Flying Squad officers who are making an arrest, because Viccei was pulled out straight through the broken windscreen.

Perhaps fearing further retribution, but with considerable savoir-faire, he told Detective Sergeant Jim Goldie, 'Right chaps, the game is up now and you have no need to be nasty. You are the winners so calm down and everything is going to be fine!'

There was loot worth more than £2 million in the Ferrari's boot.

Two other men were arrested after a high-speed car chase. The following day, property from the raid valued at £5 million was recovered from houses and other safety deposit boxes. Due to a misunderstanding of the nationalities of those arrested, the press took no time at all in inaccurately dubbing it 'The Italian Job'.

During the next eight days, twenty-six persons connected with Viccei were arrested, although not all were charged. Rubin, O'Donoghue, Pinkus and Mann had already been identified;

following Viccei's arrest, Poole was arrested at White's hotel. In all, property valued at £10 million was recovered, as were the firearms, the implements used to force the boxes and forged documents. Rubin was in the USA; work began to find him. Viccei's parents were interviewed in Teramo and later, in London. The only evidence against the father would come from Stephen Mann, and this was not enough to prosecute him. However, since Viccei considered this to be an act of humanity by the Squad, in later conversations he decided to admit, then plead guilty to, the earlier London robberies.

But by 14 August, one month after the robbery, there was evidence to arrest Parvez Latif; he joined the others on remand. Dick Leach told me:

> We were never happy with Latif, but whilst he was with us and going nowhere, we decided to bide our time. It was not until the arrest of Pinkus that we discovered regular communication on Israeli hotel telephone bills from Viccei in Israel to the Knightsbridge Centre. Latif was giving Viccei daily updates. One thing that Latif did not know (and that was kept very close) was the discovery of Viccei's identification by the bloody fingerprint.

In addition, Latif's name had been found in some of the other gang members' address books, and an examination of Viccei's radio-pager phone revealed that there had been 130 calls between the two men. Latif was also less than pleased to discover that Viccei had been bedding his mistress, with whom he was besotted.

In a highly unusual – yet perfectly legitimate – transaction, the Squad bought back five diamonds worth £3 million – one alone, weighing 40.23 carats, was worth £1 million – from a Belgian diamond dealer who had been duped into paying $1,300,000 into Viccei's Luxembourg account, before in turn selling them to an Israeli business syndicate. But when the Squad had made their arrests in London, they had discovered the secret account and frozen its assets. Again, Dick Leach takes up the tale:

> Persons in Israel were contacted and told we knew they had the diamonds and due to their specific measurements and high value they could not now be sold on the open market. The situation was very delicate, difficult, different. A high-level meeting and judicial decision decided that the Israeli syndicate should return the diamonds to us in Luxembourg in return for their payment which was

deposited in a false account in Luxembourg controlled by
Viccei. The meeting was supervised by the Luxembourg
Sûreté in the offices of an advocate and attended by myself
and other Flying Squad officers, a diamond expert, an
insurance assessor, members of the Israeli syndicate and
their bodyguards and the bank manager, outside the office.
The diamonds were produced, weighed and identified
and the money transferred to the Israelis. I stuck the
diamonds in my pocket, we all had a glass of champagne,
said our goodbyes and were escorted immediately to the
airport.

The diamonds were later reunited with their owner, the fabulously
wealthy Donatella Flick from the family of German industrialists.
It had been a stylish piece of Flying Squad work.

At the Old Bailey on 30 January 1989, for robbery and possessing a firearm, and with the trial judge telling him, 'The stakes
were colossal. Having lost, you have to pay the price accordingly',
Viccei was sentenced to concurrent terms amounting to twenty-
two years' imprisonment and was made criminally bankrupt in the
sum of £3.15 million.

For the same offences, Latif (whose unsuccessful defence
was that Viccei had 'threatened to blow his brains out' unless
he participated in the robbery) was sentenced to eighteen years'
imprisonment, Poole to sixteen years and O'Donoghue to eleven
years, for robbery. Israel Pinkus received concurrent terms of nine
and seven years' imprisonment for receiving stolen goods and five
cases of theft, and Mann, for robbery, five cases of receiving stolen
goods and conspiracy, was sentenced to five years' imprisonment.
He gave evidence for the prosecution and when he told the
jury that Viccei carried a gun and was quite prepared to use it
against anyone, Viccei leaned forward in the dock and said, 'Yeah,
especially on you.'

It appeared Mann was not well liked; he appeared in court
displaying a broken nose, smashed teeth and bruising, having been
beaten up by a fellow prisoner in Wandsworth. His assailant had
told him, 'As far as Viccei is concerned, it does not matter how
long it takes – you are gone.'

This was a typical Viccei ploy – get someone else to do your
dirty work.

Pamela Seamarks (she was described as 'an adventuress')
had been Latif's companion (she haughtily repudiated the term
'girlfriend') who had had an affair with Viccei, and after the
robbery she had met him in Zürich, then accompanied him to

Paris. She admitted conspiracy to handle stolen goods valued at £50,000, asked for one case to be taken into consideration and was sentenced to eighteen months' imprisonment, suspended for two years, plus a two-year supervision order.

The following day, Danish-born Helle Skoubon – who had met Viccei in a health club and had an affair with him – admitted one charge of receiving stolen property. Of the £5,000 she had received, all but £250 had been repaid, and she was sentenced to three months' imprisonment suspended for twelve months and was fined £750. On the same day Latif admitted fifteen counts of criminal deception and one of attempted deception and was sentenced to one month's imprisonment on each count, consecutively but concurrent with his eighteen-year sentence; he was also fined £500 on each count. Matters might have gone a little easier if he'd admitted them the previous day.

On 8 February 1989 Rosemary Jean Poole (the wife of David Poole) was convicted of handling stolen goods, was sentenced to one month's imprisonment suspended for twelve months and fined £1,750.

Abraham Bartov and Yossi Meshulam were both convicted of two cases of handling stolen goods on 27 February 1989. They ran a small smelting operation near Hatton Garden where they had rendered down all the scrap gold from the stolen coins, rings, bracelets and jewellery. In all, it amounted to 22 kilos, the weight giving an indication of the amount of property which had been stolen. Both were sent to prison: three years for Bartov, fifteen months for Meshulam.

On 19 May 1989 Viccei again appeared at the Old Bailey, where he admitted the previous five other cases of armed robbery and possessing firearms at banks and was sentenced to a total of seventeen years' imprisonment, to run concurrently with his twenty-two-year sentence.

And after extradition proceedings which had lasted for two years, Eric Rubin – he was known as 'Boris' – had been chased by the Squad to New York, where they worked with agents from the Federal Bureau of Investigation. Rubin then fled to Los Angeles, where the Squad officers worked with the State Marshals, who traced his movements to Toronto and thence to Tel Aviv. Squad officers travelled to Israel and arranged his extradition to London, where Rubin was convicted at the Old Bailey on 23 July 1991 of two cases of armed robbery and was sentenced to a total of twelve years' imprisonment.

It only remained for four people, accused of stealing £15,000 from Parvez Latif, to present themselves at Northampton police station to receive a caution, under the Attorney General's guidelines.

Following the sentencing, His Honour Judge Lymbery QC said:

> Mr Leach, most of what has to be done has been done in this matter and I think I ought to express appreciation of the efficiency and indeed the fairness of the activities of the police throughout this enquiry, both of yourself and your colleagues. I think we know that there was surveillance of a number of these people for some time before they were arrested. They were not going to get away and you got them precisely at the right moment. It is to be a matter of congratulation both to yourself and to the others on the work you have done. You brought a lot of these people to book, who should have been brought to book and through your efforts, so much of the property has been recovered. I am sure the public should be very grateful to you all for what had happened.

Afterwards, well, really predictably, Ms Skoubon and Ms Seamarks confessed everything in fairly salacious detail to the tabloids as to their couplings with the 'pint-sized' Viccei: 'I made love with a diamond in my belly button', 'Romeo robber couldn't satisfy me', etc. It was all a far cry from the sobbing, penitent, soberly dressed ladies in the dock at the Old Bailey.

Others eagerly jumped on the bandwagon: 'Tycoon spied as wife bedded sugar daddy', 'We smashed love bed making whoopee' and 'Busty juror's lust for villain' were some of the titillating articles to excite readers.

Although Viccei had the colossal cheek to demand the return of the Ferrari which he had purchased with stolen money, it was in a sorry state in the police compound; a bashed-in windscreen which would cost £900 to replace, a dented wing (which would have cost rather more) and smothered in fingerprint powder. But not to car dealer Pelham O'Reilly, who on 22 May 1990 purchased it at auction for £88,000. He believed that after the car was cleaned up he would be able to sell it for £110,000, and it could well be he was right; with only a hundred of that model being manufactured, the price was appreciating every day, and in no time at all the Ferrari might well be worth double, perhaps quadruple that sum. It was a bullish hope, but not likely – at the time of writing, almost 30 years later, such a car would probably fetch £120,000.

Two and a half years later, the last twenty lots of unclaimed jewellery and other valuables were auctioned off at Phillips'

Berkeley Square auction house for £210,000, the proceeds going to the Police Widows' and Orphans' Fund. The case docket which was in eleven parts, the seven boxes containing items pertinent to the case and the seventeen appendixes were neatly packed up and sent on their way to the Yard's repository at Hayes, Middlesex.

On 16 January 1992 Latif, O'Donoghue and Poole had their appeals against conviction rejected; it was said that Poole's contemporaneous interview notes had been altered, but although the Appeal Court agreed that that might well have been the case, there was still 'a wealth of evidence' to show that his conviction was safe.

On 11 November 1992 Viccei boarded an Alitalia Airbus at Heathrow. Under the Treaty of Strasbourg he was being transferred to a prison in Pescara to finish his sentence. He was allowed out, briefly, one month later, so that he and his wife could divorce. However, matters were not as clear cut as all that, as Dick Leach explains:

> To be able to transfer to the prison system in Italy, he had to admit to the Italians all of his criminal past. No doubt, he did a deal with the Italian prosecuting authorities. We learnt later that he had admitted numerous robberies, firearms offences and surprisingly, the murder of an accomplice by shooting. I suppose that the 22-year sentence from the UK was considered a severe sentence, and his admission to an offence which they might have difficulty in proving was also considered a result. Viccci went to a high level security prison in Campobasso, Naples, where I met him with officers of the *Direzione Investigativa Antimafia* Police Squad. He was now an informant for them and subsequently transferred to Pescara, an easy jail. He informed on Tino Vallorani, his boyhood friend who aided him in London, saying that he had received property from the vault. He was prosecuted in Rome for this and received a suspended prison sentence.

Viccei had said that he would 'break out of jail in two years' although he now tried a different tack; he said that one of the safe deposit boxes he had opened had been rented by Francisco di Carlo, who was then serving a twenty-five-year sentence for a mafia-organized heroin ring in the UK. Viccei also stated that he had found confidential documents relating to Roberto Calvi ('God's banker'), who had been found hanged under Blackfriars Bridge in 1982. An initial finding of suicide had been overturned, to be replaced with an open verdict which coincided with what the Italian authorities had always believed; that Calvi had been murdered.

Dick Leach travelled to Italy twice, to check these matters out with Viccei – and he didn't believe him. Nor did the *Antimafia* police, but they nevertheless travelled to England with a judge and prosecutor and, assisted by the Flying Squad, they interviewed first Rubin in Parkhurst prison, then Di Carlo. The latter denied any involvement with Viccei and the vault, although he apparently did provide information which later led to the arrest of Italian nationals in connection with Calvi's murder, although in June 2007 five were acquitted.

Meanwhile, Viccei's cell was bugged and conversations with his parents revealed that the Calvi information had been a ploy to enable him to escape.

But on 22 July 1996 he was released on five-day home release, and six months later, he was released during the day, to work in a publishing company in Pescara and to return to his cell at night. He had been told he would be eligible for parole in 2003 and he had been given a release date in 2007. It was not to be.

Viccei had befriended a fellow prisoner, Antonio Malatesta, a member of Puglia's mafia, *Sacra Corona Unita*, who like Viccei was a grass – a supergrass (or *penito*) in Malatesta's case. Like other supergrasses, these had been given reduced sentences and privileges, and many occupied their free time carrying out robberies and murders. Understandably, the use of supergrasses had fallen into public disrepute.

On 18 April 2000 Police Officer Enzo Baldini was one of two patrolmen who were following the orders of their deputy police chief, Giovani Grimani – to carry out routine checks of all vehicles due to a sudden proliferation of robberies in the Teramo area, quite close to Pescara.

A check on the Lancia parked by a farmhouse on one of Teramo's country roads revealed that it was stolen. Therefore, picking up his sub-machine gun, Baldini and his companion got out of their patrol car and walked towards two men standing by the Lancia. The officers were 10 metres away when the two men opened fire with their revolvers; the first shot missed but it was followed by three more, one of them hitting Baldini in the leg. The officers returned fire with fifteen rounds from their semi-automatic weapons; Antonio Malatesta was wounded but Viccei, wearing jeans and a green jacket, was believed to be dead before he hit the ground. He had been hit eight times. Both men had been wearing gloves and were in possession of rubber masks.

What were they up to – a kidnapping or a security van robbery? Who knows?

A third man in the Lancia drove away from the scene. Accomplice or set-up – who knows?

The bullet that hit Officer Baldini came from Viccei's .357 magnum revolver, with which he held a morbid fascination. The combination number for his £700 Louis Vuitton briefcase was 357. He had a gold key-ring in the shape of a shotgun. He said that he had modelled himself on Al Pacino in *Scarface*, which he had apparently seen on fifty-eight occasions.

So that was the end of the man who was referred to as 'The Gentleman Crook'. When, due to his womanizing, the English tabloid press dubbed him 'The Italian Stallion', he must have all but swooned with delight. He was less than impressed with 'Gigi', the nickname bestowed on him by his English admirers. Since this was the name of Colette's eponymous heroine who aspired to become a courtesan, it's understandable. His Italian nickname, *Il Lupo* (The Wolf), was much more to his liking.

'I had a passion for weapons, beautiful women and fast cars', he said, and it was true.

He possessed a monumental ego, 'as big as the Old Bailey' said one detective, and that was also true; when he was arrested, he grassed up everybody he could think of and he intended to plead guilty at his trial. However, it was pointed out to him that under English law, when one member of a gang pleads guilty and others do not, that person is remanded until such time as the case against the others is completed. That, as far as Viccei was concerned, was completely out of the question, so he pleaded not guilty and had the most wonderful three months in court, resplendent in designer clothing and sunglasses, winking at the jury and making smart remarks.

His memoirs, *Knightsbridge: The Robbery of the Century*, were published in 1992; although riddled with typos and grammatical errors, this didn't prevent the *Sun* from serializing it, the same year. After his death, *Too Fast to Live*, with a hastily updated account of his death, was published, and *Live by the Gun, Die by the Gun* came out in a paperback version four years later.

And what of Helle Skoubon ('*Topino*'. . . the sweetest kid in the world')? Having approached any newspaper willing to purchase an account of her adventures with 'Gigi', she was sacked from the boutique where she worked; she sued for unfair dismissal and on 11 March 1993 was awarded an out-of-court settlement of £5,000. Ten weeks later, she sent Viccei a telegram saying she was going to marry another man, following a six-week whirlwind romance.

Viccei was glum. But never mind, because one month later Helle and her paramour fell out and she took the next available plane to Italy, where she visited Viccei in prison, telling anybody who was interested – and by now there were not too many – 'I'm still in love with Valerio'.

Before returning, broken-hearted, to Copenhagen, she attended the funeral. 'He was shot so many times . . . and we don't know why.' Somebody should have explained to her that when a near-psychopathic egotist tries to murder a police officer who then has the impertinence to return fire with a semi-automatic weapon, this is often the consequence.

Pamela Seamarks who by now was a Home Counties housewife, was less moved by Viccei's demise. 'I detest everything about him and the life he led me into', she told the press. 'I'd hate the same thing to happen to any other girl searching for success and excitement.'

When veteran crime reporter James Nicholson asked Viccei how much money he had left, he had already totalled up what he thought was the correct amount: £15 million. Was that right?

'No', replied Viccei. 'It's more'.

So who managed the money for him whilst he was in prison? Who manages it now?

Who knows?

★

What caused this very clever criminal's demise? Dick Leach, the police officer who almost certainly knew him best of all, has his own theories:

> Viccei's downfall was as much due to his arrogance, vanity and total belief that he could not possibly fail in anything he did. I don't think cocaine was something he relied on. He was a fit, athletic and strong-willed person. As a kid, his family gave him everything and then allowed (and always excused) his excesses and notorious behaviour, particularly towards the authorities in Ascoli, Italy. I met all of his family, mother, father, brother and sister, some of his associates in Teramo and then at a dinner in Pescara. They were always polite and correct. During prison visits at Parkhurst, then in Italy, Viccei's attitude was always the same, amiable, confident and forthright. When you examine the gang he cobbled together, the only professional was Eric Rubin. The others were not in any

way hardened criminals. Viccei knew this. His ultimate plan was to leave the UK and live in Colombia, which he travelled to during the month after the vault job. He arranged the transfer of the Ferrari Testarossa car to go to Colombia via Florida, but the required export licence was delayed. He was about to leave the UK when we arrested him. He was ready to abandon all of his criminal partners and he knew that Rubin was probably 'lost' in the USA, and therefore safe.

There is no doubt that Viccei's life throughout had been one of manipulation, deceit and domination. He betrayed his wife, Noemi, family, his girlfriend Helle Skoubon, associates such as Latif and Latif's girlfriend Pamela Seamarks, as well as close friends such as Tino Vallorani. His way of life was always to take and gain the advantage, however big or small. The Knightsbridge job fell into his lap by accident and he took advantage of a weak individual, Latif. Whilst in Parkhurst prison, he informed on a number of individuals responsible for a number of contract murders in the UK. In Italy, he became an informant for the *Direzione Antimafia* squad. After his arrest by the Flying Squad, everything thereafter was calculated to lessen the pain of twenty-two years in the English prison system. Did he succeed? Well . . .

*

The last word on this matter must come from Viccei himself. Despite coming to this country speaking hardly a word of English, within two years he had become a prolific and fluent writer. In his letters to Dick Leach he always referred to him as 'Fred', named after Alex Graham's cartoon character, Fred Basset. Perhaps Viccei's grasp of English had not quite extended to the fact that the dog was a basset not a bloodhound, maybe it was because of the dogged way Leach pursued him or perhaps he was influenced by the 1977 publication, *Fred Basset and the Spaghetti*; but whatever the case, Dick Leach was 'Fred', and this is an extract of one of the last letters Viccei sent to him:

> I am a predator, Fred, not simply a bank robber and that's another ball game altogether. I have values and principles. I can make a point without a big gun in my hand and I do not squeak when under pressure.

I might give up the game, all the same but I want you to know that I will be around until I die. I ain't no Buster or Biggs; they were pets who put on a wolf's mask for a day or two. I am a true wolf and you know that, better than most. The world offers plenty of challenges and there is too much mediocrity about; heights are there to be taken and I feel comfortable with them.

CHAPTER 20

Prison Escapes

On 20 November 1984 three prisoners were being conveyed in a yellow prison van with barred windows from Maidstone to Parkhurst Prison on the Isle of Wight. Including the driver, five prison officers were on board. On the A217 at Reigate, the van, already followed by a beige BMW, was suddenly overtaken by a silver BMW – both cars had been stolen from Wanstead, earlier that day – which braked sharply, forcing the van into a lamppost. At the same time, the beige BMW blocked the rear of the van, and four men wearing balaclavas jumped out wielding pickaxe handles and jemmies and smashed the windscreen with a sledgehammer, ordering the prison officers to 'let these two men go or we'll beat you to a pulp'. Two men – John Kendall and Terry Smith – were handcuffed together; they leapt out of the van and into the silver BMW – the third prisoner stayed where he was.

Smith, aged twenty-five, had been serving a fifteen-year sentence imposed the previous year for a £20,000 armed robbery at Corringham, Essex; Kendall was serving a ten-year sentence for robbery and burglary. It was thought by the Surrey police that the escape plot had been engineered during a visit that Smith had received the previous week. Furthermore, it was initially believed that both men had escaped, simply because they were handcuffed to each other. Dogs were called in and road blocks were set up, all to no avail. No association between the two men was known, and Kendall was said to be less dangerous than Smith.

That's all *they* knew.

Eighteen months later, on 11 June 1986, there was a robbery on a Security Express van at Kilburn. Two men on a motorcycle demanded bags containing £35,000 from the guard and fired shots, then, having got the money, rode off towards the getaway, an alley with a post in it to prevent a car following.

Seeing what had happened, an antiques dealer driving a Ford Granada estate crashed into the motorcycle, and the rider – Terry Smith, who was carrying a .38 Smith & Wesson revolver – was trapped underneath it, unconscious and with his leg broken in several places. As Detective Sergeant Roger Smith recalled, 'His leg was almost severed.' The pillion passenger – John Kendall

– got up; a gas board man who was passing drove up to him, there was a struggle and Kendall (described by the judge at his trial as being 'the scum of society') produced his .22 pistol and shot him three times, in the chest and groin. The man, 43-year-old Barry Smith – he happened to be an ex-Para – nevertheless grappled with Kendall, tore off his motorcycle helmet and battered him unconscious with it. Both Smith and the antiques dealer were later honoured at a ceremony in London.

As Detective Sergeant Terry Allen, who at the time was serving in the Finchley Flying Squad office, told me, 'The arriving troops from Kilburn had little to do but take them into custody for armed robbery, freeze the scene and take possession of the firearms and money.'

Smith was taken to the Central Middlesex Hospital, Kendall to Kilburn police station, both men initially refusing to give their particulars until their identities were revealed by their fingerprints.

The following year at the Old Bailey, their trial was stopped after Kendall's barrister said he had been 'professionally embarrassed' by his client and withdrew from the case. One of the jurors arrived late, saying she'd been approached at Northolt railway station and offered £5,000 upfront, plus another £5,000, for a not guilty verdict. The trial was again halted and the jury was discharged. Both men were returned to the prison system since they were still serving sentences for other offences.

On several occasions in December 1987 one Andrew Russell hired a helicopter from Stansted airport and, on a number of pretexts, flew over the Leicestershire countryside, obtaining good aerial views of Gartree prison. Opened in 1965, Gartree was a training prison, catering for 707 Category 'C' prisoners. That was about to change.

On 10 December at 3.16 pm Russell, who had paid £640 in cash to hire the Bell 206L helicopter in order to fly to Leicester airport, ostensibly for 'a business trip to the Midlands', drew a handgun and forced the pilot to land within the confines of the prison during the recreation period.

'This was Kendall's chance', said Allen, 'and he took it.' So, too did Sidney Draper, serving life for the murder of the security guard in Glasgow. 'Draper, who had nothing to do with the plan, took the given opportunity with open arms and took flight', Allen told me. This was his third escape. It took just 30 seconds to airlift the men to freedom.

'It was like something out of James Bond', said Stephen Gravett, the rather bemused junior governor of the prison.

The pilot was told to fly to a nearby golf course – where, almost certainly, getaway cars awaited them – but mist forced them to land at Welland industrial estate in Market Harborough. There they handcuffed the pilot, hijacked a transit van from Hugh Ellis and drove on the A427 towards Corby, before forcing a woman out of her red Fiat Uno near Dingley. They abandoned that car in Corby, before taking the driver of another car hostage and driving to Sheffield.

'Whilst Leicestershire Constabulary were dealing with the job themselves, the best way for the Squad to get involved was to list the case for trial immediately,' Allen told me. 'With Kendall failing to appear at court, a bench warrant was issued so we could then take the helm and move it forward.'

The resultant news coverage gave this unique escape the maximum publicity, and Kendall's face with his distinctive glasses was plastered all over the newspapers and on television. The same applied to Draper, because it was initially thought that the two men were in it together. However, that was wrong. The men had gone their separate ways, and Draper was re-arrested thirteen months later

Within a few days there was a robbery, when a Brink's-Mat van making deliveries to Lloyds Bank at Archway was ambushed by two men. Terry Allen takes up the tale:

> The guard was oblivious to what was happening. He had made one or two deliveries to this very busy bank, and on his third visit Kendall appeared behind him; as he negotiated an airlock-effect of double doors, Kendall shot him at point-blank range, without warning, straight through the back. He then calmly stepped forward, picked up the cash bag of £20,000 and decamped. I attended the scene. Miraculously and thankfully, the internal injuries sustained, despite the shooting, were non-life-threatening. Quite unbelievable, given the circumstances. The resultant photofit from one of the main witnesses to the offence showed that apart from a beanie hat, the description of the assailant could only be Kendall – an amazing piece of evidence.

Russell, together with Kendall's wife Lorraine, had been a frequent visitor at Gartree, and now Russell was followed to an address in Dagenham, where Lorraine Kendall was found. She, in turn, was followed to a flat in Chelsea. An OP was found overlooking the flat, and over a period of three days Mrs Kendall was seen coming and going, as was Russell; but it was decided to wait until such time as it was known that the three of them were together before the attack could be given, once it was assumed they'd had a couple of hours sleep.

And that happened on 31 January 1988. The three returned to the flat, 'looking', as Terry Allen told me, 'as though they had a few beers'. King's Road was closed off, and during the next two hours PT17 (the firearms unit) was summoned and drew up in a van with a considerable amount of firepower; a sniper was also positioned on the roof of the premises opposite. Dragon lights were switched on, fully illuminating the flat, and as Detective Constable Dennis Walkington told me, 'Kendall came to a window, looking like a rabbit caught in a searchlight.' The door of the flat was breached, commands were shouted and Kendall swiftly came to the conclusion that shooting an unarmed security guard was one thing, but arguing with someone in possession of a carbine pointed straight between his eyes was quite another. So he decided not to utilize either of the handguns found in the flat (one of which was shown by ballistic tests to have shot the guard), and they, together with a shoulder holster and a scanner, plus the proceeds left over from the robbery, accompanied him, his wife and Russell to the local nick.

As well as threatening the helicopter pilot, Russell was also charged with the offence of embracery, in other words trying to bribe the juror at the previous trial, and at Leicester Crown Court in 1988 the Judge said everyone was to be searched. To his annoyance, this included the eminent barrister Rock Tansey QC, who objected to removing his shoes.

In 1989, after three separate trials, Kendall was sentenced to a total of thirty-five years' imprisonment, which was later reduced to twenty-nine years on appeal. Russell got ten years for the helicopter escapade and embracery. He was later charged with being the second man on the Archway robbery and in 1992 was sentenced to ten years, to run consecutive to the existing ten. This offence he denied, saying that he believed this charge was brought because they thought the sentence for the helicopter rescue had been 'too lenient'.

⋆

Russell was moved to the brand new Whitemoor prison with its Special Secure Units (SSU), which were considered to be prisons within a prison and pretty well escape-proof. Nevertheless, a loaded gun and some Semtex were successfully smuggled into the SSU, with the result that in September 1994 Russell, together with five IRA men, managed to escape, having fired shots at the pursuing prison staff and hit one of them in the ribs. They were all recaptured.

The wounded prison officer, John Kettleborough, was awarded £14,000 in compensation for his injuries. Compensation was also paid to two of the escaped prisoners, Russell being one of them. Mr Justice Crane, sitting in London, accepted Russell's account that he had been kicked and punched following the escape and awarded him £2,500. Russell did not attend the hearing, which was funded by legal aid and which, it was believed, cost the taxpayer £500,000.

★

And what of Terry Smith, who recovered from his leg injury following the Kilburn robbery? On 29 September 1987 he pleaded guilty to the Kensal Rise robbery and was sentenced to fourteen years' imprisonment plus, for escaping from custody, another two years, consecutive but concurrent to his existing, albeit interrupted sentence of fifteen years. He was quite pleased with the result until realization crept in that he had to serve fourteen years and two months, which was equivalent to a twenty-year sentence.

He was finally released on 29 August 1995 and became a 'reformed character', a television personality and the author of several books, including *The Art of Armed Robbery*. Then on 5 June 2001 he was arrested and charged with possessing an Uzi sub-machine gun, 376 rounds of ammunition, a shoulder stock and silencer. He claimed he was 'set up'. In May 2002 he was acquitted of all charges by a majority verdict. When he was arrested for conspiracy to rob in May 2008, with his brother, he stated, 'This is outrageous!' – but it all came to an end when on 27 February 2010 he was convicted at Chelmsford Crown Court of conspiracies to rob and possess firearms between 2006 and 2008; his brother was acquitted. One such offence was at Rayleigh, Essex, where during the course of a robbery which netted £250,000 a commuter who tried to intervene was shot by another of the gang.

A police officer described Smith as 'A violent, cynical individual with no regard for the law who was prepared to go to frightening ends to ensure his demands were met', and Judge Charles Gratwicke passed an indeterminate sentence, saying Smith should serve twelve years before being considered for parole.

In May 2016 Smith unsuccessfully appealed against the indefinite jail term; at the time of writing he's still behind bars.

CHAPTER 21

The Speckled Plate Team

Ever heard of 'The Speckled Plate Team'? No, neither had I, but when Detective Sergeant Ron Heal arrived at the Finchley office of the Flying Squad in the summer of 1987, that was the name of the file he was handed by Detective Chief Inspector Bob Melrose, who told him, 'Sort this lot out.' What followed was a gem of criminal investigation to grace Heal's debut with the Squad, and it's best described in his own words:

> Having spent all my service in the North-East of London and the West End, I sat and read the docket which listed various armed robberies on security vans in places I had never been before as they operated all over North-West London.
>
> It was apparent that this three-man team were very professional. There was no intelligence on them and no clues as to who they might be. The title of the file derived from the fact they used at least three stolen vehicles during each crime. All were plated to identical cars in the area of the attack, and their number plates were sprayed with fine mud to disguise the fact that they were brand new.
>
> They always wore full-faced crash helmets and gloves, and the two attackers were armed, but no shots were ever fired. They would attack the security guard as he made his first drop across the pavement and demand his 25 grand bag and two further bags from inside the van. The getaway car would be in an adjoining street accessible through either an alleyway or footbridge where the robbers would run off to. The first getaway car would be abandoned after a short while, likewise the second. Depending on police attendance, the third would be used or left in situ.
>
> These were the days when DNA was in its infancy and CCTV was not as widespread as now and not particularly good, either. The abandoned getaway cars yielded no forensic clues to go on.

There were various descriptions of the three men which seemed to suggest two older suspects and one younger. The age range was 40–55 for the elder two and 25–35 for the younger. From their accents it was believed they were white Londoners. That was it. So, where to start? Having read the reports of the previous robberies, of which there were many, I decided to give my eyes a treat and visit the various scenes to see what I could glean and acquaint myself with the area. I chose a Squad driver called Trevor ('George') Washington, who had been on the Squad for many a year and knew the area like the back of his hand.

Having made my visits and got to know the area, I formed the opinion that this was a family team, local to the North-West of London and so tight-knit that no information leaked. I picked George's brain as to how I was going to break this case. 'Simple', he said. 'Find the cars.' During my investigation I had discovered the stolen cars had been laid down within a half a mile of the registered owner of the real vehicle. On one occasion I spoke to a witness who had reported a car left outside his address in Wembley for a week. He was told by police not to worry as it belonged to a neighbour a few streets away. Bingo! Find the cars! Where do I start? The robbers had hit all different parts of NW London from Hendon to Greenford. My plan was to visit all the night-duty teams across that area and look out for the speckled plates. I also mentioned a few bottles of champagne to the successful relief. This was time-consuming but ultimately rewarding, as a speckle-plated car was spotted in Kingsbury.

Then there followed a round the clock surveillance, and after a couple of days, one of the team turned up to move the car to a new location. He was then collected by his companion in his own vehicle. Two of the three were identified as long-time muckers, 'Billy the Blagger' Harding and 'Gorgeous George' Jones. However, the next few weeks were taken up by trying to identify the third team member. This would later prove to be Jones' nephew, David Adams, who lived in New Barnet. The two oldies and the younger nephew. 'Gorgeous George' was a renowned getaway driver who lived in Mill Hill, and Billy was a prolific blagger who had evaded capture for many years and resided in Hatch End. My initial theory was right up to a point.

Eventually they went to work again, and we were with them every step of the way. The two oldies collected the nephew en route to the robbery. We watched as they put on their crash helmets and gloves and headed for a Securicor van delivering to Lloyds Bank in The Hyde, West Hendon. It then dawned on me this was one of their previous hits I had surveyed. I remembered the getaway was an alley behind the bank where the driver would be waiting for his mates. I radioed to units to cut off the escape route and readied ourselves for the attack. To my horror, the guard refused to hand over the money, and Harding shot him in the leg. All hell then broke loose as the two robbers collected the bags thrown out by his colleague who feared further gunshots, and we pounced, bringing them to the ground. 'Gorgeous George' was apprehended in the road off the alley. I was then relieved to see the guard had not been seriously injured as the shot in the cartridge fired had been replaced by rice.

All three appeared at the Old Bailey in the summer of 1988 and pleaded guilty to various robberies and wounding. Jones received fifteen years, Harding twelve and Adams, eight.

The officer in overall charge of the operation had been Detective Inspector David Kelly (of Walthamstow fame) who, Heal told me, 'Stood by me every inch of the way, authorized anything I wanted and was there on the day; top man!' It was Kelly who told the court that the four robberies that Jones confessed to had resulted in £192,000 being stolen – but outside court, he stated that he believed that the gang had been involved in fifteen similar robberies which had netted half a million pounds. Kelly and Heal were two of the four officers commended by the commissioner for courage and detective ability.

*

As the second hand of Ron Heal's watch swept past midnight, it proclaimed that the new date was 1 April 1989. Just at that moment, as Heal and Ray Summerbee were watching a stolen Ford Sierra on false plates from an OP in Cricklewood, they saw a large man approaching the car.

Believing this to be Detective Sergeant Dave Cant, one of the officers on surveillance, Heal said to Summerbee, 'I don't believe it; Canty's playing an April Fool on us. Look, he's only getting into the car – what's he up to?'

But it wasn't Dave Cant. It was John Gorman, a 49-year-old armed robber whose convictions for robbery and firearms offences stretched back over thirty years; he was not dissimilar in appearance to Cant.

Time was running out for Gorman; he had barely a fortnight of freedom left.

Detective Sergeant Mick Petra had arrived on the Squad at Finchley in 1988 and together with Detective Constable Pam Miller got to work on what became known as 'Operation Char'. A gang had been employing the unusual technique of using an RSJ (a steel roof-supporting joist) bolted to the floor of a van to ram the rear doors of National Westminster Banks, because the banks inevitably had a car park at the rear. Sometimes they used it on security vans, and on one occasion they had the ram protruding from the side of the van and used it rather like a lance in a medieval jousting tournament to rip open the side of a passing Group 4 cash-in-transit van. This was inventive but unsuccessful, since those vans had quadruple skins to protect them from chainsaw attacks. There was no intelligence regarding the gang and no forensic evidence to tie them to the raids.

Resources were tight; half the Squad was working with DCI Bob Melrose on the murder of a security guard, the other half was hard at work on 'The Speckled Plate Team'.

But what Petra and Miller did know was that the gang always used stolen Ford Sierras and Granadas, as well as double wheelbase vans. Quarter-lights would be smashed and tax discs would be stolen; index plates to match the registration on the tax disc would be obtained from Jepson & Co. and fitted to the stolen vehicles. So the officers went to the crime desks of all the stations of the area – 'T', 'S', 'E' & 'Q' Divisions – where they obtained details of stolen Sierras and reports of stolen tax discs. Sometimes losers did not report the theft of their tax disc to police but to the DVLC, in order to obtain a replacement; the officers maintained liaison with them as well. Street searches were carried out, and eventually the officers struck lucky.

As Mick Petra told me, 'A doctor parked her Sierra overnight; I can even remember the index number – W512 OPP – and the following morning, she found that her tax disc had been stolen. A week later, a couple of PCs discovered the plated vehicle parked in a side street at 3.30 in the morning. I got a phone call and came down right away.'

An OP was set up, an associate of the gang collected the car and the trail led to Gorman and then to James Farrell, aged fifty-two, whose criminal career had commenced in 1959. He had been released from prison the previous year, having served ten years of an eighteen-year sentence for robbery.

Gorman had a flower stall outside the Crown public house at Cricklewood Broadway. There was an enclosed yard at the rear of the pub and it was there that he kept his flower stall. Courtesy of the police helicopter, it was ascertained that this was where the latest ramming van was kept.

So as a result of lengthy, painstaking police work, that was how Heal and Summerbee came to be keeping observation on the Ford Sierra.

By 13 April 1989 it had been determined that the gang's next target was to be the National Westminster Bank at Rayners Lane; the stolen Sierra had been put down in a nearby car park the night before. Other getaway 'switch-over' vehicles had been similarly put down in the vicinity. The Squad officers were augmented by the specialist firearms officers, PT17 Department; this was necessary since the gang had taken to discharging guns to reinforce their threats. Two armed officers would be allocated to what was termed a 'gunship'; this car was also crewed by two unarmed Flying Squad officers, there to make the arrests once the situation had been contained by their armed colleagues.

The gang arrived in the vehicle fitted with the ram; as well as Gorman, wearing a balaclava and armed with a sawn-off shotgun, there was Farrell wearing a black crash helmet and in possession of a .45 Colt revolver. The third member of the team (who was not identified until that day) was Terence Dewsnap, who was aged forty-eight and who had received an eight-year sentence in 1980 which had been reduced on appeal to six years. Wearing a white crash helmet, he was in possession of a 9mm Luger pistol.

So here was a highly dangerous gang, fully armed and ready for business – except their target was not the bank at all; it was the Post Office, situated opposite, which had £76,000 to pay out in state pensions. Having made their preparations, they managed to get their venue as wrong as the Squad had – instead of hitting the rear doors of the Post Office, they smashed into the building next door, which, with the ram fully extended firmly jammed the van into the building line.

Jumping into the Sierra, the team made off, with the Squad and the Firearms Unit in hot pursuit. Abandoning the Sierra, they ran across a footbridge, then down an alleyway, where they had put down a changeover vehicle, a stolen Ford Granada. Telling the Squad officers to stay back and shouting, 'Armed Police!', two firearms officers emerged from the alley, whereupon from a distance of 5 metres Farrell and Dewsnap opened fire, hitting one of them. They returned fire, the injured officer from a sitting position; both men were hit twice in the chest, with Dewsnap receiving an extra round in the leg. Gorman was within reach of Dewsnap's dropped Luger and his own sawn-off, but in the brisk series of shots from PT17 he was hit in the side of the head and his arm and foot. He lived to be sentenced to thirteen years' imprisonment on 15 January 1990 – but his two associates did not survive, and the inquest concluded that Farrell and Dewsnap had been lawfully killed.

The two firearms officers had acted with great courage during the close-quarter gun battle in which the robbers fired twenty rounds at the police, who returned fire with eighteen shots. The officer who had been shot by Dewsnap was later awarded the Queen's Gallantry Medal; his companion received the Queen's Commendation for Brave Conduct.

CHAPTER 22

Operation Yamato

Professional armed robbers do not restrict themselves to one target. They will have several plans on the go; if one job blows out, too bad, they'll go on to the next one. It is possible that at a future date the initial plan will be inspected, resurrected and turn out to be viable. Again, it might not. The permutations are endless.

That was the way of what became known as 'Operation Yamato'. In 1990, Detective Inspector (later Detective Superintendent) Michael Brooker was in charge of the surveillance unit – 12 Squad – at the Tower Bridge office of the Flying Squad. He believed that a series of armed robberies carried out across counties abutting the southern perimeter of the Metropolitan Police Districts was the work of core targets at that Squad office; principally, members of the notorious South London Turkish-Cypriot Arif family.

'The manner of commission showed a certain level of skill', Brooker told me. 'The robberies would occur in one force area, and whilst that force was tied up in the investigation, the subsequent week, another of a similar style was committed in a neighbouring area.'

It was not until the surveillance team was deep into the operation that they saw that multiple venues had been scoped by the gang, while vehicles were stolen to support the potential robberies and were all in place prior to the operational phase of each robbery.

Photographic surveillance was used at the outset to cover as many venues as possible, until officers witnessed meetings between members of the gang, and then actual surveillance was brought to bear. The intended dates of the potential robberies also became clear.

Using other surveillance assets, the team began to get a clearer picture of what was intended, but it became obvious that unless they received some other form of assistance from intelligence they would be alone in their efforts to counteract the gang. But as if that were not enough, the officers had to contend with the huge distances involved, inter-force politics regarding armed operations and the gang's element of surprise.

Nevertheless, by using technical surveillance the Squad officers were able to track the gang and observe them watching security vans making deliveries at three venues in Kent, Surrey and Sussex. The task was to understand when the robberies were to occur, which – if any – of the vehicles the team were aware of were to be used and what would be the venue attacked – but might it possibly be another venue, one which the Squad had not discovered? Stolen vehicles to be used for the robberies were kept 'alive' on original plates, and in order to do this, someone regularly moved them from location to location. The person the gang used for this turned up to park the cars and move them at around seven in the morning, wearing a business suit in order to give the impression of being a commuter parking his car on the way to the station.

Detective Sergeant Terry Hobbs was one of the surveillance team and he told me, 'We were looking at two or three different plots – we didn't know which plot or when. We used to get up at ridiculous hours to go and sweep the area of the plot, to see if the Arifs were about – they would go out with scanners.'

Short of any other intelligence, there was no alternative but to cover potential venues on already featured anniversaries whilst in full attack mode with armed vehicles and countless observation posts.

'In anticipation of this I was grateful for the intervention of Assistant Chief Constable of Kent, Ian Johnston, who coordinated meetings between the Met and all the affected forces', Brooker told me. 'The difficulties of managing the coordinated armed responses against such a mobile operation, between forces, was understood, and an agreement was hammered out which permitted the Flying Squad to provide the armed response using PT17 resources.'

The first indication of the possible target came at 5.00 pm on 26 November 1990 – but it was then that the Squad lost control of all their known targets. Vehicles which they anticipated would be used by the gang did not feature in the last 24 hours of surveillance. It would later transpire, on the day of the attack, that not just new vehicles but new targets had emerged.

This highlighted the obstacles to maintaining full surveillance against a determined gang who were conversant with most police methods and knew how to avoid leaving unnecessary traces of their activity.

Michael Brooker now takes up the story:

The day before the robbery was an evil day, raining heavily, and this in itself was causing difficulties with our clear objective, which was to regain control of what we knew, addresses and lost or stolen vehicles.

Contact with the targets was regained at an address in Mitcham. This along with the fact that some preparations were being made on a Tuesday night gave us a clear indication that the Surrey venue, at Woodhatch near Reigate, was going to be active the following day.

To add to this certainty the gang took the most unlikely of the vehicles we had under surveillance and placed it in, presumably, a getaway route near the venue of the intended attack. The venue was Barclays Bank in a parade of shops, where we had watched the gang observe a delivery some weeks earlier.

It is worth noting, as you will be well aware, Dick, what a logistical nightmare this operation had been. Quite apart from the fact it was a purely surveillance-led operation utilizing whatever other intelligence assets we could gather, there were no freebies here. We stood or fell by what we managed to glean and interpret. In addition, our response was always going to need to be a heavy one, and there was a massive requirement to keep the lid on what we knew. Leaks were feared but never transpired.

Each week for the best part of a month I had the responsibility of mobilizing two transit vans full of PT17 officers and all their kit, four squad cars full also of PT17 officers and a fleet of surveillance cars to locations in Kent and Surrey (a venue at Crawley in Sussex was not receiving the same amount of attention from the gang).

Observation posts needed to be obtained and maintained in secrecy; arrangements with the forces of Kent and Surrey were having to be renewed and also kept under wraps whilst using facilities from both. Not a day went by when I didn't fear that, given the pedigree of the targets and their history, our work would go down the pan through the malicious acts of others.

At around 4.00 am we took up our usual positions in observation posts, mine in a TV and radio shop opposite the bank, and in a garage forecourt next to it. The delivery time was around 10.00 am; the intended target a Securicor van. The guards had the habit of leaving the van to get tea at a café next to the bank. The robbers knew this, having watched them.

We were obviously conducting limited sweeps of the area without showing out too much. The venue was complicated by the fact that the parade of shops had a service road behind. This was difficult to keep under control as access would have been seen by anyone who was hanging around.

In the last hour things were fraught. We were aware that the robbers were making their way toward the intended robbery venue, but control in that vital hour was lost and hence information as to what they were exactly going to do was limited.

We had no alternative but to sit, wait and hope to see activity ahead of the attack to give us early warning. In the event none came. The minutes ticked towards 10.00 am and still no contact was gained with the robbers.

Suddenly, from an observation post, a Squad photographer thought he had a sighting of one of our targets in an unknown pickup truck. Moments later, the Securicor van containing £750,000 arrived and the guards – a man and a woman – got out to collect their refreshments.

As they returned to the van, the pickup truck swung around on the service road, a tarpaulin cover on the rear was flung back and two men jumped out. One was Kenny Baker, a serial armed robber and the latest addition to the gang; he was wearing a caricature Ronald Reagan mask. The other was Anthony Downer, wearing an Afro wig. Both men held handguns. Two others then emerged from the pickup truck: Dennis Arif was wearing an 'Old Man' mask, his brother Mehmet Arif had his face covered in boot polish and also wore an Afro wig; they, too, were armed. Dennis Arif shouted at the guards to get back into the van, otherwise they'd be shot, and he followed them into the van. Meanwhile, Downer got into the driver's seat of the Securicor vehicle, having forced the driver on to the passenger's seat, while Baker and Mehmet Arif got back into the pickup truck.

As soon as the pickup truck arrived, so Brooker had given the 'attack', but first on the scene was Detective Sergeant Terry Hobbs in an unmarked car.

As he told me, 'I was driving around and saw the blaggers marching the Securicor crew into the vehicle. I blocked it in so they couldn't get out. I got clear because I was unarmed – earlier, I'd bought bacon rolls for the PT17 team and I was glad I did, because they must have recognized me when the shooting started.'

And the shooting certainly had started. Vince Payne, then a detective constable told me:

> I watched as Mehmet Arif, resplendent in Afro wig and black makeup, took aim at two colleagues as they ran on to the forecourt. He was directly in front of me. I wasn't armed so I couldn't engage. However, before he could fire he was hit in the shoulder by one of the other PT17 officers, who had deployed alongside us and shot Kenny Baker, then Mehmet.

Police Constable William Hughes had wrenched open the pickup's passenger door, to be confronted by Baker pointing a 9mm self-loading pistol directly at him. Hughes opened fire with an MP5 machine pistol, hitting Baker in the stomach; then immediately, seeing Mehmet Arif pointing a handgun at him, Hughes fired again; the bullet travelled along the length of Arif's back, between his shoulder blades – the fact that he was wearing body armour probably helped to save him.

At the same time, Police Constable John Benson had arrived at the offside of the truck; having no doubt that Hughes was in imminent danger of being shot by Baker, he opened fire, the bullet passing through the windscreen and hitting Baker just below the eye and to the left of his nose. Baker toppled on to the ground, face-downwards, but he still had his handgun underneath his body, so a firearms officer put his foot on his back to prevent him from using it.

'I went forward to formally arrest him', Hobbs told me, 'but he was already dead.'

Meanwhile, a firearms officer who had been in Payne's Squad vehicle, seeing Downer sitting in the Securicor van's driver's seat holding a handgun, fired five shots at him; the windows and doors were armoured, which prevented penetration, but it was sufficient to frighten the living shit out of Downer who, like Mehmet Arif, hit the pavement. That left Dennis Arif, still in the back of the Securicor van with the custodians and still armed. The attack mechanism having been activated, all the doors were locked and there was no immediate means of access. The matter was resolved by a firearms officer, who with astonishing bravery climbed into the money access hatch at the rear of the vehicle and not only disarmed and arrested Arif but also unlocked a roof escape hatch.

The scene had been videoed and photographed, and now the evidence was amassed: at the scene, a 12-bore pump-action, sawn-off shotgun, a .38 revolver, a .45 self-loading pistol and a 9mm self-loading pistol. Elsewhere, there were getaway vehicles parked at specific locations, a radio-jamming device and, at a safe house, three more sawn-off shotguns and a sub-machinegun. There were also the photographs and surveillance logs which had been accrued over a three-month period. It was slightly amazing that the time which had elapsed between the guards being threatened and the arrests carried out was just two minutes.

Meanwhile, Vince Payne takes up the story:

> I remained at the scene and assisted in the arrest of Dennis Arif once he was pulled out through the roof of the Securicor van. Me and a DS took him in to the local nick, where the station officer/custody sergeant nearly fell off his chair. Dennis had a loaded gun and his pockets were full of ammunition. We were then kept in a room and not allowed to get on with things – Flying Squad officers together in the station bar area (closed) and PT17 separate.
>
> There was a bit of a misunderstanding with the Surrey police. They maintained at the time that we had a fixed plot on their ground rather than a mobile one and that we hadn't told them. It didn't affect the authorities required in any way, but protocol suggests that the host force deals with a fixed plot (if they are capable and wish to). Post-incident procedures were still being developed, and even though the officers who had fired shots declared as much, the host force wanted to take possession of all the firearms in police possession. PT17 would have run out of tools, carrying on like that!
>
> Eventually, Bill Hatful (a Flying Squad detective superintendent) along with a senior officer from the Firearms Unit arrived and we were effectively 'released' and allowed to get on with dealing with the aftermath and the prisoners. All was OK, once the dust had settled.

Superintendent Bob Bartlett of Surrey Police was in charge of a firearms team to ensure that no attempts would be made to rescue Mehmet Arif, who had been taken to the local hospital ('a sullen little man, not happy at being there') to receive treatment for his wound. A representative of the Police Complaints Authority attended the force headquarters, and a local senior officer, Superintendent Pat Crossan, was appointed to investigate the shootings.

In November 1991, at the Old Bailey, Mr Michael Stuart-Moore QC asked for (and was granted) jury protection, citing a previous case of jury-tampering in a case which involved the Arif family. Dennis Arif – he had previously been sentenced to eleven years' imprisonment for conspiracy to rob in 1981 – pleaded not guilty. His defence was one of duress; Baker – his nickname was 'Crazy' – to whom he owed £60,000 had allegedly threatened to shoot him unless he participated in the robbery, in order to use part of his share to pay off the debt.

It seemed an incredible story, only made possible since Baker was dead; the jury certainly thought so. A few months prior to the robbery, it was revealed that both Dennis Arif and Baker had attended an Arif family wedding reception at the Savoy Hotel, the cost of which came to £32,000. It was also attended by the glitterati of the North and South London criminal families, and after the jury heard that despite this display of beneficence, Dennis Arif lived in a council house, any credibility he might have possessed evaporated, and it took less than an hour to convict him. Mehmet Arif and Anthony Downer (he was the common-law husband of the Arifs' sister) had both pleaded guilty, and on 9 December 1991 the trial Judge, Her Honour Heather Steel, told the trio:

> You are each dangerous, ruthless, greedy and clever men from whom society must be protected for a very long time. You were going as four armed men to take care of three unarmed security guards in charge of a large sum of money. I have no doubt when you went out that morning, you were each prepared to shoot and be shot at. The way you went armed and prepared, you anticipated armed police may be involved and you were prepared for an armed shoot-out.

Dennis Arif was sentenced to twenty-two years' imprisonment and brother Mehmet and Downer to eighteen years each.

After the jury at Baker's inquest returned their verdict of 'lawful killing', Superintendent Crossan's investigation supported the actions of the firearms officers: 'There was every possibility that the gang would try to shoot themselves out of trouble.'

Detective Inspector Ian Robertson assisted Crossan in the investigation and his comment was, 'From a police officer's perspective, I thought they did a superb job'.

Now in retirement, Michael Brooker still retains this recollection of 'Operation Yamato':

> Despite the months of planning, achieving great intelligence gains which helped us try to understand at that time what the robbers intended, with so many unknowns and a gang who were used to keeping police in the dark, it was always going to be an uphill task.

CHAPTER 23

Tiger Kidnaps

Between December 1989 and November 1991 five robberies occurred in which Post Office remittance cash-in-transit (REM) vans from the Eastern District Office at Whitechapel were targeted, resulting in the loss of over £750,000.

Initially, there was no clue as to the identities of the attackers, who often worked under cover of darkness and always with the element of surprise. Furthermore, the way in which the robberies were carried out bore no similarity to anything the Flying Squad had dealt with before; they were known as 'Tiger Kidnaps'.

In each case – and these robberies only occurred on a Wednesday, when there was the most money in the REMs – a crew member of the REM van would be kidnapped at gunpoint and bundled into a car as he made his way to work. He was put in fear for his own safety and that of his family who, he would be told, were being held hostage. Having been given instructions on what to do after the REM van had been driven out of the depot, the postman was fitted with a transmitting device to enable the gang to overhear his conversations after he had been sent on his way.

The driver would be told to follow a motorcyclist, who would take the van to a cul-de-sac or alleyway. The motorcyclist would then leave. Other members of the gang would keep the van under observation from nearby buildings 'borrowed' for that purpose. They were looking for police vehicles, as well as using scanners to detect police activity in the area. Only when they were satisfied that the coast was clear would two gang members carrying holdalls approach the van, take the cash and retrieve the bugging device.

Neither the motorcycle nor any of the vehicles were stolen; all were purchased legitimately and cheaply via a local newspaper by a junior member or associate of the team.

There was obviously an inside agent at the Post Office, but no one knew who the intended victims would be. These robberies would usually occur twice a year, perhaps one in the spring to provide the gang with luxuries such as exotic summer holidays, then another in late autumn to give them a comfortable Christmas. By acting in this fashion, committing only intermittent robberies and not becoming too greedy, the gang obviously thought they were being very clever and would be too difficult to catch. They were right.

This scenario was completely different to the usual Squad investigation where, once a robbery team were identified, the Squad would keep them under observation, following and photographing them, determining where and from whom the robbery was going to take place; then, on the day of the robbery, with all the main players appearing on the pavement, gathering them, their stolen vehicles, firearms and other robbery paraphernalia, all in one hit. Easy. But not this team.

However, the gang leader, Terrence Agombar, *was* identified. He ran a pub near Victoria Park, Bow, which was used as a business premises to meet other gang members and plan further strategies; and his associates were also identified. However, with an operation being set up from the Rigg Approach office, under the direction of Detective Chief Inspector (later Superintendent) Albert Patrick, a decision was made not to conduct random or lifestyle surveillance on a team who were not operating on a regular basis.

Consequently, it would be necessary to try to capture the gang all together in one hit; to pick them off one at a time might result in a half-hearted conspiracy charge, which in all probability would not survive inspection by the Crown Prosecution Service.

However, Agombar lived just around the corner from the Crook Log swimming baths, Bexleyheath, and Albert Patrick also lived in the vicinity at that time. So for a period of six months, every Wednesday morning at 4 o'clock, Patrick would check Agombar's car to try to determine if he was out plotting up a robbery.

So whilst overt surveillance was seldom used, covert means were; in mid-1990 this resulted in successful identification of the inside agent at the Post Office, and as a result it appeared that a robbery would occur the following day. Therefore, it was necessary to house the gang members that night, but they were nowhere to be found; they had borrowed cars from their associates and stayed in different premises to avoid detection.

The following morning, an observation was carried out outside the Post Office; a gang member wearing an earpiece was in the street outside. Clearly, a postman had been kidnapped, and the gang member was testing the bugging device to ensure his compliance. The robber was driven back to a block of flats in Bethnal Green to meet up with the rest of the gang for the next stage; then the motorcyclist would go to the Post Office to meet the van on its departure.

But on the return journey to Bethnal Green the gang's suspicions were aroused; a junior member of the team was sent out with a scanner to try to detect a police presence, and he did. He was then excluded from any further involvement with the gang.

The robbery was aborted; there was insufficient evidence to justify an arrest, but when the kidnapped postman came forward, still wearing the microphone which had been taped to his chest, it was found to be a viable listening device.

'With only a limited number of covert surveillance operations that we could run in a day, it was decided to stand the operation down for a while', Albert Patrick told me.

But on 13 November 1991 the gang changed its tactics. Rather than utilize an early morning kidnap, a postman was kidnapped late that afternoon and made to hand over a van's contents in a Bethnal Green alleyway. This was a massive blow to the morale of the 'Operation Wooton II' team members; it had been their last chance.

Or was it? The team knew of an address in Wenvoe Avenue, Bexleyheath, South-East London used by the gang – would they go there to divide the proceeds? It was worth a try, and at 8 o'clock that evening a bungalow in that quiet residential street was surrounded. Outside were known vehicles, and into them, from the bungalow, got known members of the gang, carrying holdalls. Two of the gang members (one of whom was Agombar) experienced a 'hard stop' at traffic lights in East India Dock Road, E14; when pulled out of their Mercedes, its boot was found to contain two holdalls, each containing £25,000. The other car was also stopped and the driver arrested; in his holdall was found cash, plus Post Office packaging, wrappings and seals from the stolen cash bags.

'The money wrappers had writing on them that was identified by the Post Office staff as their mark when counting the money that was collected by the REM that morning', Patrick told me.

A search of the bungalow's attic revealed a bag containing 10 per cent of the cash for the inside agent. Unfortunately, the occupant of the bungalow, John Henry, escaped over the back gardens and was not arrested until over a year later at his building society in Lewisham.

During the five-week trial at Southwark Crown Court, several thousand exhibits were produced and 117 witnesses were called; these included a woman who had seen two men take bags from the crew of a REM van. She stated that they looked like brothers and resembled the Mitchells in the television soap, *Eastenders*. In fact, a copy of the *Radio Times* which featured the brothers on its front cover was used as an exhibit during the trial; it helped to convict Mark Cummings.

At the conclusion of the trial on 18 December 1992 Agombar was sentenced to fourteen years' imprisonment. Cummings was similarly sentenced to fourteen years, to run concurrently with a four-year sentence imposed earlier for dishonestly handling £35,000. A third gang member, Gary Hutchings, was sentenced to twelve years, to be served concurrently with a ten-year sentence imposed in January for handling £65,000, the proceeds of a robbery. John Henry, convicted of dishonestly handling cash, was sentenced at a later date.

His Honour Judge Victor Watts said:

> The public can rightly feel indebted to the police for the work they have done under the leadership of Detective Superintendent Albert Patrick.

Additionally, due to the amount of attention generated by the press, no more robberies using this particular method were attempted.

'Operation Wooton II was a great team effort: SO11 surveillance, SO19 firearms teams, the Post Office investigators and the hard-working Flying Squad officers based at Rigg Approach', Albert Patrick told me. 'Patience prevailed and another armed gang was brought to book.'

★

Mark Burdis came to the Squad at Rigg Approach in 1990; and before being appointed to the surveillance team two years later he worked in the office, carrying out investigations into reported armed robberies as well as targeting men suspected of carrying out those raids. What follows was a bit of both.

'Operation Epinal' investigated the activities of three such robbers, two black, one Asian. They targeted jewellers' shops, pistol-whipped the staff and removed the cassettes from the CCTV cameras to protect their anonymity; that was, until the plucky owner of 'The Golden Mantella', Green Lanes, N13 fought back. He was badly beaten but he retained the cassette; and now the Squad had clear pictures of all three.

Next, the owner of a shop in Dagenham's Heathway was speaking on the telephone to her solicitor when the gang burst into her premises; hearing the commotion, the solicitor immediately called the police.

'The whole job', Burdis told me, 'then turned into one of those "you wouldn't believe it" ones.'

Two uniformed police officers – one male, one female – were on patrol, looked through the shop's window, saw what was happening and rushed in. Just as quickly, the alarmed blaggers rushed out of the back, where a minicab was waiting for them. At that moment, a vanload of TSG (Territorial Support Group) arrived. Trained to high levels of fitness and used for crowd control, as well as stop-and-search and evidence-gathering under hazardous conditions, they now proved their worth by smashing every window in the mini-cab and dragged out two of the armed robbers, Thomas and Bhyatt. The third miscreant, Reid, hi-jacked the TSG carrier and was chased until he reached a block of flats near Dagenham police station, where he kicked in the door of a family flat and got up on the roof.

Burdis had heard the commentary on his police radio and went straight to Barking police station, where Thomas and Bhyatt were detained – neither had anything to say.

By now, Reid had been talked down from his rooftop eyrie and was taken to Edmonton police station, where tape-recorded interviews on video had just been introduced; he was invited to participate in one and made a full confession.

At the Old Bailey, the solicitor for Reid was taken to task by his defence barrister for giving his client the wrong advice, i.e. permitting him to confess; a member of the jury walked into court wearing a T-shirt with the logo 'Justice? What Justice?' and threats were made to witnesses. During the retrial the defence was one of duress; all of the defendants stated that they owed money to a Jewish jeweller and that he had forced them to carry out the robberies. His name was mentioned in court – it was an unusual one, and Burdis found it in a telephone directory. The jeweller, who lived in Kent, was interviewed, admitted that he knew the gang, who had tried to get him to receive stolen jewellery, and said he was terrified of them. He repeated this at the Old Bailey, which led to the gang receiving double-figure prison sentences.

There was also a knock-on effect from 'Operation Epinal'.

A collection of violent low-lifes, so utterly devoid of personality that they were compelled to refer to themselves as 'The Wrens Park Massive', on 1 September 1994 rushed into a shop in Green Lane, Dagenham where a CCTV fitter was finishing off installing cameras. He was made to lie down on the floor with a shotgun in his back. The gun went off, killing the fitter, but the images were recorded – as Burdis told me, 'Unfortunately, he basically filmed his own death.'

The case was investigated by Detective Superintendent Iain Malone of the Squad who told me, 'There were two circular marks like brand marks on his body from the heat of the barrels.'

When Burdis saw the CCTV images he recognized one of the gang. Whilst he was investigating 'Operation Epinal' he had visited Bhyatt's home address; they were, he told me, 'a pretty decent family'. But now he realized that the person on the tape was Bhyatt's brother.

The flat was put under surveillance; four days later, the brother emerged, was tailed off and led the officers to the rest of the team, who were charged with murder.

★

Although Detective Sergeant Gordon Livingstone was running a very successful surveillance team at the Rigg Approach office he still maintained his links with underworld informants. After two years work on a North London team of robbers, pen pictures of a number of targets were compiled. The gang were shrewd and not greedy; they would carry out perhaps two or three robberies per year, but these, on average, would net them £250,000. But Livingstone's persistence and hard work paid off. When he established that some of the gang were going to hit a Royal Mail van containing £250,000 at the Sub-Post Office at Crouch End on the morning of 22 February 1993, he, his surveillance team and officers from SO19 Firearms Unit[1] were ready for them.

As the Royal Mail van drew up at the Post Office at 10.13 that morning, 'Operation Odense' got underway.

A white Transit van screeched to a halt and two men armed with handguns leapt out. This location had been specially chosen by the gang because railings outside the Post Office prevented the van from parking close by; therefore the guard would have to walk a short distance from his van. Steven Charalambous aged twenty-six, dressed as a uniformed police officer and wearing a false moustache, and Loukas Menikou aged thirty-one, dressed in black and wearing a black balaclava, rushed at a Post Office employee.

'Steve Collins' was in charge of the SO19 'Black Team' in a flat opposite to the Post Office. He told me, 'When Charalambous pitched up, we went down the stairs to the door that led directly on to the street and waited for the attack to be given. I had a sniper on a flat roof further up the street to dominate the scene, which was to become rather cramped.'

---

[1] The Firearms Unit had changed its designation from PT17 to SO19; additionally, the Flying Squad's description had been changed from C8 to SO8.

The order to attack was given and surveillance officers disguised as taxi drivers, road-sweepers and deliverymen moved in; but by now Charalambous had grabbed hold of the guard, pushed his gun into the man's chest and demanded that the custodians throw out the £250,000. Challenged by the SO19 officers, he unwisely refused to drop his gun.

As 'Steve Collins' told me, 'He saw me and levelled the pistol. Conscious of the fact that I was between him and the sniper I ducked back, and "Nigel", who was in a better position with an MP5, shot him.'

In fact, Charalambous was shot three times, twice in the chest and once in the chin which, as Livingstone pointed out to me, 'stopped him in his tracks'.

'Get on the floor, on the fucking floor!' shouted 'Steve Collins' to Menikou, who wisely dropped his gun before being assisted to the ground.

The driver escaped, and the Transit van was later found abandoned nearby.

Charalambous, with gunshot wounds to the chest and shoulder, was taken by air ambulance to the Royal London Hospital. His gun turned out to be an imitation, but Menikou's was not; it was loaded, with one in the chamber.

This was the fifth time in twenty-five years that the Crouch End Post Office had been targeted by armed robbers. The sub-postmistress, 57-year-old Mrs Pushpa Patel, was surprisingly phlegmatic about the incident: 'I am now used to it', she said.

At the Old Bailey that September, both men pleaded guilty to firearms offences and conspiracy to rob, and each received the rather lenient sentence of five years' imprisonment, Recorder Anthony Arlidge QC telling them, 'You were both involved in a very serious offence. Next time, you can expect to get between fifteen and twenty years.'

There was a full enquiry presided over by the Police Complaints Authority which completely exonerated the firearms officers of any wrongdoing.

Charalambous was due for release in June 1996 when, on Wednesday 28 February, he absconded from Hollesley Bay prison. He had been granted legal aid to fund suing the police for the injuries he had received during his arrest. The figure he had in mind as proper compensation for 'the unlawful assault and trespass to his person, plus excessive and unreasonable force' was £250,000, precisely the sum he would have received had the police not had the insolence to intervene during his morning's work. For good measure, he also mendaciously claimed that he had been shot whilst he was on the ground and he demanded an additional £335 for the damage the shots had caused to his clothing. However, the legal aid board had, in the light of the public furore which followed the granting of the bursary, suspended their decision.

Two days after his unofficial parole, Charalambous telephoned the *Evening Standard*, telling them, 'I am not on the run, officially. I have taken three days away and am going to hand myself back.' He was, he said, 'shocked and outraged' at the way that the media had publicized the situation, telling them, 'I just want to clear my name.'

Since he had pleaded guilty to some serious offences, this statement did appear to be illogical; he surrendered the following day.

Legal aid was withdrawn on 30 April, and three days later, an investigation was carried out to determine precisely why it had been granted in the first place.

Charalambous was returned to prison but not to the place from where he had absconded, which was reserved for Category 'C' and 'D' offenders nearing the end of their sentences – the prison authorities decided he needed somewhere rather more secure than that.

On the lighter side, Detective Sergeant Mick Carroll, who had worked for months on this case with Gordon Livingstone, had realized at one point that the foliage on trees in the street had grown so rapidly that it would be difficult to see from the OP; therefore, early in the morning, the officers decided to cut some branches away. Unfortunately, this attracted the attention of a local resident, who telephoned the local police station to complain that men were stealing tree branches.

'The local bobbies couldn't be told the reasons why Flying Squad officers were cutting branches off a tree at 3 o'clock in the morning', Carroll told me. 'They left, thinking we were either drunk or mad!'

CHAPTER 24

Funny Business

Time now to take a short break from the rough and tumble of Flying Squad operations, because humour, unintentional or otherwise, played a significant part in Squad work.

Mike Bucknole recalled the arrest of five desperadoes, one dressed in police uniform, who had gone to rob someone who had allegedly received some of the proceeds of the Bank of America job. The miscreants were leapt upon, and one of them had a sawn-off shotgun concealed down his trousers leg. Unfortunately, at the time of being apprehended his finger was on the trigger, which resulted in him shooting himself in the foot.

A Magistrates' Court was hastily convened that morning, with three lay magistrates in attendance. In the interests of security, the prisoners were brought in one at a time, each handcuffed to a Squad officer. Since the raid had been assembled at very short notice, the officers had come straight from a boxing dinner at Quaglino's famous restaurant in St James' and were still dressed in their dinner suits. This incongruous sight appeared to unnerve the magistrate, who visibly trembled and shook. Upon being told the prisoner's name was 'Buxton', he told him in a quavering voice, 'Mr Brixton, you will be remanded in custody to Buxton for seven days.'

Taken to the cells, the aggrieved prisoner asked, 'Where the fuck is Buxton?' Told it was in Derbyshire, he expostulated, 'How's me missus going to visit? She won't know where that is!'

★

The late Judge Michael Argyle MC, QC was a hard-line and controversial judge at the Old Bailey who retired in 1987 after being bollocked by the Lord Chancellor for his comments about foreign immigration being out of control and about wishing to re-impose the death penalty. He admired the Flying Squad, and that approbation was fully reciprocated. After an attempt was made by defence counsel to attack the probity of a Squad officer (which Argyle swiftly kicked into touch), the officer sent a Flying Squad tie to the judge's chambers, together with his thanks.

The following day, Argyle phoned the Squad office and told the telephone operator that he had worn the tie the previous evening and hadn't paid for a single drink!

*

Former Detective Superintendent Duncan MacRae (who served in all but one rank in the Flying Squad) told me an amusing story of when he was a detective constable on the Squad. Information had been received that a gang were going to help themselves to the contents of a security van in Garston, Liverpool. Two of the gang travelled to the location by car at night; to assist in keeping it in sight, someone helpfully broke one of the car's rear lights; a car showing one red and one white light was then comparatively easy to follow at a safe distance. The men met up with the gang leader at Lime Street Station; he had travelled up by train, bringing with him the 'happy bag'[1] necessary for the robbery, which was a way of improving the odds should those in the car get pulled by police.

The two car travellers were arrested, but the third man escaped, jettisoning the distinctive tartan 'happy bag' as he went, and found temporary sanctuary underneath a jacked-up car before escaping completely.

He was later picked up after he went to sign on for bail regarding a different case at Wood Green police station. An OP was set up opposite and he was identified after dozens of pedestrians had walked past the police station's entrance – which I feel sure that the most sceptical, left-wing, tree-hugging, do-gooder would agree was the fairest type of identification parade.

At the trial at Liverpool Crown Court, Detective Sergeant Alan Johns gave evidence of overhearing a highly incriminating conversation between the three suspects at Lime Street railway station, and this resulted in fierce cross-examination from the defence. How, it was demanded, could he possibly have been able to hear what was being said on one of Lime Street's busy eleven platforms against the noise of the incoming and outgoing trains, plus announcements being made to passengers over the loudspeakers?

A nice point, as you'll agree, but Johns was up to it. 'Ah', he replied. 'Well, this was very familiar territory for me. You see, I used

---

[1] The term 'happy bag' was used to describe a holdall into which all the impedimenta for an armed robbery had been placed.

to work on the footplate on the railway and I was very well able to differentiate and block out the various background noises and give my full attention to what was being said by the defendants.'

This response caught the judge's attention, and he demanded to know more of Johns' background; when it was revealed that he had also served as a rear gunner – or 'Tail-end Charlie' – on Lancaster bombers during the Second World War, at a time when life expectancy in this position was two weeks or five operations, he could do no wrong.

Seeing the way the wind was blowing, the defence barrister wisely shut up and sat down, but he was up on his feet again when Duncan MacRae gave evidence, especially with regard to the tartan holdall containing all the robbery impedimenta which, he stated, the third man had been carrying before abandoning it in his flight. The lawyer produced three different coloured tartan holdalls and suggested it was one of these that his client had been carrying.

MacRae – of Highland crofting stock – was up for that as well. 'Och, no', he replied. Pointing to the court exhibit – the 'happy bag' – he said, 'That's a MacLaren tartan – in fact, it's a MacLaren hunting tartan – I couldn't be mistaken about that, and that's what your client was carrying.' Indicating the other three offerings from the defence, he added dismissively, 'Those aren't genuine tartans at all; in fact, I believe they were manufactured in China!'

MacRae was quite right; there are 500 varieties of Scottish tartan, woven cloth in criss-cross patterns known as setts. Furthermore, each clan has different official or unofficial versions of the tartan; the MacLarens have twelve.

The judge was as impressed with MacRae's knowledge of his native Scotland's tartans as he had been with Johns' footplate and aircrew experiences, and as the unhappy trio descended to the cells to commence long prison sentences, they had learned a valuable lesson in life – never double-dare a Flying Squad officer!

★

The ways of subduing an armed blagger and getting him to comply with a direction to get down on the ground are many and varied; some recalcitrant robbers need to be helped. One method that I found particularly efficacious was to grip hold of their clothing at the nape of their neck, half-turn them and then stamp on the area at the back of the knees, causing them to buckle and fall forwards. The grip on their clothing was, of course, necessary to prevent (or at least minimize) facial damage when they encountered the pavement.

One officer told me about the time that he and his partner made a decision to burst into a bank to take out a pair of armed robbers before matters escalated into a siege situation. They did so, quite successfully, although the officer's partner kicked one of the robbers to get him to the ground. He was then admonished for his actions by one of the customers, who until then had been held at gunpoint; but, as I was told, 'She was a proper South London girl!'

★

Disapprobation was certainly not limited to ladies from south of the River Thames; I once experienced condemnation from a source far closer to home.

I was in a Flying Squad car being driven through the West End in August 1981 when a robbery occurred at the Diamond Gallery, George Street, Mayfair. Two armed men had burst into the premises, stealing jewellery valued at £740,000 before being disturbed and escaping in a stolen Mercedes driven by a third man, leaving a scattering of jewellery across the pavement. We heard the call on the radio, but by the time we arrived the blaggers had long gone. The staff were busy picking up the rather expensive items, and as I walked towards them, I suddenly noticed something sparkling in the gutter; it was a starburst diamond ring with emeralds. I knelt down to pick it up and as I did so I glanced up; in front of me was a dazzlingly beautiful apparition, the Polish manageress of a nearby hairdresser's salon.

Instinctively, still in the kneeling position, I held out the ring and said, 'Will you marry me?'

'Vell', she replied in her deliciously husky, rolling accent, 'you've got the r-r-ring – vhy not?'

It was a bit of light amusement on a sunny, Mayfair day, and after I handed the ring over (to the owner of the Diamond Gallery, not the hairdresser), we went on our way and I forgot about the incident.

The affair was reported in an extremely modest fashion by *The Times*, but all I can say is, the *Daily Express* must have been seriously short of copy that day because they gave a great deal of prominence not only to the robbery, but also to the beauteous Polish popsy and our conversation.

I suppose the story caused a modicum of amusement to some of the readers of the *Daily Express*, less so to the proprietor of the Diamond Gallery and at the breakfast table of a premises in Upminster, Essex, not at all to a certain Mrs Ann Kirby.

'*HOW BLOODY DARE YOU!*' she screamed, and before physical molestation could commence, I was saved by the arrival of my driver, Tony Freeman, who since he had been present at the previous day's light-hearted exchange immediately grasped the substance of this domestic situation.

'Don't upset yourself, Ann!' he cried. 'I was there; she was middle-aged and ugly as sin!'

'*SHE BLOODY WASN'T!*' shrieked the mother of my children, flourishing in his face the offending article, which included a photograph of the lady in all her loveliness.

Tony and I beat a hasty retreat; East End girls, rather like their South London counterparts, can be difficult to control when their blood's up; armed blaggers are a lot easier!

CHAPTER 25

Automatic Weapons

Right, a light-hearted break over, because Tuesday, 17 August 1993 was an important day for the Flying Squad; it was the first time that Squad officers pursuing robbers were shot at with an automatic weapon.

The operation had commenced several weeks earlier. Detective Sergeant Barry Nicholson from 10 Squad at Tower Bridge had been investigating a series of armed robberies which had occurred in South-East London between 1991 and August 1993; but these had been carried out so professionally that not one witness was able to identify the perpetrators.

Nicholson received word from an informant that two men – Steven Farrer aged twenty-five from Greenwich and Anthony Pendrigh aged twenty-six from Eltham – were responsible. Since neither man possessed a criminal record, this on the face of it seemed unlikely, but a full surveillance operation was carried out on them, and within three days both men were photographed in six stolen vehicles and were seen taking a great interest when cash-in-transit vans delivered to Post Offices. It became clear that the men intended to attack a Security Express van on 17 August when it made a delivery to the Post Office at Blackfen, South London. It was thought both would be armed.

It was a joint operation between 10 and 11 Squads, as well as a C11 surveillance team; the Post Office had been covered several times in the previous weeks, and both targets had been seen at the vicinity checking it out. Everyone on the team was confident the information was accurate, and the subjects having previously been seen on the plot went a long way to confirming it.

Detective Constable Peter Redford was the front nearside passenger in a Squad Vauxhall Carlton driven by Police Constable John Macaskill. The rear nearside passenger was Detective Sergeant Michael Stubbs and the offside passenger was Detective Sergeant John Swinfield. Other than Macaskill, all the officers were armed.

The briefing was for two Squad vehicles to keep close to the Post Office to await the van and the suspects' arrival. The position for the car containing Redford and Co was 'floating', keeping away from the Post Office and aiming to close in behind the subjects.

C11 had picked the two up that morning and were making their way towards the plot. Redford takes up the tale:

> Where we were parked, we had a decent view of the main road. A security van drove past us. It just didn't feel right. (Dick, you know what I mean. I just can't explain it.) We didn't inform the Officer in Charge but decided to just move our position and generally follow after the box[1] and in the opposite direction to the Post Office.

The robbers arrived in a stolen red Vauxhall Astra and hit the guard from the van as he was on the footpath, stealing £17,000. Unfortunately, right at the time of the attack, the watchers' view was obstructed by a high-sided vehicle. But C11 were close behind them and Redford's car was just around the corner. The robbers made off in their car; a C11 vehicle was coming face on to their vehicle and had to swerve on to the pavement to prevent being rammed. However, the Squad car driven by PC Macaskill was right behind them within seconds, and once again, Redford relates what happened:

> One of the subjects leant out of the front nearside window with a sub machine gun and emptied it at us. I remember one bullet hit the windscreen right in front of me. The windscreen cracked in a circle but held. I later found out that the bullet had hit the rubber covering of the washer jet and had lost a lot of its force. Result for me! The next bullet had come through the windscreen just under the internal mirror. The glass apparently deflected it past my right ear and across DS Stubbs' forehead.
>
> Blood from Stubbs flew about the car, and I think he may have then collapsed. Swinfield started to look after him and rendered a bit of first aid as our car rocked about. Where the rest of the bullets went, I can't recall. What really worried us was when the shooter tried to reload the machine gun with another magazine. Luckily, in his haste, he jammed the gun. He moved back into his vehicle for a few seconds and then leant out of the window again with a rather large revolver, which I believe was a .44 magnum.

---

[1] 'Money box', slang term for a cash-in-transit van.

One bullet from it came through the radiator and entered the engine compartment, took out some important wiring and lodged behind the force radio. Our vehicle was rendered useless.

There was a photo journalist who saw the aftermath and took a photo of Stubbs, who we had got out of the car and laid on the floor, with me looking like I was doing cardiac massage but was actually removing his firearm, and Swinfield who was trying to stop him bleeding. I think the image was in the *Mirror* the following day.

Although three of the officers in the Squad car were armed, never once did they consider returning fire; they were in a built-up area, and the risks of hitting someone were far too great to take. It was not a consideration which occurred to the robbers, however; as Denise Freshwater, a local hairdresser, said:

The man was hanging right out of the car window and firing a machine gun along the street. He wasn't aiming at any one thing, he was just firing everywhere. Anyone on the street could have been hit. I couldn't believe it. There was this man just shooting all over the place.

Twenty-nine-year-old Andy Merrill said, 'There were red flames and sparks coming out the muzzle of the gun. The shooting was indiscriminate.'

John Wiggins, a panel beater, said, 'The red Astra was up on the kerb and this bloke was hanging out of the back, blazing away with a gun. It looked like an Uzi, one of those things you see on Rambo.'

The first civilian on the scene was Paul Duffett who, seeing Stubbs, said:

He was lying on the ground with a bandage around his head, writhing and wincing with pain. Others were standing about him, telling him, 'Hold on, hold on'. I counted at least fifteen rounds of rat-a-tat gunfire. One of the bullets hit the outside wall of my house. My son Tom, who is only nine, and his five-year-old brother were playing in the garden.

The other Squad cars from the Post Office saw the Astra as it raced down a road towards the A2, where there was a barrier. The robbers abandoned their vehicle, ran past the barrier and hijacked a Ford Capri from a woman at gun point. Holding a gun at 48-year-old Marie Gilhooly, one of the heroic pair screamed, 'Get out the car, ya fucking bitch!' Ms Gilhooly, who had just returned from a doctor's appointment, staggered weeping to her father's house a few doors away, before collapsing.

No vehicle could follow them; it was unfortunate that the C11 team had not brought a 'Four-two' with them. As the robbers abandoned the car, they fired shots at two police constables who approached them; they were unharmed.

It was highly likely that the robbers were unaware that the Squad knew their identities. However, the house at Eltham was soon surrounded, Farrer and Pendrigh were arrested and they, in company with another man and a woman and together with the machine pistol, two other firearms, ammunition and the stolen cash, made their way to the local police station.

Stubbs was rushed to hospital to have the wound to his left temple treated; he was placed sick for six months. The other occupants of the Squad car had been struck by flying glass. Of the nineteen rounds which had been fired, eleven from the machine pistol had struck the pursuing Squad car; the twelfth, from the .44 Magnum, had finally disabled it.

On 2 June 1994 Farrer and Pendrigh appeared at the Old Bailey. Naturally, they denied attempted murder, with one of the defence counsel crooning, 'They were only trying to stop the car and not trying to hurt anyone' and adding that the charge of attempted murder was 'ridiculous'. Try telling that to the residents of Blackfen who witnessed the whole disgraceful episode. However, they admitted using the machine pistol to resist arrest, other firearms charges and robbery. For that offence, they were each sentenced to twelve years' imprisonment, and for using the machine pistol to resist arrest, another six years, making a total of eighteen years' imprisonment each.

Almost two years later, the four officers received the Queen's Commendation for Brave Conduct. PC Macaskill had driven brilliantly, and all of the crew had shown great resolution in pursuing a dangerous foe who had sprayed them with automatic fire. It was slightly amazing that apart from Sergeant Stubbs no other member of the crew (or any member of the public) had sustained serious, if not fatal injuries.

Speaking to me twenty-five years after the incident, Michael Stubbs said, 'I was told that my injury was minor because the bullet hit my left temple, then ricocheted off my skull.' He added, 'It didn't feel minor!'

There are always touches of humour in every serious situation; when the chase began, Redford alerted the team on the small set (as opposed to the main RT set) used for communications over a limited area of 2–3 miles. However, at the same time, there was an ongoing operation by a team in North London who were following armed men believed to be dealing in large quantities of firearms. The North London team heard broken parts of the radio transmissions and thought it was they who were under attack. In such a fraught situation, it is not recorded how they responded!

Once Stubbs was discharged from hospital, in accordance with new guidelines at the time, the four officers were instructed to attend a meeting with psychiatrists from the Force's Medical Branch who wanted to know firstly what happened and secondly, 'How the officers felt'. As Redford told me, 'They were not at all happy with what we told them!'

And when the officers were invited to a reception at the House of Commons by Jack Straw MP, the commissioner was late and missed most of the function. As Redford told me, 'Jack Straw slagged him off mercilessly in front of everyone; I don't think there was any love lost between the two!'

With the court case out of the way, what used to be known as 'The Black Museum' (now the politically correct 'Crime Museum') laid claim to the machine pistol. Originally used as a property store from 1869, the museum has since 1875 housed a collection of interesting criminal artefacts. Since that time, the collection and the size of the museum have expanded; some objects have of necessity been removed and replaced with others, but there is always room for a unique item.

That weapon was a necessity for the collection; it was 'a Flying Squad first'.

CHAPTER 26

Joint Operations

M any Squad cases were the result of joint operations with different constabularies: the Squad provided the knowledge and expertise in dealing with sophisticated criminals from the London area; the constabulary supplied man-power and expert local knowledge. They were good amalgamations.

One such case was 'Operation Cockburn', which was run by Detective Chief Inspector Dave Ryan from the Finchley office. It commenced in 1996 and concluded on the M11 motorway on 11 July 1997, and what happened was as follows.

Since 1994 there had been a total of eleven armed attacks on cash-in-transit vehicles in North and South London and the Home Counties. Although they were investigated by different Squad offices throughout London, plus constabulary offices, they were believed to be linked. Not all of the attacks were successful, but between 2 April 1994 and 25 July 1996 those that were earned the gang £1,048,167.30p.

The main type of subterfuge employed by the four-man team was to use a stolen and plated British Telecom van, disguising themselves as BT engineers and lifting manhole covers, in order to get very close to a cash-in-transit van. The guards were invariably approached from behind by one or two of the gang, and in this way they were able to gain immediate access to the van, hi-jacking the guards and permitting one of the gang to drive the van away to a quiet area, usually a warehouse in a disused industrial estate, where they would help themselves to the money at their leisure, before driving off in other stolen vehicles. Communication between the members of the gang in the hi-jacked van and those in the warehouse would be by radio.

The guards would be restrained, occasionally with handcuffs or more usually with plastic cable ties or masking tape. The heavy duty tape would have the top of the roll folded back on itself so that the gang could use it wearing gloves and not leave tell-tale forensic evidence. Similarly, after each attack, the gang would either get new rolls of tape or be very careful to ensure that no exact match of the end of the rolls of tape could be made from one offence to another.

In the same way, crowbars were used to force open secure cash boxes in the van; but since the gang were obviously very forensically aware, after each raid these crowbars would be filed or honed down, to prevent forensic linkage.

The stolen BT van would either be left at the scene of the robbery or sometimes used as transportation to the warehouse; but whatever the case, it would be abandoned thereafter and a fresh one stolen for the next raid.

What was abundantly clear was that the gang did a lot of homework in choosing the best locations and examining in great detail the routines and movements of the security vans and the guards at a variety of locations, in order to pick the best site and opportunity to strike.

It was after the last robbery on 25 July 1996 that information was received by the Finchley office that those responsible for the raid included a Bobby Stubbs, someone named 'Gary' from South London and an older man known only as 'Granddad'.

Stubbs was easy to identify as Robert Patrick Stubbs aged forty-seven from Camden Town; he had a long criminal career, having been convicted of mainly petty offences. His only sentence of imprisonment was one of six months' duration; however, he had been acquitted of armed robbery on four separate occasions.

He had associated with James Albert Hampton, aka 'Granddad' because at sixty-two years of age he was the oldest of the team. His criminal career had commenced in 1961 with a series of offences which had been dealt with by means of fines, until 1974 when with two other gang members and two stolen and plated getaway cars he stole £9,000 at gunpoint from the custodians of a Security Express van. The getaway was unkindly thwarted by the Flying Squad, and Hampton went to prison for a total of four and a half years. Released in 1976, he next appeared at the Old Bailey three years later for attempting to bribe a detective, for which he received a suspended sentence. He had stolen cars on several occasions – he was regarded as an efficient 'wheelman' for robbery teams – and in 1983 he received a further suspended sentence for stealing another vehicle.

But in 1988 at the Old Bailey he was sentenced to a total of eleven years' imprisonment. He, together with three others in possession of disguises, loaded firearms and a number of stolen and plated vehicles, had waited for a cash-in-transit vehicle to arrive so that they could take a custodian hostage and demand cash. However, they were caught, once more, in a Flying Squad ambush, and Hampton told Squad officer Bob Fenton QGM, 'Be careful with the guns, Guv, they're loaded!' Hampton was released in August 1993.

As Detective Sergeant Terry Allen told me:

> By February 1997 we had collated as much relevant information as was needed to move forward to the next phase and actively conduct surveillance in its many and varied forms to enhance and advance the intelligence we had and produce and advance an evidence-gathering exercise required to arrest them. This meant catching them in the act across the pavement, guns and money in hand; easier said than done, as you know.

The Squad had identified the next gang member as being 50-year-old William Robert Griffiths, who had once run the infamous Bluecoat Boy public house at City Road, a centre for many of North London's assorted villains.

The fourth member of the team, 'Gary', was finally identified as Arthur Gary Edney from Carshalton, Surrey. His main role was as part of a team of organized shoplifters in different parts of the country, and he had just been released from a six-month sentence when he was arrested, with two accomplices, for a £40,000 armed robbery at a jeweller's. At Canterbury Crown Court in 1982 he was sentenced to eight years' imprisonment and was released five years later in 1987, whereupon he was sentenced to fifteen months' imprisonment at Chelmsford Crown Court for acting as a lookout/driver for a team of professional shoplifters in Essex. He was released in October 1989.

It was during this time of surveillance and evidence-gathering that two of the gang (together with seven others) were involved in an overnight raid on a GPO sorting office in Reigate, Surrey, in which £3,000,000 was stolen. Their total haul now exceeded £4 million.

In April 1997 Edney was followed to Norwich, where he met up with Hampton and Griffiths. The three men observed various Securitas vehicles leaving their depot close to Norwich airport before following an old-style security van across the county to Great Yarmouth. The gang concentrated on the movements of the guards, particularly around Sainsbury's, Marks & Spencer and a Kentucky Fried Chicken premises, before driving to a disused industrial estate and checking out an unused warehouse, as well as routes into and out of town.

By now it was necessary to inform Norfolk's chief constable of the Flying Squad's interest in his county, and he eventually came down on the Met's side, permitting them primacy in all that followed.

On the following two Mondays, Griffiths and Hampton were seen watching the same routines as well as checking out the disused industrial estate, but by the time intense surveillance was carried out it became clear that Great Yarmouth had been rejected as a target by the gang.

During the next eight weeks the gang were observed carrying out surveillance in the Norwich area, particularly around Callenders Restaurant in the Bowthorpe district of the city. It was there that the cash-in-transit van stopped after making a number of pick-ups at bank premises.

As the weeks went by, two of the gang 'walked the plot' around the area of Callenders Restaurant, closely scrutinizing cars, people and shops, especially the upper levels of premises, and looking for any signs of movement or reactions from people. They then checked the restaurant itself, examining the front door area and its immediate environment, until the time of the security van's arrival drew near, whereupon they went and hid in bushes on a nearby roundabout to await it.

It was clear to the Squad that the van would be hit outside the restaurant. The gang had visited the area on so many occasions, studied the manhole covers in the immediate area, reconnoitred Costessey Retail Park, just to the north-west of the city (which was clearly where the hi-jacked van and its crew would be taken to) and appeared very satisfied.

'We'll meet you at the first one after the blue' was the cryptic message issued to the gang members; this was a reference to the lay-by at Stump Cross, by junction 9A of the M11 motorway, and it certainly appeared that on 11 July 1997 the game was on. Four stolen and plated vehicles were in use by the gang: Stubbs in a Ford Sierra Estate, Griffiths in a Ford Escort, Edney in a Mercedes 190 and Hampton – naturally – in a BT van.

The Squad from the Finchley, Rigg Approach and Tower Bridge offices were in attendance; so were Norfolk officers, as were the helicopters of both forces. But there was no need for conventional surveillance; the Squad knew where the miscreants were headed and so they let the gang come to them; their progress was charted by a series of OPs, en route and throughout the city. Squad vehicles were parked up around the vicinity and out of sight.

And then – the job was aborted. The Securitas van which arrived was not the usual old rust-bucket – it was a brand new, state of the art vehicle with all the latest, up-to-date security equipment, including tracking devices; this was something the gang were quite unused to and they headed for home.

The Squad had to cut their losses and arrest them for conspiracy. They had sufficient surveillance and photographic evidence and were sure that this was no 'dry-run' – that the gang were in possession of firearms.

'All four stolen cars were on the M11 heading back towards London', Dave Ryan told me. 'They had to be arrested before they reached the M25, because if they had split up, there wouldn't have been the resources to arrest them simultaneously.'

There was a hard stop on the motorway; the gang were all arrested.

In the back of Hampton's van were found two revolvers, a pistol and a sawn-off shotgun and ammunition, as well as other robbery paraphernalia: handcuffs, plastic cable ties, masking tape, knives, crowbars, hammers, wigs, gloves, BT engineer's overalls, BT equipment – trellis and box guards and BT cables – and two-way radios.

During the next six months the case papers had to be prepared, and there were a total of 120 identification parades for the substantive offences. Eight strong positive identifications were made and all of the defendants were picked out, with Stubbs and Edney being identified the most.

The matter was dealt with at Woolwich Crown Court in 1999, when the gang were found guilty of conspiracy to rob Security Express of £293,000 and of possessing firearms with intent. Edney was sentenced to fourteen years' imprisonment, Stubbs to twelve years, Hampton to eleven and Griffiths to ten.

For Hampton to have received that length of imprisonment in his sixties must have come hard, but when he was arrested he must have known it was coming.

Still, he managed to retain his composure. Recognizing Detective Sergeant Terry Allen on that windy motorway as one who had previously dealt with him as a client of the Flying Squad, he appeared to accept the inevitability of the situation. 'Mr Allen', he said sadly. 'We should stop meeting like this!'

However, his contrition was not quite as genuine as one might suppose, because when Allen told him that they were going to search the van and photograph the contents, Hampton responded with a combination of injured innocence and surprise, 'What van?'

'They were not the last, by any means, of the 'old-school' security van robbers', Terry Allen later told me, 'but their calibre was, by 1997, a dying art form.'

CHAPTER 27

Operation Magician

From the early days of the Flying Squad it has been the practice for officers who had served in a junior capacity to return as they rose through the ranks, and that made sense. Wise in the ways of the Squad, they could bring their expertise to others, and many of them rose to the very top of the Flying Squad. Other top line officers were thrust into positions on the Squad to which they were unsuited, since they had never before served on the Squad in any capacity, and that often proved disastrous. But there are exceptions to every rule: Peter Wilton and the late Dave Little were posted to the Squad for the first time as detective chief inspector and detective superintendent respectively, and they proved to be enormous successes. The same applied to Detective Superintendent Jon Shatford who, with twenty-five years' service, arrived on the Flying Squad in 1998 as its operational head. He, too, proved a success; but the widely publicized case – 'Operation Magician' – which brought him to everybody's attention was a baptism of fire.

★

In February 2000 there was an attempted robbery at Nine Elms, in South-West London on a Securicor van containing £10 million by an armed gang of ten men. A BMW blocked the path of the van, two men emerged from a white Ford Transit van with cutting equipment and a flatbed lorry with a sharp spike welded into the vehicle's chassis was preparing to ram the back doors of the Securicor van. The plan was frustrated after a commuter took the ignition keys of the ramming vehicle, and to the sound of approaching police sirens the plan was aborted.

As the gang left the scene, two things happened which were highly unusual in the world of armed robbery.

The first was that the three vehicles used by the gang exploded, one after the other. And the second was that the gang got into a high-speed inflatable speedboat waiting for them at Battersea Pier, which then sped off with the miscreants safely on board.

It was rather like the successful conclusion of a Special Forces military exercise.

*

The investigation was taken up by the Flying Squad at Tower Bridge, and then, five months later, it happened again. Shortly after a Securicor van containing £8,796,000 left the depot at Maidstone it was ambushed by men in a 40ft long articulated lorry with a metal spike wielded to the chassis, together with four other vehicles. Shots were fired, but again the attack was aborted, and this time the gang fled to the River Medway. As the police approached, a gang member fired at them before he and the rest of the gang escaped – once more in a speedboat. Since the two offences were obviously linked, a joint investigation was launched by the Squad and Kent police.

Due to some clever intelligence work by a Kent detective carried out prior to the aborted raid at Maidstone, Tong Farm at Brenchley, owned by a scrap metal dealer, Lee Wenham, became the focus of attention after it was discovered that two of the vehicles there had been used in the attack.

Officers from the C11 surveillance team 'dug in', and anyone who visited the farm was photographed, together with their vehicle. On 2 August a JCB digger was seen arriving at the farm, and two weeks later came the Squad's first breakthrough. Terrence Millman, aged fifty-six, had convictions for armed robbery. He was stopped for a drink/drive offence, and the van he was driving proved to be stolen; but because he was a regular visitor to Tong Farm, whilst he was being detained for the drink/drive matter, Squad officers raced down to Tonbridge police station to examine the vehicle.

Shatford told me, 'I found a screwed-up piece of paper in the back of the van with five telephone numbers on it.'

More than that, Millman's fingerprints were found on items from vehicles used in the attempted Maidstone robbery, but he was released from custody. In the meantime, telephone intercepts in respect of those five numbers were requested from the Home Office and granted. But there was very little action on the intercepts or on the surveillance, and two weeks went by.

Sensibly, Shatford called for a meeting between the two forces, so that all of the intelligence data – or lack of it – could be discussed and mulled over.

Lee Wenham had been visiting the Millennium Dome, going to pubs and chatting to various people about nothing in particular.

There was a building site where he and others might be doing some work – all very vague, and nobody knew the location of the site. That was probably why the JCB digger at Tong Farm had been acquired. Wenham had been discussing getting some tickets for something or other: £20 for a single, £57 for a family one, and he had opted for the latter. So what? As the intercept operators were prone to tell the 'line handler': 'Just general traffic – nothing of interest.'

Or was there? Wenham had been to the Dome twice – why? What was there? Well, there was an exhibition of the fabulous De Beers diamonds, among them the Millennium Star, weighing 200 carats and worth £250 million. Then someone checked – the cost of a single ticket to the exhibition was £20, with £57 for a family ticket. Last of all, the Dome was situated on a 180 acre site, a peninsula protruding into the Thames with a possible three-way escape route on the river. There was no building site – that was the code name for the Millennium Dome – and it was the diamonds which the gang were after.

When Wenham went to the Dome on 25 August 2000, together with a woman and a little girl, and went into the diamond display area with a camcorder, looking at the display cabinets, making a call on his mobile phone, videoing the entrance area and looking in all directions up and down the river, he had no idea that he was being observed for the three hours and two minutes he spent there.

It was decided to replace the Millennium Star with a fake made out of plastic and zircon; and on 1 September – a Friday, the same day that the other two attempted robberies had been carried out – two Brink's-Mat vans arrived at the Dome. The diamond was placed in one of them and they drove back towards the De Beers headquarters. The whole operation was overseen by 300 police officers, including members of SO19 firearms unit. A van being driven erratically joined in the procession; so did a lorry which suddenly appeared from a side road. However, the Brink's-Mat vans reached their destination safely. But no sooner was that operation concluded than the gang turned up, inside the Dome.

Ray Betson was one; Bill Cockram was another. Both were career criminals who associated with Terrence Millman. They were joined by another of the gang, Aldo Ciarrocchi. With Lee Wenham, that made five.

Repeated surveillance had convinced Shatford that the robbery was going to take place inside the Dome. When, he didn't know. How they were going to get the diamonds, he didn't know. He believed it would happen in the morning, probably as the Dome opened for visitors, and thought it extremely likely that a speedboat would be used as the getaway, especially now that he knew that there was a one at Tong Farm.

Therefore the plan was to permit the gang access to the vault. There, if they were armed (and Shatford believed they almost certainly would be), they would be contained and not a danger to the public – then they could be arrested. It was as simple as that – or was it?

There were problems with the chairman of the Millennium Dome, who quite properly had concerns about the safety of the staff and customers, but these were overcome.

Now there was more activity at Tong Farm. The speedboat was tested at Whitstable but it appeared it was not functioning properly, the controls of the JCB digger were checked and a Hilti DXA-41 cartridge gun capable of penetrating one inch of steel was purchased, using a false name.

Shatford was receiving a series of shocks: one was when a disgruntled former employee of the Dome acquired plans of the vault and took them to the *Daily Mirror* to show how bad the security was. Then there was a terrorist attack on the MI6 building. Both incidents heightened security. On 22 September two of the gang entered the Jewel House in the Dome. This was it – except that it wasn't. After an hour, they left.

Five days later, Millman purchased a Picton 180 speedboat, capable of 55 mph – the other boat was clearly unsuitable – and another robber, Robert Adams, joined the team.

September passed into October, and the speedboat and the JCB were made ready. On 6 October a hundred police officers were deployed inside the Dome, the JCB digger was on the move – and then it returned to whence it came. Everybody stood down. Now there were queries from senior officers at the Yard. Was the operation too risky? Should it be shut down?

The next of Shatford's shocks was when the whole plan (including the use of the JCB digger) was leaked to the *Sunday People*; mercifully, the paper's editor agreed not to do anything to compromise the operation.

The gang member who was to drive the speedboat dropped out, and a new member, Kevin Meredith, came in.

Every indication was that the job was on for 6 November – it wasn't, and 250 police officers stood down. Then it was scheduled for 7 November – this was the sixteenth occasion – and this time it was.

'All five of those telephone numbers that had been on that crumpled up bit of paper lit up', Shatford told me, 'and we knew the job was on.'

The JCB, driven by Betson, together with Ciarrocchi, Cockram and Adams, armed with smoke grenades, ammonia and bolt croppers, was heading for the Dome, a white van containing Millman was across the other side of the Thames and Meredith was in the speedboat. And just when everything was coming to fruition, Shatford had the last of his shocks. As he told me, 'A coachload of schoolchildren turned up – we quickly ushered them into McDonald's.'

And then it happened. The JCB crashed through, firstly, a metal fence, then a gate and then, at 9.33 am, the Perspex shutter of the Dome; it came to a halt by the Jewel House. A smoke grenade exploded and Adams and Cockram, using the Hilti gun and a sledgehammer, smashed open the case containing the huge stone, then turned their attention to the other case containing eleven rare diamonds. Ciarrocchi was still letting off smoke grenades, and Betson, Meredith and Millman, the getaway drivers, were in position. Cockram, his arms swathed in bandages to protect them from the shards of glass, reached in to seize the Millennium Star – and with that, Shatford gave the command to attack.

It was pandemonium, with SO19 officers getting the gang down on the floor at gunpoint. Adams and Cockram refused to leave the vault, but they did so after stun grenades were thrown into the area. The Marine Support Unit with three boats and SO19 officers on board roared down the Thames to intercept and arrest Meredith.

By the time the trial at the Old Bailey started on 8 November 2001, Millman had died of cancer. Betson, Adams, Cockram and Ciarrocchi pleaded not guilty to conspiracy to rob, arguing that they had only conspired to steal the diamonds; Meredith's defence was that he had been coerced into the conspiracy.

It was a dirty trial; it was suggested that a serving police constable, working with a former Dome employee, had set the gang up, something that was fiercely denied by the officer in the witness box. 'He wasn't involved', Shatford told me. 'It was a mud-slinging exercise', as it was when it was alleged that Shatford had carried out the operation to regain credibility for the Flying Squad. This was because five members of the Squad at Rigg Approach had been jailed for serious dishonesty, and the resultant publicity had thoroughly dented the Squad's reputation.

The defence by Betson, Cockram and Ciarrocchi (Adams did not give evidence) was that they were the ubiquitous cheerful, chirpy, cheeky chappies incapable of using violence, although Betson did himself quite a bit of damage after he not only committed perjury in the witness box but was obliged to admit it.

Convicted of conspiracy to rob on 15 February 2002, Betson and Cockram were each sentenced to eighteen years' imprisonment (reduced on appeal to fifteen), with Ciarrocchi and Adams each receiving fifteen years (Ciarrocchi's sentence was later reduced to twelve years); Meredith, convicted of conspiracy to steal, was sentenced to five years.

In a separate case, Wenham pleaded guilty to conspiracy to rob Securicor at Aylesford in 2000 – he was the only one to be convicted of that offence – and was sentenced to nine years' imprisonment with four years concurrent for conspiracy to steal in the Dome plot.

Although the gang were keen to stress that they had not used violence during the offence, that did not stop one or two of them alleging that the police had behaved violently towards them. One or more of them alleged they had been hit in the face by the firearms officers with rifle butts, causing facial injuries; one of them had a fractured cheek/eye socket. Vince Payne, who had taken no part in the Dome investigation but had returned to the Squad as a detective inspector shortly afterwards, now takes up the tale:

I was trained as a Civil Litigation Officer and was not involved in the case, so I volunteered to access the case and produce a factual statement. The factual statement is used when the Job [i.e. the police] decides whether to pay up or defend itself.

I read all the evidence, reviewed all the videos and read the cross-examination transcripts from the trial.

The outcome was that I identified multiple areas where the injury/ies described could have been sustained.

When the vehicle carrying the offenders drove through the exterior of the dome, the exhaust pipe crashed through the windscreen into the cab. When the lead offender was attacking the glass casing of the diamond, a second robber was immediately behind and could have been struck. When challenged by the armed officers, all the subjects fell face-down on the floor. The medical examiner – in cross-examination, I think – had said that the facial injuries could be consistent with hitting the floor while wearing gas masks. I was also able to say that from the briefing given to the officers it was clear that their actions would all be subject to visual recording. It was therefore inconceivable that any of them would have acted as alleged or that others not acting that way would have omitted it from their recollection. The

Job agreed to robustly defend the action and this was communicated to the bad guys' lawyers. The litigation was then withdrawn.

'The Boatman' who dropped out of the conspiracy was traced to Spain, but the Crown Prosecution Service relinquished the case against him prior to extradition proceedings.

'I think there was credible evidence to convict "The Boatman",' Shatford told me. 'It would have been well worth a run.'

The driver of the white van on the day of the raid was never arrested, neither was the vehicle ever recovered. This could give rise to all sorts of speculation, but on that matter Shatford is adamant. 'No,' he told me. 'No snout was ever involved.'

To have devised such an elaborate plan, there must have been a buyer involved. But who was that person? On that matter, none of the gang are saying anything.

CHAPTER 28

Hatton Garden

The Hatton Garden Safe Deposit Company, founded in 1954, is situated at 88–90 Hatton Garden, EC1. Its vault is home to 996 security boxes, and on Good Friday, 3 April 2015, 562 of them were occupied. No one can possibly say how much in the way of valuables was stored in those boxes, stashed there by the great and the good, the old and the bold, but during that Bank Holiday weekend the company was entered. A Hilti DD350 diamond-tipped drill took two hours and twenty minutes to make three concentric holes through a 50cm wall, and of the seventy-three boxes which were opened, twenty-nine contained nothing. The other forty-four, it was initially estimated, contained property worth £14 million, although that figure was later revised upwards. This offence was to be the largest burglary in English legal history.

The burglar alarm was activated at twenty-one minutes past midnight on 3 April, but it was of little use. Kelvin Stockwell, the company's security guard, arrived, had a look round, could see nothing wrong and left. At least Mr Stockwell had made an effort; when the alarm from the Southern Monitoring Alarm Company was noted at Scotland Yard, due to a misinterpretation of the detail absolutely no action was taken.

'It is too early to say if the handling of the call would have had an impact on the outcome of the incident', said the ubiquitous Scotland Yard spokesperson, but by 8.10 am on Tuesday, 7 April, when the burglary was reported to police, it was clear that it would have been, and the renters of the forty-four emptied security boxes were furious.

'This investigation is being carried out locally', simpered the Yard's representative, but of course it wasn't; the Flying Squad was called in.

There appeared to be no sign of forced entry on the outside, but CCTV footage revealed that six men had entered the vault over that weekend; they had left and then returned, before getting into a white Ford Transit at 6.37 am on Sunday, 5 April and disappearing. The scene was carefully inspected, and some four hundred exhibits were removed for examination.

And then everything went quiet. Those who had suffered losses (and there were over forty of them) were now raving at the incompetence and inactivity of the police, and the soubriquet 'Keystone Cops' was probably the least offensive of the terms used to describe them.

But because the Squad was quiet, it did not mean they were indolent; they were beavering away at the case. A week afterwards, clearer CCTV images were made available to them. On Saturday, 4 April a distinctive Mercedes had been seen in the vicinity; and after detailed analysis of national ANPR (Automated Number Plate Recognition) data, together with painstaking street searches, it was soon traced to 74-year-old John Collins, whose criminal career had commenced in 1961 and who had notched up convictions for burglary and handling stolen goods. This was the breakthrough the Squad needed; cell site analysis and intensive covert surveillance of Collins led them to 67-year-old Terry Perkins, who had received twenty-two years' imprisonment for his part in the 1983 Security Express robbery. The cars of both men were electronically bugged, and the Squad listened in to their conversations and to those of the others involved in the crime, deploying undercover officers and lip readers to monitor their activity. They now knew who was involved; they also knew that much of the loot had not been disposed of. As a result of the Squad's dogged investigations, the artisans and tradesmen of Hatton Garden who had used the vaults to safeguard their life's work now had at least some hope of justice.

On 18 May Collins' Mercedes was covertly filmed in a car park in Enfield, where he met Hugh Doyle. The next day, Collins was again seen, as was 60-year-old Danny Jones, a man with a chequered criminal career, including convictions for robbery and burglary. They were joined by 59-year-old William Lincoln – he, too had convictions for burglary – who arrived in his nephew's taxi and placed three holdalls in the boot of the Mercedes.

Twelve premises were simultaneously raided. One of the addresses searched was that of 76-year-old Brian Reader, acquitted of the murder of John Fordham but convicted and jailed for receiving gold stolen from the Brink's-Mat robbery. Property worth £4,324,437 was recovered; so was a drill, gloves, overalls and face masks. Jewellery and cash were found behind skirting boards, in cupboards and in lofts. A smelter was found, together with crucibles and tongs, for melting down gold. Carl Wood, aged fifty-eight and with many convictions, was brought in and he, Doyle, Jones, Perkins, Lincoln, Collins and Reader were all charged with conspiracy to commit burglary, appeared at

Westminster Magistrates' Court on 21 May and were remanded in custody. When questioned, Collins, Jones, Perkins and Reader played their usual 'no comment' defence which had sometimes served them well in the past. Not, however, on this occasion. When their recorded conversations were played to them, when they were shown the photos linking them together, they rolled over and confessed.

There was one member of the gang missing. He was known simply as 'Basil the Ghost'. He had used a key to enter the building, had temporarily disabled the alarm system and had been one of the two raiders who crawled through the hole to ransack the security boxes. He had not been arrested, simply because the Squad did not know who he was.

Jones tried to be extra clever by telling Sky News and the police that he was willing to lead them to where his share of the loot was hidden. 'But for some reason I don't know, they're not that interested', he told the media. He was wrong; they were very interested indeed.

In mid-October the police did take Jones out of prison, to Edmonton Cemetery, and he directed them to plot GB177 where, under the memorial stone for a family member, one Sidney John Hart, they found a bag containing a small amount of jewellery. Was there any more, asked the detectives. 'That's all I had', virtuously replied the penitent Jones. 'The rest of it you got on the day.'

It was a clever ploy – a plea of guilty, the return of his share of the loot, some fulsome mitigation in court – all of which could well lead to a substantially reduced prison sentence.

But Jones was less than penitent and was certainly being less than truthful, and the apparent lack of interest on the part of the Squad was a delaying tactic. They had their own separate interest in the residents of Edmonton cemetery. One week earlier, the Squad officers had inspected the headstone of Sidney James Hart, at plot GB800. This was the final resting place of the father of Jones' partner, Valerie Hart, the mother of their three children. Underneath were two bags, each containing jewellery with a total value of £110,000 – a nice little pension to come out to.

On 16 November 2015 the trial got underway at Woolwich Crown Court, and Wood and Lincoln pleaded not guilty. But on 9 March 2016 they were found guilty; Lincoln was sentenced to seven years' imprisonment and Wood, to six. Doyle received a twenty-one-month sentence, suspended for two years, and Collins, Jones and Perkins, all of whom had pleaded guilty, were sentenced to seven years each, with Reader receiving six years and three months.

Perkins and Jones thanked the judge. Later, they could be heard cheering. They would certainly be released within three years – and of course, there was still loot valued at £10 million – or possibly more – outstanding. However, they were celebrating what would be a hollow victory.

In November 2017 Carl Wood was ordered to pay back £50,000 in three months or face an additional eighteen months in jail.

On 30 January 2018 Judge Kinch ordered the gang to pay back £27.5 million between them – the total amount estimated to have been stolen had by now risen – or face additional terms of imprisonment. Terry Perkins was ordered to pay back £6,526,571 or serve an additional seven years' imprisonment; he died one week later.

Danny Jones failed to pay up £6,599,021; he was sentenced to an additional six years and 287 days.

John Collins was ordered to pay £7,686,039 or serve another seven years.

Brian Reader, at seventy-nine the oldest of the gang, was released from prison in July 2018, having served just half of his sentence. He was in very poor health, suffering from prostate cancer and having had a series of strokes. He appealed against a decision to repay £6,644,951 (which included the sale of his £639,800 house plus development land worth £533,000), but in October 2018 the Court of Appeal rejected his application, saying, 'he had no arguable grounds'.

Three years after the burglary, on 27 March 2018, the tenacious Squad officers raided a flat on the Mersey Estate, Islington. It was situated less than two miles from Hatton Garden. They found 1,000 items of gems, jewellery and gold ingots stolen from the heist, valued at over £143,000, as well as home-made mobile phone jammers and other electronic equipment. They also found 58-year-old Michael Seed, aka 'Basil the Ghost'. On 15 March 2019, after deliberating for 35 hours and 35 minutes, the jury at Woolwich Crown Court convicted Seed of conspiracy to commit burglary and conspiracy to hide the proceeds. Telling him, 'In my judgement, this must rank among the worst offences of this type', Judge Christopher Kinch jailed Seed for ten years on the first charge and a concurrent term of eight years on the second.

The Freemasonry of 'the chaps' were naturally staunch in their support of the gang with their predictable, imbecile comments: 'No one got 'urt, did they? . . . Yer. Good luck to 'em . . . got themselves a nice little pension, didn't they? Diamond geezers, ain't they . . . ?'

Not really. Given their ages and general decrepitude, they were more like 'diamond wheezers'. They successfully carried out the job using twentieth century methods, but they were caught because the Flying Squad 'in the finest traditions of the Scotland Yard detective' were now using twenty-first century technology, in addition to their proactive investigation methods.

Commander Peter Spindler, head of Specialist Crime Investigations and the officer in overall charge of the investigation, summed matters up succinctly when he told me: 'They were analogue criminals operating in a digital world, and no match for digital detectives.'

Detective Superintendent Craig Turner, then head of the Flying Squad who directly oversaw the investigation, told me:

> This was one of the most audacious crimes that has been carried out in the capital in recent times, impacting upon victims and the very heart of the diamond district in London. As a result of their consummate professionalism, tenacity and detective ability, officers from the Flying Squad obtained overwhelming evidence, leading to the conviction of those involved and the recovery of property.

Epilogue

In 1988, at the Barnes office of the Flying Squad, information was received that a gang comprised of three black Londoners and one white Glaswegian had carried out a number of raids on cash-in-transit vehicles over a period of ten months. If the information was correct, the gang had accrued £349,000, their levels of violence had escalated – one guard had been shot in the base of the spine and almost died, and another's leg had to be amputated – and they were exceptionally surveillance-conscious.

Information was received that Dennis 'Duke' Claudius Ellington, a man with convictions for armed robbery, was involved; he was known to drive a BMW with personalized number plates. A sweep of the area was carried out which resulted in Ellington being 'housed', and with the resultant surveillance his associates Louis Anthony Miles and Hartgeald Emmanuel McLeod were identified. However, nothing occurred which would have justified the team being arrested.

But on 21 June information was received that two of the gang had stolen a Ford Transit van and left it in the Harlesden area. Therefore, a further sweep of the area was carried out by the Squad officers, noting the registration numbers of every Transit until one which had been reported stolen from Cricklewood was discovered. All surveillance was now concentrated on this vehicle, and it paid off; the following day, one of the gang drove the vehicle away, followed by McLeod in a similar stolen Transit which had been fitted out like a police observation van; later, false plates were seen being affixed to the Transit.

During July, August and September, this van was moved to different locations throughout West London, and on each occasion the gang carried out anti-surveillance manoeuvres, doubling back on themselves and monitoring police radio frequencies. But it did them no good; the Squad had now set up observation points to monitor the gang's addresses, log their movements and photograph them together and with the stolen vehicles.

By 20 September 1988 the gang had control of six stolen vehicles: three vans and three Sierras. One of the gang in a white Transit picked up the other three and they drove to Preston Road,

Wembley, where they concealed themselves in the back of the van, which had had its rear windows blanked out. The Transit was on top of an incline, overlooking a branch of the Abbey National Building Society; the other stolen vehicles had been spotted on a line between Wembley and Harrow, and the gang had taken advantage of cul-de-sacs, alleyways and bridges to use as changeover points.

It seemed almost certain that the attack on a cash-in-transit van would be carried out that night; due to the gang's propensity for violence, PT17, the firearms unit, had been called in.

The immediate and surrounding area, including the getaway vehicles, was now under intense police surveillance.

At 10.35 pm a Securicor vehicle containing £720,000 arrived outside the building society, the gang drove their Transit alongside and the 'attack' was given. But whereas previously they had held a custodian hostage while the van was emptied, this time there was a change of plan. They bundled the female guard into the back of the Securicor van with three of the gang, who drove off, and Ellington followed in the stolen Transit.

They were challenged by the officers, but although a Squad car rammed the Transit, it was no match for the heavier vehicle, which drove off pursued by other officers. Ellington then abandoned the van and ran on to the railway track between Kenton and South Kenton stations, where he was arrested. In the abandoned Transit was found a single-barrel sawn-off pump action shotgun containing six 20-bore cartridges. One was in the breech, and nine more cartridges were found in the van.

Meanwhile, the Securicor van containing three of the robbers had mounted the pavement before turning into Grasmere Avenue, where it was rammed by a Flying Squad car. Two of the gang leapt out and kicked in the front door of No. 4. Carrying firearms but dropping a full Securicor cash box, they dashed through the house and out into a dark, unlit service road. Dog handlers eventually found one of the gang, Louis Miles, still wearing a balaclava, hiding on the embankment. Close to him was a loaded sawn-off shotgun; wisely, he made no effort to use it. The other man who escaped through the house with Miles was never caught.

McLeod, who had also been in the Securicor van, ran off along Grasmere Avenue pursued by Detective Sergeant Alan Knapp, who had been part of the surveillance team and was consequently unarmed. Knapp shouted, 'Stop – armed police!' for this was a ploy that had worked before, but it did not on this occasion. McLeod pointed a Luger at Knapp and telling him to 'Back off!' disappeared into a dark alleyway. Despite this, Knapp chased after McLeod, who fired at him before fleeing.

There was nothing Knapp could do; to continue, unarmed and without armed back-up, would have been suicidal.

There was a hasty debrief; the Squad officers were furious. Eight months' work had resulted in a robbery, a kidnap, two smashed-up Squad cars, a shot fired at one of their own and just two out of four prisoners!

McLeod was later spotted leaving an address in Greenford on his motorcycle, a very powerful Honda CBR 600 Sports capable of speeds of up to 130mph. Knapp decided to take the route which he thought McLeod might well take if he was heading for his Harrow address, so, still unarmed and in an unmarked police car, he set off. Suddenly spotting the motorcycle, Knapp gave chase, reaching 80mph at times. McLeod slowed before turning into a side street, and Knapp, braking over a brutally short distance, turned into the same street, resolving to knock McLeod off his motorcycle – and he did just that.

Knapp then grabbed hold of McLeod and wrestled him to the ground. But the robber was not going to give up easily; his frequent gym visits made him a formidable opponent, and a violent struggle ensued. The sound of the crash and the subsequent fight had woken some of the local residents.

'Keep that noise down!' shouted Lindsay Weller. 'I'm a milkman and I've got to get up, early – clear off, or I'll call the police!'

'I *am* the police!' shouted Knapp. 'Come and give us a hand!'

Mr Weller did just that – and it would later earn him the thanks of the High Sheriff of Greater London and a £250 reward.

Among the firearms recovered was McLeod's loaded 9mm Luger; he had tried to fire a second shot but the pistol had jammed – fortuitously for Knapp. Forty premises were searched, and seven more firearms were recovered.

The trial at the Old Bailey commenced on 20 January and was completed on 11 May 1990. At its conclusion, prosecuting counsel Mr Nigel Sweeney praised the officers in capturing 'the most professional, ruthless gang of Division One robbers that I have ever encountered'; and Her Honour Judge Nina Lowry sentenced Ellington to eighteen years' imprisonment, Miles to seventeen years and McLeod to twenty-one.

Addressing the prosecution counsel, the judge commended all of the officers and, singling Knapp out for special mention, she said, in part:

> Sergeant Knapp was unarmed. He knew the man he
> was chasing was armed and likely to fire. He was told to
> back off but he continued on and he followed McLeod

into the alleyway, still trying to effect an arrest. After he had been fired at, he remained on duty and continued to pursue McLeod, ultimately taking part in effecting his arrest. He behaved with the greatest courage. I should like my observations to be brought to the attention of the commissioner.

They were. Following his award of a commissioner's high commendation, Knapp's Queen's Commendation for Brave Conduct was gazetted on 15 May 1992 – that was the day after he was gazetted for receiving the George Medal for his actions which are mentioned in the prologue to this book.

Author's Afterword

Today's Flying Squad is rather different to the Squad of yesteryear. No longer will a Squad officer at the Magistrates' Court hear those encouraging words from a prisoner, 'Guv, I need a bit of help', and be reasonably confident that there's a snout in the offing. This is for two reasons. First, thanks to the existence of the Crown Prosecution Service, the officer wouldn't be attending court in the first place.

Second, a snout is a snout no longer – he or she is a Covert Human Intelligence Source or CHIS – pronounced CHIZ. Oh, it's an absolute minefield of ifs, ands or buts. When is a CHIS not a CHIS? Have they been asked to establish or maintain a relationship? There's a whole set of buzzwords: necessity, proportionality, balancing, explaining, reasonable and best of all, 'considering whether the activity is an appropriate use of the legislation'. The controller (usually of detective inspector rank) and the handler (perhaps a detective sergeant or constable) from the dedicated source unit of that area or the central unit concerned make application to a superintendent for authority to use the snout; any forthcoming information is disseminated via intelligence logs to the unit concerned.

An officer attending court will apply to a judge to protect the identity of a CHIS using a P11 certificate, to justify its use under the public interest immunity rules.

It's the Regulation of Investigatory Powers Act 2000 (RIPA) which deals with CHIS handling, as it does with surveillance. An officer wanting to carry out surveillance on a suspect submits his application electronically via gatekeepers who 'quality assure it' before authorization by a superintendent. Each individual who is the subject of surveillance is named in the authority, which lasts for three months but is reviewed more frequently than that. On a Flying Squad surveillance, individuals will be added or deleted on an authority on a daily basis, as circumstances change. At court, the defence may well ask for the documentation proving that the authorities were in place at the time it's said they were. The application will stipulate what sort of surveillance is contemplated, such as using visual aids or camera/video.

Using probes in buildings or tracking devices on vehicles requires a higher authority.

The Crown Prosecution Service (CPS) not only conducts the case at court, it will also inform the Custody Sergeant in writing what charge, if any, there is going to be. The prosecution case file is completed electronically and contains all the information to allow the CPS to make a decision. This applies 24 hours a day, and usually, although as I'm reliably informed not always, on Flying Squad cases there will be a lawyer pre-briefed to be contacted for the authority.

When the Assistant Commissioner (Crime) Sir Basil Thomson KCB asked Chief Inspector Wensley all those years ago in 1916 if the CID could be made 'more fluid . . . more streamlined and flexible', he was probably making polite conversation. Thank goodness, Wensley took him at his word; he went on to become the Chief Constable of the CID – and Sir Basil went on to be convicted of outraging public decency in Hyde Park with a prostitute exotically named Miss Thelma de Lava. By then, the Flying Squad was well established, so any impetus that Sir Basil might claim to have provided towards its creation could be quietly brushed under the carpet.

Because the Squad *was* streamlined – Wensley made it so, ridding it of all the nonsensical rules and regulations which had inhibited detectives in the past.

And what a pity that the politicians have introduced more and more stifling legislation to hog-tie police officers in their pursuit of dangerous criminals whose response when caught is inevitably, 'I want my brief.'

Check out every Home Secretary of the past few decades; whenever a criminal crisis appears which might well threaten their job, they roar or shriek (according to gender), 'I'm going to slash the red tape that stops the police from getting out on the streets!' Of course, they never do; they increase it, to demonstrate their 'openness and transparency', and it's the police – and, of course, the public – who suffer.

It's amazing that any proactive police work gets done at all, especially in the case of the Flying Squad who, dealing with the major villains, come under the greatest scrutiny and criticism from their fawning lawyers, who are very well paid in cash, itself the proceeds of crime.

But the fact is, the Squad does carry out impressive work – and they do it consistently and they do it well.

★

There are now two main offices: Putney, which deals with the matters which were dealt with by the Barnes and Tower Bridge offices, and Eagle House, which covers the areas originally dealt with by Rigg Approach and Finchley.

There are forty officers allocated to each office (including Squad drivers), with three teams, all of which are multi-skilled, including in the use of firearms – Glocks and MP5s – and surveillance. However, due to the chronic shortage of detectives in the Metropolitan Police, they may be loaned out for other investigations – the Grenfell Tower enquiry, for instance. There were three detective inspectors at each office; there may now only be two. There is one detective chief inspector who covers both offices, a detective superintendent in charge of operational matters and a detective chief superintendent in overall charge of the Squad.

In fact, the Squad is not, it seems, the Squad any more; at the moment it is part of 'Specialised Front Line Policing' – but that, of course, may change.

There are constant policy changes; it is proposed that there may be offices not only at Barking and Putney as there are at present, but also at Lewisham and Hendon.

So what does the modern day Squad deal with? Complex serious and organized crime across London, allegations of robbery involving cash-in-transit attacks, banks, Post Offices, casinos, bookmakers, building societies, removal of ATMs (Automated Teller Machines) and smash-and-grabs at jewellers' during business hours. They also deal with robberies and burglaries where a firearm is involved (or intimated) in residential or commercial premises and cases where a firearm and ammunition has been stolen, plus 'Tiger Kidnaps'.

They deal with moped robberies and, I was initially told, aggravated burglaries – these are when the occupant of a premises is threatened or attacked with an offensive weapon during the course of a burglary. A week later, aggravated burglaries were taken off the list.

So matters are still pretty fluid, just as they were back in 1919 – things, of course, are different, but the Flying Squad can and does adapt to the changing face of crime; and it fills, as its title suggests, a really specialized role in front line policing.

*

Just the other day, I was speaking to former Squad Detective Superintendent Duncan MacRae when, in a voice rather charged with emotion, he said, 'Oh Dick, didn't we have the best years in the Job?'

He was right; we did.

To anyone who wasn't a member of the Flying Squad and wore the Squad tie with its swooping eagle motif, it's difficult to express on paper how exciting it all was. When I went to 12 Squad at the Yard in 1981 as a detective sergeant, I thought I'd died and gone to heaven. At that time I had fourteen years' service, I knew criminals, how to run informants, how to put a job together and give compelling evidence at court. But this was something different; I was now one of 170 officers inhabiting the world of the crème de la crème.

There was an air of urgency about the place, and everybody was doing something: telephoning informants, gathering together exhibits and case papers to take to the Old Bailey or getting search warrants and informants' reports typed up. Others would be leant over tables studying maps of areas where it was thought that an armed raid was going to be carried out, checking the streets to be blocked off and deciding how many personnel would be needed. Inevitably, there would always be someone picking up one of the green internal telephones to call the drivers in their room G.40 on the ground floor with the command, 'Get it up!' It would lead to a rushed exodus from that office on the 4th floor, Victoria Block, down to the concourse, where a sleek Flying Squad car would be waiting, engine ticking over; and as the toughly built officers crowded into the car, the driver would be told, 'Romford Road, Forest Gate, Ron – like the clappers!'

And 'Ron', who knew the streets contained in the 787 square miles of the metropolis better than any black cab driver, would set off, sirens wailing, steering the car effortlessly and safely at fantastic speeds (double-declutching the manual gearbox, all the way up and all the way down) to whatever adventure awaited the Squadmen. I used to say, 'Without the drivers, there wouldn't be a Flying Squad' – and I still adhere to that.

How thrilling it was to tear down Charing Cross Road, through the busy traffic at 70mph, and as we approached the junction with Oxford Street, for the uniform Police Constable on point duty to stop the oncoming traffic and wave us through, with a big grin on his face.

And when the denouement came – a wrenched-open car door, the bashed-in door of a flat, together with the no-nonsense shout, 'Flying Squad! YOU'RE NICKED!' – it was good to know that several more villains were in the bag.

The Squad had earned a reputation for toughness over the years; as one villain was heard saying to another, 'The last thing I want is to have the Sweeney breathing down me Gregory!'[1]

And if the Squad knew how to nick villains, they knew how to enjoy themselves as well. The annual 'Mums & Dads' dinner and dance would be held at one of the more prestigious West End hotels – usually the Dorchester – and only death or hospitalization would keep the Squadmen and their wives from it. But apart from that, each of the Squads had its own private watering hole – in 12 Squad's case, the Barocco Bar in Moor Street, just round the corner from Cambridge Circus. 'The Baroc', as it was known, was a small family-run café that served delicious Italian food. It was also frequented by male dancers from the Cambridge Theatre who thought it acceptable to spend hours there nursing a solitary cup of coffee, so the management were pleased when a dozen or so intimidating men came in and frightened them away. Political correctness was then in its infancy. As they left, telling us, 'Well, we wouldn't stay here now if you *begged* us!' bottles of wine were brought in from a nearby off-licence, the food would be ordered and after a 'Closed' sign was put up on the door, plans would be made for our next coup. Messages from informants would be redirected by telephone from the Yard, and some officers would hurriedly leave, only to return later with high-value information.

Unless a raid or an ambush was planned, nobody knew what would happen on a day-to-day basis. Work could arise simply from keeping one's eyes open during the morning's journey to the Yard; it could be a telephone call from an informant in the middle of the night – or perhaps an anonymous voice from the Yard's Intercept Room (or Confi Section) saying, 'Your man's on the move tomorrow at 8.30.' In either case, any further sleep was out of the question; it meant telephoning round other Squad officers to be at a certain place at a certain time.

Of course it wasn't Utopia – there were upsets, blown-out observations, irrational acquittals at court and other drawbacks – but believe you me, being a Flying Squad officer was the cat's whiskers. Then there were the office staff: the women in Divisional Office who made sure the Squad's administration ran like clockwork, the typists and the operators who manned the switchboard and the radio, 24/7. The Flying Squad was like a family, and I'm very grateful that I was part of it.

---

[1] Rhyming slang: 'Gregory' = 'Gregory Peck' = 'Neck'.

In conclusion, I needed some information to illustrate the modern-day running of the Squad. Since I'd been retired for over a quarter of a century I spoke to a serving officer, explaining that my ignorance of the current situation was due to the fact that I'm a dinosaur.

'I'd like to be a dinosaur as well, Dick', he replied sadly, 'just like you!'

Bibliography

Ball, John, Chester, Lewis and Perrott, Roy	*Cops and Robbers*	André Deutsch, 1978
Beveridge, Peter	*Inside the CID*	Evans Brothers Ltd., 1957
Bowers, Gordon	*The Great Diamond Heist*	John Blake, 2016
Burt, Leonard	*Commander Burt of Scotland Yard*	Heinemann, 1959
Capstick, John with Thomas, Jack	*Given in Evidence*	John Long, 1960
Clarkson, Wensley	*Public Enemy Number 1*	Blake Publishing, 1997
Collins, Steve	*The Good Guys Wear Black*	Arrow Books, 1998
Cornish, G.W.	*Cornish of the Yard*	Bodley Head, 1935
Fido, Martin and Skinner, Keith	*The Official Encyclopedia of Scotland Yard*	Virgin Books, 1999
Forbes, Ian	*Squadman*	W.H. Allen, 1973
Foreman, Freddie	*The Godfather of British Crime*	John Blake, 2008
Frost, George	*Flying Squad*	Rockliff Publishing Corporation Ltd., 1948
Gillard, Michael and Flynn, Laurie	*Untouchables*	Cutting Edge, 2004
Gosling, John with Tullett, Tom	*The Ghost Squad*	W.H. Allen, 1959
Greeno, Edward	*War on the Underworld*	John Long, 1960
Hatherill, George	*A Detective's Story*	André Deutsch, 1971
Higgins, Robert	*In the Name of the Law*	John Long, 1958
Hinds, Alfred	*Contempt of Court*	Bodley Head, 1966

Hogg, Andrew, McDougall, Jim and Morgan, Robin	*Bullion Brink's-Mat: The Story of Britain's Biggest Gold Robbery*	Penguin Books, 1988
Johnson, W.H.	*Surrey Villains*	Countryside Books, 2004
Kelland, Gilbert	*Crime in London*	Harper Collins, 1993
Kirby, Dick	*Rough Justice – Memoirs of a Flying Squad Detective*	Merlin Unwin, 2001
Kirby, Dick	*The Real Sweeney*	Robinson, 2005
Kirby, Dick	*You're Nicked!*	Robinson, 2007
Kirby, Dick	*Villains*	Robinson, 2008
Kirby, Dick	*The Guv'nors*	Pen & Sword, 2010
Kirby, Dick	*The Sweeney*	Wharncliffe, 2011
Kirby, Dick	*Scotland Yard's Ghost Squad*	Wharncliffe, 2011
Kirby, Dick	*The Brave Blue Line*	Wharncliffe, 2011
Kirby, Dick	*Whitechapel's Sherlock Holmes*	Pen & Sword, 2014
Kirby, Dick	*London's Gangs at War*	Pen & Sword, 2017
Kirby, Dick	*Operation Countryman*	Pen & Sword, 2018
Kirby, Dick	*Scotland Yard's Gangbuster*	Pen & Sword, 2018
Knight, Ronnie, Knight, John and Wilton, Peter with Sawyer, Pete	*Gotcha! The Untold Story of Britain's Biggest Cash Robbery*	Sidgwick & Jackson 2002
McLagan, Graeme	*Bent Coppers*	Orion Books, 2004
Millen, Paul	*Crime Scene Investigator*	Robinson Books, 2008
Morton, James	*Supergrasses and Informers*	Warner Books, 1996
Morton, James	*East End Gangland*	Warner Books, 2001
Morton, James	*Gangland, Volumes 1 & 2*	Time Warner, 2003
Morton, James and Parker, Gerry	*Gangland Bosses*	Time Warner, 2005
Morton, James	*Gangland Soho*	Piatkus, 2008

Murphy, Robert	*Smash and Grab*	Faber & Faber, 1993
O'Mahoney, Maurice with Wooding, Dan	*King Squealer*	W.H. Allen, 1978
Pearson, John	*The Profession of Violence*	Panther Books, 1973
Read, Leonard and Morton, James	*Nipper*	Macdonald & Co, 1999
Sharpe, F.D.	*Sharpe of the Flying Squad*	John Long, 1938
Shatford, Jon with Doyle, William	*Dome Raiders*	Virgin Books, 2004
Short, Martin	*Lundy*	Grafton, 1991
Slipper, Jack	*Slipper of the Yard*	Sidgwick & Jackson, 1981
Smith, Terry	*The Art of Armed Robbery*	John Blake, 2003
Sparks, Ruby and Price, Norman	*Burglar to the Nobility*	Arthur Barker Ltd., 1961
Swain, John	*Being Informed*	Janus Publishing, 1995
Thomas, Donald	*Villains' Paradise*	John Murray, 2005
Viccei, Valerio	*Knightsbridge: The Robbery of the Century*	Blake Hardbacks Ltd., 1992
Viccei, Valerio	*Live by the Gun, Die by the Gun*	Blake Publishing, 2004
Waldren, Michael J.	*Armed Police: The Police use of Firearms since 1945*	Sutton Publishing, 2007
Wensley, Frederick Porter	*Detective Days*	Cassell & Co, Ltd., 1931

Index